1970

This book ma be kept

JOHN LOCKE

by

D. J. O'CONNOR

Professor of Philosophy
University of Exeter
England

x

DOVER PUBLICATIONS, INC.
NEW YORK

This Dover edition, first published in 1967, is an
unabridged republication with minor corrections of the work originally published by Penguin
Books, Ltd., London, in 1952. This edition contains
a new Preface by the author and a revised list of
Suggestions for Further Reading.

Library of Congress Catalog Card Number: 66-28363

Manufactured in the United States of America
Dover Publications, Inc.
180 Varick Street
New York, N.Y. 10014

Preface to the Dover Edition

THIS book was originally published in 1952 in the Pelican Philosophy Series edited by Professor A. J. Ayer. The present edition differs from that one only in the addition of some minor corrections. If I were rewriting the book today, I would not want to make any significant changes in my exposition of Locke's doctrines. Critical comments on those doctrines would be substantially restated. But these changes would elaborate and qualify my criticisms rather than withdraw or replace them. I am therefore very glad to see the book republished in its present form.

A good deal of important critical work on Locke has been published during the past fifteen years, and any rewriting of the book would have to take this into account. The revised Suggestions for Further Reading lists some of the outstanding items of this work. In particular, Professor Yolton's investigations into the contemporary background of the theory of innate ideas seem to have settled the historical question left open in Chapter II.

D. J. O'CONNOR

June, 1966

Preface to the First Edition

THE general plan on which this book is written is explained in the first chapter and does not need any further comment here. But I should perhaps explain that my criticism of Locke is inevitably directed by my own philosophical outlook, a moderate empiricism which is not, I hope, too far removed from Locke's own position.

It may be useful to say something about the system of references I have used. Quotations from the *Essay Concerning Human Understanding* are by book, chapter, and section, so that 'IV.21.4', for example, means 'Book IV, Chapter 21, Section 4'. References to the introductory parts of the *Essay* appear as 'Epistle to the Reader' or 'Intro. 4' for 'Section 4 of the Introduction.' In noting quotations from the *Treatises on Civil Government*, 'ii. 95', for instance, means 'Section 95 of the *Second Treatise*'. Quotations from other works are referred to by sections where the work is so divided; *e.g.* '*Examination of Malebranche*, 10'.

I am glad to acknowledge the help I have received from the editor of this series, Professor A. J. Ayer. His very patient and careful criticism has removed a great many mistakes and obscurities. I have also to thank Mr Maurice Cranston who corrected a number of inaccuracies in the biographical note in Chapter I, and Dr E. E. Harris and Mr D. S. Livingstone for some helpful advice on Chapter IX.

Suggestions for Further Reading

It is not possible to get a sympathetic understanding of a philosopher's point of view without reading his works. There are two standard editions of the *Essay Concerning Human Understanding* in two volumes, one by A. C. Fraser (Oxford, 1894; Dover reprint, 1959), and a recent and more convenient edition by J. W. Yolton (London, 1961). The abridged single volume editions of A. S. Pringle-Pattison (Oxford and New York, 1924), and Raymond Wilburn (London, 1947) are more suitable for a first reading. The *Second Treatise on Civil Government* and *A Letter Concerning Toleration* have been edited by J. W. Gough (Oxford and New York, 1946). The standard biography is *John Locke: A Biography* by Maurice Cranston (London, 1957).

The following books and papers are important contributions to the understanding of Locke's theory of knowledge.

Aaron, R. I., 'Locke's Theory of Universals'. *Proc. Aristotelian Society*, N.S. xxxiii (1932–33).

——, *John Locke*, 2nd ed. Oxford and New York, 1955.

Ammerman, R. R., 'Locke's Concept of Substance'. *Theoria*, Vol. 31 (1965).

Bennett, Jonathan, 'Substance, Reality and Primary Qualities'. *Amer. Philosophical Quarterly*, Vol. 2 (1965).

Broad, C. D., 'Locke's Doctrine of Substantial Identity and Diversity'. *Theoria*, Vol. 17 (1951).

Flew, A. G. N., 'Locke and the Problem of Personal Identity'. *Philosophy*, Vol. xxxvi (1951).

SUGGESTIONS FOR FURTHER READING

Gibson, J., *Locke's Theory of Knowledge*. Cambridge and New York, 1917.

Jackson, R., 'Locke's Distinction between Primary and Secondary Qualities'. *Mind*, Vol. xxxix, N.S. 153 (1930).

von Leibniz, G. W., *New Essays Concerning Human Understanding* (trans. by A. G. Langley). New York, 1896.

Ryle, G., *Locke on the Human Understanding*. Tercentenary Addresses. Oxford, 1933.

Warnock, G. J., *Berkeley*. London, 1953. (This book, though primarily an exposition of the philosophy of Berkeley, contains some valuable critical passages on aspects of Locke's theory of knowledge.)

Yolton, J. W., *John Locke and the Way of Ideas*. Oxford, 1956.

CONTENTS

CHAPTER ONE

Introduction

The Purpose of this Book

THERE are many different ways of writing about a philosopher's work and I would therefore like to make clear what I have tried to do in the following chapters. The writings of a great philosopher do not go out of date in the way that scientific writing must do. Newton's *Principia Mathematica* or the *Celestial Mechanics* of Laplace are not used today as authoritative text books on astronomy. The discoveries and methods first published in these books have become, to a large extent, part of the established body of science. But students of philosophy still read Plato, Descartes, Locke, Hume, and Kant. This is because the objects and methods of philosophers and natural scientists are quite different and their work has accordingly to be judged by different standards.

When we are criticizing the work of a philosopher, we are not primarily concerned with the 'truth' of what he is saying. This is shown by the fact that the refutation of a philosopher's theory does not render his work out of date or valueless. No scientist is interested nowadays in the phlogiston theory of combustion or the caloric theory of heat except as curios in the history of science. But Hume's theory of causality or even Plato's theory of universals are not dead for the philosopher. Critics of philosophy have suggested that this respect for outmoded theories is due to the essentially sterile and unprogressive character of philosophical endeavour. Scientists, it is asserted, advance by making new discoveries and leave their predecessors' errors behind them: philosophers are content to make their most constructive work little more than a variation on themes by earlier writers.

It is true that the progress of philosophy is of a very different kind from the progress of science. It consists largely in the progressive clarification of difficult and elusive ideas. And the task is made more difficult by the lack of any sure method of procedure such as the experimental method of science or the axiomatic method of geometry. Nevertheless, progress is made. It is, however, largely of a negative kind, consisting in the *elimination* of unproductive or erroneous lines of thought. Most of the advances in philosophy lie in finding out the mistakes of our predecessors and avoiding them ourselves. Solving a philosophical problem is often rather like trying to find our way to the centre of a very complex maze by identifying the blind alleys and putting a mark at the entrance to each so that no one will make the same mistake again. It is, of course, not nearly so simple as it sounds in this metaphor because the vagueness and ambiguity inseparable from ordinary language can disguise the same error in many different forms.

But progress in philosophy is not entirely of this negative kind. Or perhaps it would be better to say that destructive criticism and positive insight are complementary activities. Constructive ideas are suggested by criticism and themselves point the way to further criticism. Thus we read the works of the classical philosophers not to gain information but to make our ideas clear about subjects like causality, free will, the relation between mind and body, and so on. We find their works valuable for this purpose in so far as we find them suggestive and stimulating. When we read philosophy, we are not going to an authority for information but to the product of a lively mind which will stimulate us to philosophize for ourselves. There is no necessary connexion between the philosophical fertility and suggestiveness of a writer and the consistency of his system or the logical rigour of his demonstrations. Few philosophers have had a wider influence than Plato. Yet his writings are marred by obvious fallacies and trivial quibbles to an extent unparalleled by any other serious philosopher. But it would be captious to dwell on the mistakes of a great philosopher who was a pioneer in a number of different fields with practically no predecessors to guide him.

I do not intend to give an account of what Locke 'really meant'. Nobody but Locke himself could give such an account, and he is dead. Nor do I intend to give more than a casual mention to the influences which moulded his thinking or the intellectual background of his time. This has been done by others and, in any case, is not philosophy but history. What I shall try to do is to give a reasonably orderly and simple account of what Locke actually said. I shall also enlarge and defend his views where they seem defensible and try to reduce them to some sort of order where they seem confused. And where they seem indefensible, I shall criticize them and give my reasons for supposing them to be wrong. This will necessarily involve a certain amount of 'interpretation' but, as I mentioned above, I shall not claim the interpretation to be 'correct'. What a certain philosopher 'really meant' is of no importance, being undecidable. What interests his readers is the extent to which his actual words excite their interest in philosophical thinking and suggest lines of thought which will help to elucidate their own philosophical puzzles. And Locke's philosophical writings are, in this sense, still as alive and fertile as they ever were.

Of course, the only satisfactory way of learning what a philosopher has to say is to read him. But not all philosophers can be read with equal ease, especially by beginners. Some, like Descartes, Berkeley, or Mill, wrote clearly and concisely and their writings form perhaps the best introduction to philosophy. Others, like Aristotle, Kant, or Hegel, are confused, prolix, and almost incomprehensible on a first reading. They are best approached through the simplified version of some friendly commentator. In this respect, Locke is nearer to Berkeley than to Hegel. He writes reasonably clearly though in a clumsy pedestrian style, only occasionally enlivened by a forceful or elegant phrase. But his careless use of technical terms is a source of great confusion. And the manner in which the *Essay Concerning Human Understanding* was written ('by incoherent parcels; and after long intervals of neglect, resumed again, as my humour or occasions permitted')

13

; it a poorly constructed, ill-balanced and repetitious
Even when we read the *Essay* in a shortened version,
the manner in which Locke expands trivial points and passes
hastily over points of great importance makes the *Essay* a
rather tiresome book and by no means ideally suitable for a
beginner in philosophy. I shall therefore try, in what follows,
to provide an introduction to the study of his philosophy
which will make the approach a little easier than through a
reading of his own words. But what I have to say here is, of
course, in no sense a substitute for Locke's own writings.

Biographical Note

John Locke was born in 1632, during the reign of Charles I,
and died in 1704, two years after the accession of Queen Anne.
His life covered an unusually turbulent period of English
history and his fortunes were affected by the stresses of
the times in which he lived. He was born at Wrington in
Somerset, the son of a West Country lawyer. The Civil War
broke out when young Locke was ten years old and his father
joined the Parliamentary army. Locke spent his childhood in
Somerset and at the age of fourteen was sent to Westminster
School where he stayed until his election to a junior studentship at Christ Church, Oxford, in 1652. From his *Thoughts on
Education*, published in 1693, Locke seems not to have been
favourably impressed either by the curriculum at Westminster
or with the savage discipline of the English public school of
his time.

At Oxford he was introduced to philosophy. The characteristic conservatism of that university restricted philosophical
studies at that time to a particularly arid form of medieval
Aristotelianism, 'perplexed', as Locke described it, 'with
obscure terms and useless questions'. But though he thought
little of the rather debased form of scholasticism which he had
to study as an undergraduate, he absorbed more of it than he
realized. Many of the suppressed premises of his own thinking were derived from medieval scholasticism and he never

quite succeeded in reconciling the unacknowledged influence of his scholastic training with the natural trend of his own thought. But his interest in philosophy seems to have been excited not by his official studies at Oxford but by his private reading of Descartes. The rather artless clarity of Descartes' writing impressed him by its contrast with the scholastic 'unintelligible way of talking' and made him realize that philosophy could be more than pretentious verbalizing and term-shuffling.

But though he admired Descartes' way of writing he was not greatly impressed by his philosophical opinions. Here again, however, he found it difficult, as all philosophers do, to keep his thinking unaffected by contemporary influences and the fourth book of the *Essay* in particular shows a strong Cartesian influence.

Locke took his B.A. degree at Oxford after four years' study and his M.A. two years later. In 1659 he was elected to a Senior Studentship at Christ Church tenable for life. He became lecturer in Greek the following year and subsequently Reader in Rhetoric and Censor of Moral Philosophy. After he had laid down the office of Censor in 1664, Locke seems to have been in some doubt about his future. The usual consummation of a university don's career would have been to take holy orders. Locke did not wish to do so, partly perhaps because his rather liberal religious opinions, combined with his natural sincerity, made such an equivocal acceptance of orthodoxy impossible for him, but also because he was much more attracted to the study of medicine. He had some difficulty in taking a medical degree and it was not until 1674 that he was granted a faculty by the Chancellor of Oxford to practise medicine. By this time he had secured his B.M. degree and he was now given the degree of Doctor of Medicine. He continued to practise from time to time but he did not take up medicine as a regular profession.

An alternative career was opened to him by the offer of an appointment as secretary to a diplomatic mission to the Elector of Brandenburg. This was the beginning of an active interest in public affairs which was to involve Locke rather embarrassingly in the uncertainties of seventeenth-century politics. The mission, headed by Sir Walter Vane, left England in November 1665. After two months of diplomatic man-oeuvres, the Elector refused to sell, at the price offered, either his alliance or a promise of neutrality in the Dutch war, and the mission returned to England empty-handed. On his return, Locke declined a further diplomatic post and took up resi-dence in Oxford again to continue his medical studies.

In the summer after his return, Locke made the acquaint-ance of Lord Ashley, later to become the first Earl of Shaftes-bury. Acting for a medical friend, Locke attended Ashley who had come to Astrop near Oxford to drink the local medicinal waters. Each man seems to have been impressed with the abilities and personality of the other and the meeting was the beginning of a friendship which lasted until Shaftesbury's death in 1683.

Shaftesbury was one of the most influential men in politics during the reign of Charles II. No one has ever doubted his abilities but his character is not so well attested. Dryden satirized him savagely in *Absalom and Achitophel*. Macaulay, a fellow Whig, said of him that he was a man 'in whom the immorality which was epidemic among the politicians of that age appeared in its most malignant form'.[1] He had, indeed, the most useful of all politician's talents, an unerring intuition of the right moment to change sides. But this seems to have been the worst that can be said of him, and as much can be said of distinguished men of the twentieth century now dignified and honoured under the title of statesmen. No doubt Locke's affection for him was founded on less public qualities. In any case, they had in common a strong and sincere hatred of religious and political absolutism.

Locke entered Ashley's service in 1667 and lived with him in London. His duties were various. He acted as his medical adviser and is said to have saved his life by an operation for an abscess in the chest. He also performed some of the duties of a

1. *History of England*, Everyman Edition, Vol. I, p. 168.

political secretary, assisting him, among other tasks, with the drafting of a constitution for the new colony of Carolina.[1] In addition he acted as tutor to Ashley's son and even undertook the task of finding the boy a wife.

In 1672 Ashley became the first Earl of Shaftesbury and Lord Chancellor of England. Locke, sharing his patron's success, was given an official secretaryship in charge of the ecclesiastical business under the Lord Chancellor's control. Within a year, Shaftesbury was out of office again, having alienated the king by supporting the Test Act, a measure designed to secure civil and military offices from the supposed treasonable activities of Roman Catholics. Locke's fortunes did not suffer from this political reverse. He resumed his life as a student of Christ Church, drawing an annuity of £100 from Shaftesbury together with the income of some property of his own. He was now financially independent and, for the time, free from official duties.

His health, however, had never been good and at the end of 1675 he left London for a long stay in France. He went first to Montpellier where he took the cure and met the leading medical men. Some fifteen months later he moved north and spent a year in the stimulating intellectual atmosphere of Paris. One of Locke's friends in Paris was Bernier, a pupil of the scientific philosopher, Gassendi, whose work undoubtedly influenced Locke's thinking. Locke was also able to meet leading exponents of the Cartesian philosophy, then at the height of its *succès de scandale*. (It had recently been prohibited by ecclesiastical influence from being taught in French colleges or universities.) After another visit to Montpellier, he returned to Paris in November 1678 and in the following April crossed the Channel after an absence of over three years.

He found the political situation as dangerous and uncertain as it usually was in Stuart times. Shaftesbury was out of office and in disgrace when Locke left and had actually spent a year in the Tower of London in 1677–8. The ostensible pretext for

1. The constitution proved to be quite unworkable.

his imprisonment was the comparatively minor one of refusing
to retract an indiscreet suggestion that the reigning parliament
was illegally constituted.

In 1678, however, Shaftesbury again returned to power as
president of a newly constituted privy council, and when
Locke returned from France he re-entered his patron's service.
This time his activities were of a more political and a more
secret kind. Shaftesbury was now engaged on extremely
delicate political issues. He used his new office to press a bill
for the exclusion of the Roman Catholic Duke of York, later
James II, from the succession to the throne. But he had over-
estimated the strength of his position and in October 1679 he
was once again dismissed. He now turned to support the Duke
of Monmouth, a natural son of Charles II and a Protestant
aspirant to the throne of England. Unless he was legitimatized,
Monmouth had, of course, no constitutional claim to the
succession, but he was young, charming, and popular. The
king, to ease the political tension, dismissed Monmouth from
his army command and banished him temporarily to Holland.
Shaftesbury organized clubs all over the country in support of
the Duke and used his own considerable prestige and abilities
to engage popular opposition to the legitimate successor to
the throne.

Locke's part in these dangerous activities is not too clear.
His health was still bad and he spent a good deal of time in the
comparative peace of Oxford. But extracts from the letters of
a political opponent who was a fellow member of his college
are interesting.

'*March* 14, 1681. John Locke lives a very cunning and unintelligible life here, being two days in town and three days out;
and no one knows where he goes or when he goes or when he
returns. Certainly there is some Whig intrigue amanaging . . .

'*March* 19, 1681. Where J. L. goes, I cannot by any means
learn, all his voyages being so cunningly contrived . . . I fancy
there are projects afoot.'

And indeed there were, though we do not know how much
Locke knew about them or how far he was implicated. At

Oxford he seems to have been extraordinarily discreet about expressing his political opinions. A political opponent, the Dean of his college, later wrote of him: 'I have for divers years had an eye upon him; but so close has his guard been on himself that, after several strict inquiries, I may confidently affirm that there is not anyone in the college, however familiar with him, who has heard him speak a word either against or so much as concerning the government'. Shaftesbury continued with his intrigues on behalf of Monmouth and Locke could hardly have failed to be aware of what was happening. In July 1681, Shaftesbury was arrested in London on a charge of high treason. After a few months in the Tower he was brought to trial before a jury packed by his political associates and acquitted, amid popular rejoicing. In the following year Monmouth was arrested and Shaftesbury, anticipating further charges, went into hiding. A few weeks later he escaped to Holland where he died at Amsterdam in January 1683.

After Shaftesbury's flight and death Locke began to feel unsafe in Oxford and in the autumn of 1683 he fled to the safety and tolerance of Holland. His long association with Shaftesbury did not go unnoticed. In the following year the king demanded his expulsion from his studentship at Christ Church. In the spring of 1685 Charles II died and the accession of his brother provoked Monmouth's ill-fated rebellion. Locke's name was given to the authorities as one of Monmouth's supporters and the Dutch government was asked to extradite him. The request was not openly refused but the Dutch made little effort to oblige a government with whom the House of Orange had such small sympathy. Locke went into hiding for a time under the alias of Dr van der Linden. This is probably the only historical case of a great philosopher hiding from the law under an assumed name.

However, he does not seem to have been in any real danger. His friends in England actually obtained for him the offer of a royal pardon which Locke declined, no doubt distrusting a king whose beliefs were supposed to dispense him from the obligation of keeping faith with heretics. He replied to the

Earl of Pembroke who conveyed the offer that 'having been guilty of no crime, he had no occasion for a pardon'. In the following year his name was removed from the list of wanted persons and, though he did not return to England, he was able to resume his normal life.

Locke was able to use the leisure and security of his stay in Holland for writing. He was now fifty-four years of age and had yet published nothing important. He had been working for some years on his famous *Essay Concerning Human Understanding*, which he began in earnest at Utrecht in 1684. This material was now worked up into a form suitable for publication and in 1688 a French abstract of the *Essay* was published in the *Bibliothèque Universelle* by his friend Jean Le Clerc. Moreover he had spent his time while in hiding from his political enemies in writing the Latin version of his first *Letter on Toleration*.

Meanwhile plans were maturing to remove James II from the English throne and Locke was once again drawn into politics. In 1687 he moved from Amsterdam to Rotterdam where he came in touch with William of Orange and his English supporters at The Hague. In November 1688, William landed in England, James fled and the 'glorious revolution' was accomplished. Three months later Locke ended his five years' exile and returned to England. He did not leave Holland without some regrets for its civilized tolerance. 'In going away', he wrote to a Dutch friend, 'I almost feel as though I was leaving my own country and my own kinsfolk.'

On his return to England he went to live in rooms at Westminster where he spent the next two years. During this time he was hard at work preparing for publication the philosophical books on which he had been at work in Holland. King William tried to tempt him back into public affairs, offering him the post of ambassador to the Elector of Brandenburg. Locke declined the post, perhaps somewhat reluctantly, for reasons of health. He says in a letter to Lord Mordaunt that he feared the 'cold air' and the 'warm drinking' of Germany. He accepted instead a sinecure as Commissioner of

Appeals which gave him a modest £200 a year in return for some nominal duties.

He was thus enabled to spend most of his time on his philosophical studies. In 1689 the Latin version of *A Letter Concerning Toleration* appeared. It was published anonymously, both the author's name and the name of the friend, Philip a Limborch, the liberal theologian, to whom it was dedicated, being indicated by initials. Locke seems to have been nervous about acknowledging his liberal views on so controversial a topic and only in his will did he confess to have written the *Letter*. The publication excited a good deal of controversy and it is not easy to realize that views on toleration which to-day seem commonplace became so largely through Locke's efforts. In the course of the controversy Locke published a second letter in 1690 and a third in 1693, restating and clarifying his position. In 1690 he also published the *Two Treatises on Civil Government* and the *Essay Concerning Human Understanding*.

In 1691 he left Westminster to take up permanent residence at Oates in Essex, some twenty miles from London. Oates was the country house of Lady Masham whom Locke had known before his exile in Holland and with whom he corresponded during his stay there. Here he stayed, as the guest of Lady Masham and her husband, Sir Francis, until his death in 1704. He lived there as part of the family, visited by his friends and occupying his time with philosophical controversies and biblical studies. His writings both on political and philosophical subjects were the subject of lively comment and dispute as soon as they were published and most of his work issued between 1691 and his death consisted of answers to his critics. He also published short books on education and economics and a slightly unorthodox defence of the reasonableness of Christianity.

However, he did not live in complete retirement. In 1696 he accepted office as a Commissioner of Trade and for the next four years until ill-health compelled him to resign he spent most of the summer and early autumn at his duties in London. In 1700 he published the fourth edition of the *Essay*, the last of his works to be published in his lifetime. His health was now failing and he spent the last years of his life in the friendly domestic comfort of the Masham household. His critics pursued him to the end and in 1702 the University of Oxford formally condemned the *Essay*. Locke wrote to a friend: 'I take what has been done there rather as a recommendation of the book'. In fact, the *Essay* had already made its mark on philosophy both in England and abroad. He died at Oates on October 28th, 1704, and was buried in the churchyard of the parish church at High Laver where his grave may still be seen.

Locke's character can be seen in his writings. Cautious, patient, and tolerant, a firm believer in the powers of the disinterested human reason and a fierce hater of authoritarianism and its associated bigotry, both in religion and politics, he embodies the virtues that most of Europe in the seventeenth century so conspicuously lacked.

CHAPTER TWO

The Aim and Method of Locke's Theory of Knowledge

ALL of us would agree that we know a number of different things. If challenged to give a catalogue of what you know, you might say, for example, that you know the English and French languages, how to swim, how to drive a car, how to analyse a chemical substance, that you know some history and some geography, that you know a number of different people, and so on. The list even in general terms like this would be a very long one, and it would not be possible, for practical purposes, to set out such a catalogue in detail. But one thing is obvious from the few examples I have given: the word 'know' is commonly used in many different senses. Some of the different uses are so distinct that they are assigned to different words in languages other than English. In French and German, for example, we use one word for 'know' in the sense of being acquainted with a place or a person and another for knowing a fact or being aware of something. But this is only one of the ambiguities. Consider the differences between 'I know English', 'I know how to play the violin', 'I know that arsenic is poisonous'. The first two sentences use 'know' in the sense of habit-knowledge. If I know English or how to play the violin it means that if I am put in a certain situation I am able to act in the appropriate ways, whereas a foreigner who did not know the language or a man without any musical training could not produce the noises appropriate to talking English or violin playing. These are cases of what Professor Ryle calls 'knowing how', knowledge of techniques which are the result of training and practice. They are quite different from knowing that so-and-so is the case, that arsenic is poisonous, that two plus two is four and so on. These kinds of knowing are not entirely the result of training and practice;

23

they call also for observation, inference, testimony and, in general, *evidence* of various kinds.

It is with knowledge in this last sense that John Locke was concerned in the *Essay Concerning Human Understanding*. But it will easily be seen that even what I have called 'this last sense' is not a uniquely determined and unambiguous sense of the word 'knowledge'. It is true that, in this sense of the word, we say that we know whatever we take to be established by evidence. But we recognize that evidence can be of many different kinds and, what is equally important, of many different degrees as well. Certain propositions we are commonly prepared to accept as self-evident. Euclid's first axiom, for example, 'Things which are equal to the same thing are equal to one another' would normally be accepted as so obviously and intuitively certain that it does not require any extrinsic evidence to establish it. Other propositions like 'the square root of 2 is irrational' or 'the angles of a plane triangle amount in total to 180 degrees' we may be persuaded to accept as certain by a process of proof in which these propositions are shown to be the logical consequence of others which we do accept as 'self-evident'.

It will be seen that the three examples I have just quoted are instances of what are called general or universal propositions, whose character can be made explicit by prefacing to the proposition the phrase 'in all cases' or some synonymous expression. But we are also familiar with general propositions which are not established in this way. All the ordinary commonsense generalizations which we rely on to guide our day-to-day experience, together with the laws of nature established in the natural sciences, are of this kind. 'Bread is nutritious', 'unsupported bodies fall to the ground', 'lead is heavier than iron', are all statements of this type. Like the mathematical statements mentioned above, they are general statements but unlike them they are established not by an appeal to logical self-evidence or by deduction from self-evident premises but on the evidence of repeated observation of particular instances. Such a method of establishing general propositions raises well-known philosophical problems which we need not consider here. It is sufficient to say that the reliability of general statements about matters of observable facts and the degree of certainty we feel about such statements varies widely from one case to another. In many cases we are so sure of the conclusion that we are prepared to say that we are certain. In others, our degree of confidence in the proposition may vary from a lively belief through scepticism to utter disbelief.

But general propositions, whether they are mathematical or factual, are not the only or the most interesting of those we are said to know. Our experience consists in a succession of particular events and it is our knowledge of these which forms the basic ingredients from which our other sorts of knowledge are developed. They form both the *evidence* for our factual generalizations and the *occasion* of our logical and mathematical knowledge. That the sun is shining as I write, that there is a breeze blowing, that there is a blue book on the table before me, are all particular facts which are part of my knowledge. Such statements may, of course, be about the past, present, or future. Nor are these the only sort of particular statements. There are also more elementary and primitive ones like 'I feel hot', 'I hear a noise', 'I see a blue patch' which, unless we are doing philosophy, we rarely have occasion to make because they are usually of little interest.

But even now, we have not finished listing the different types of propositions which we are said to know. Many people claim to know or at least to believe in various ethical or theological statements: 'There is a God', 'cruelty is evil', 'there is a future life', and so on. And although such statements raise special difficulties, they are statements which, if they can be made clear and shown to be true, are very important. And when we are discussing the various sorts and degrees of human knowledge, we must take them into account. It is obvious, then, that even if we restrict ourselves to knowing in the sense of *knowing that*, it is possible (*a*) to have a good many different *kinds* of knowledge, and (*b*) to know those things with a great many different *degrees* of confidence. And

25

when our degree of confidence is not very high, we tend not to use the word 'know' at all but to say instead that we have a certain opinion or believe or doubt and so on.

This hasty and very rough review of the ways of knowing will serve to introduce the problem which Locke set himself in the *Essay*. He explains that his purpose is 'to inquire into the original, certainty, and extent of *human knowledge*, together with the grounds and degrees of *belief, opinion*, and *assent*'.[1] He wants to determine, in other words, the ways in which we come to know, the different sorts of things we can know, the types of evidence by which different sorts of statements can be established and the degrees of certainty appropriate to the different varieties of statement and different weights of evidence. It should be noted at once however that Locke uses the words 'know' and 'knowledge' in an even narrower sense than that of 'knowing that'. No form of 'knowledge' is worthy of the name for him unless it satisfies at least two conditions: (*a*) I must be absolutely certain of what I am said to know; (*b*) I must be *justifiably* certain: that is, I cannot properly be said to know anything if further evidence can show my certainty to have been unfounded. 'What we once *know*, we are certain is so: and we may be secure, that there are no latent proofs undiscovered, which may overturn our knowledge or bring it in doubt.'[2]

Ways of knowing which do not satisfy these very stringent conditions Locke refuses to call 'knowledge': he uses instead the words 'belief', 'faith', 'judgement' or 'opinion' to refer to them. This is, of course, not in accordance with our present English usage. We do, indeed, demand a greater weight of evidence and have a correspondingly higher degree of certainty for those propositions which we are said to know, but we do not insist that our certainty should be absolute or that the propositions themselves should be incorrigible by further evidence. It would, in any case, be difficult to say when we were justified in saying that, in this usage of the word, we *know* a given proposition. I shall discuss this difficulty later

1. Intro. 2.　　　　　　　2. IV.16.3.

when we come to consider Locke's theory of knowledge in detail. For the present it is sufficient to remember that Locke's use of the words 'know' and 'knowledge' is restricted in this way.

By thus raising the nature of knowing as a problem, Locke was introducing a new point of view into European philosophy. And this point of view, for good or ill, has dominated philosophy since his time. This is not to say, of course, that previous philosophers had taken no account of knowledge. The Greek philosophers and the medieval scholastics after them had had plenty of useful things to say on the subject, but it had not been for them a *primary* problem. They had, in general, begun with other questions and had allowed their theory of knowledge to grow out of a general philosophy of nature. Locke was the first important philosopher to develop a suggestion implicit in the work of Descartes: that philosophy should begin with epistemology. He thought that a study of the human understanding and its functions would enable us to find out the sort of enquiries for which our minds are naturally fitted. If we could do this we could effect enormous economies of intellectual effort, by directing our minds only to those lines of enquiry which we know to lie within the capacity of the human intellect. 'If by this enquiry into the nature of the understanding, I can discover the powers thereof: how far they reach: to what things they are in any degree proportionate: and where they fail us, I suppose it may be of use to prevail with the busy mind of man to be more cautious in meddling with things exceeding its comprehension; to stop when it is at the utmost extent of its tether: and to sit down in a quiet ignorance of those things which, upon examination, are found to be beyond the reach of our capacities.'[1] If we fail to examine the capacities of our minds in this way, we are in danger, Locke thinks, of engaging in speculations which are far beyond those capacities. 'Thus men, extending their enquiries beyond their capacities, and letting their thoughts wander into those depths where they can find

1. Intro. 4.

no sure footing, it is no wonder that they raise questions and multiply disputes, which, never coming to any clear resolution, are proper only to continue and increase their doubts and confirm them at last in perfect scepticism.'[1]

It is, indeed, obvious enough that a great many of the points men dispute about, especially in subjects like religion, morals, politics, or philosophy, are never finally settled to everyone's satisfaction. They are argued afresh century after century and when we read to-day what the Greeks wrote on these subjects over two thousand years ago we realize how little progress has been made in settling them. The reason for the difficulty is easy enough to see in outline. Questions of scientific fact, like the cause of diphtheria, the distance of the moon from the earth, or the chemical composition of water can be settled by *observing* the relevant facts and, where possible, sifting them by *experiment* and making our findings exact by *measurement*. Where questions can be settled in this way, they are amenable to scientific treatment. Other factual matters may be questions of history which can be decided by consulting and comparing the relevant documents, inscriptions and so on. Questions in dispute in mathematics or logic, on the other hand, are settled by calculation, *i.e.* by reasoning according to accepted rules from generally accepted premises. But it is precisely the source of our difficulty in finding definite and final answers to disputed questions in religion, morals, politics, or philosophy that there does not seem to be any agreed procedure for finding the answer, such as we have in science, history, or mathematics. One cannot prove that God exists in the way that one proves that the duck-billed platypus exists, or that men are immortal in the way that we prove that the square root of 2 is an irrational number; or that representative government is better than tyranny in the way that we can show that one make of motor car is more economical than another. Now Locke wished to suggest that many questions of this type could not be answered, not because we do not know the right way to set about the problem but because they

1. Intro. 7.

lie altogether beyond the reach of the human understanding. Our minds are tools which are efficient for certain limited purposes, but if we try to use them for purposes for which they were not designed, we are bound to fail. Our minds can no more solve the mysteries of theology and metaphysics than our bodies can run a mile in two minutes. This, then, is his assumption, and he proposes to test it by an examination of the nature of the human mind. He hopes that the result of his examination will tell us what we may reasonably hope to know and what is altogether beyond our mental powers.

The method by which Locke approaches his problem will be made clear in subsequent chapters, and we need not discuss it in detail here. He himself calls it an 'historical plain method'. The old-fashioned use of the word 'historical' here is intended to convey that Locke's method is *descriptive* and gives a factual account of the functions of the mind and of its objects. In other words, he intends to deal with subjects which would nowadays be considered proper to psychology and therefore a matter for the scientist rather than for the philosopher. The border line between science and philosophy, as we know it to-day, was not clearly drawn in Locke's day and we should not look for twentieth-century distinctions in his writing. But though he does deal with some topics which belong to psychology, these are not the largest or the most important parts of the *Essay*. The deficiencies of untrained and casual observation and introspection are too obvious. The greater part of the *Essay* is not descriptive psychology at all but theory of knowledge or epistemology.

What is the 'theory of knowledge' and what sort of questions does it consider? The most important of them are included in the list given above of the questions which Locke wants to decide in the *Essay*. (1) What are the ways in which we come to know or believe? What, for example, are the respective places of sense perception, memory, and reasoning in the origins of our knowing? Are they equally important? (2) What sort of things can we know? We talk of knowing facts but also of believing false statements. What sort of thing is a false statement and what does it mean to say that a statement is true or false? We talk also of having ideas or concepts. What account are we to give of ideas or concepts? What are their different varieties and how are these varieties related to one another? (3) How many different types of statement or proposition are there? And what sort of evidence is appropriate to each type before the statement in question can be regarded as established with certainty or with a reasonable degree of probability? Consider, for example, the following four propositions: (*a*) It will rain in London on May 1st, 1960; (*b*) Smallpox is caused by a virus; (*c*) There are an infinite number of prime numbers; (*d*) Cruelty is evil. It is obvious that these are proved, where they are provable, by evidence of very different kinds. One observation will establish (*a*); a large number will be required for the second; and (*c*) could not be established by any number of observations, however large. It needs proof of quite a different kind.

All these questions and many others of the same type are discussed in the theory of knowledge. Clearly such questions are closely interconnected and, as is usual with philosophical questions, the answer we give to any one of them will affect and be affected by the answers we give to the others. It is clear also that the theory of knowledge has fairly close connexions with some parts of psychology. Psychology is the science which takes for its subject-matter human experience and human and animal behaviour. Thinking and knowing are features of our experience and affect our behaviour. Nevertheless, the interest of the psychologist in thinking and knowing is very different from that of the philosopher. The psychologist wants to study thought processes and their associated behaviour as they actually occur, and tries to describe and analyse them as features of the natural world. The epistemologist is concerned rather with the *standards* to which thinking and knowing ought to conform if they are to be valid and justifiable by reason. He is interested in what has been called, by Professor Carnap, the rational reconstruction of thinking.

Locke tries in the *Essay* to give a rational reconstruction, in this sense, of the nature of the human understanding and of the content and process of thinking. But because psychology, in his time, was not an independent science and was still treated by philosophers in so far as it was treated at all, he does not always distinguish clearly between psychology and epistemology.

This is unfortunate. It is never an objection to an epistemological statement that it does not conform with the actual processes of our thinking. But it is a valid ground of objection to a statement in psychology. Conversely it is not always a valid ground of objection to a psychological description of a mental process that the alleged process does not conform to the laws of logic; for our actual thought processes are often fragmentary, incoherent and illogical. But that a rational reconstruction of the nature of the mind and its functions should be logically inconsistent or should entail conclusions which contradict observed facts would be a ground for rejecting the reconstruction. Thus when we read Locke, it is not always perfectly clear what sort of criticism is appropriate as he does not always make it obvious what type of statement he is making.

There is a further difficulty against which Locke has not safeguarded his theory. It is easy for a sceptic to point out that the purpose of Locke's work, *as he states it*, is self-refuting. He was trying, in the phrase of a modern philosopher, to 'draw a limit to thinking' and in order to be sure that he really had drawn such a limit, he would have, as it were, to think on both sides of the boundary he had drawn. And in doing this he would, of course, overstep the very frontier which his theory declared to be impassable. However, this difficulty is not in practice a serious one for Locke. His actual procedure in indicating the boundaries of human knowledge is largely empirical in character. His conclusion is, therefore, not intended to be more than probable and draws no sharp line between what can be known and what cannot. It is more in the nature of a warning to proportion our convictions to the available evidence and to respect the limits of expression imposed by the deficiencies of language.

It should be noted also that Locke's pretensions were of the most modest kind. He did not suppose that the *Essay* was a positive contribution to knowledge but considered it rather as a piece of preliminary criticism which would help to ensure that the constructive efforts of others would not be wasted on insecure foundations. 'It is ambition enough to be employed as an under-labourer in clearing the ground a little, and removing some of the rubbish which lies in the way to knowledge.'[1]

The concluding chapter of the *Essay* is entitled *Of the Division of the Sciences* and Locke here sets out his views on the possible varieties of human knowledge. His reason for giving this statement at the end of the *Essay* rather than at the beginning is presumably to make it appear as the conclusion of his enquiry, though it is not, in fact, very closely related to the preceding argument. He divides the field of human knowledge into three sections: (*a*) 'The knowledge of things as they are in their own proper beings, their constitutions, properties and operations.' This Locke calls 'Natural Philosophy'. It includes knowledge of 'God himself, angels, spirits, bodies, and any of their affections as number, figure, etc.', *i.e.* what we should nowadays call the natural sciences together with psychology, natural theology, and mathematics. (*b*) 'Secondly, that which man himself ought to do, as a rational and voluntary agent, for the attainment of any end, especially happiness.' Locke is thinking chiefly of moral philosophy here though the category includes knowledge of ends of any kind and of the means whereby we can attain those ends. Part of this knowledge, as Locke recognizes, would not be knowledge of facts but of skills or techniques 'for the attainment of things good and useful'. (*c*) The third section is what Locke called the 'doctrine of signs', or, in the wide sense of the word, 'logic'. It is this 'doctrine of signs' with which Locke is concerned in the *Essay*. It is for him a study of the ways and means by

1. *Epistle to the Reader.*

which the other two kinds of knowledge are attained and communicated.

Signs may be of two kinds, *ideas* and *words*. 'For since the things the mind contemplates are none of them, besides itself, present to the understanding, it is necessary that something else as a sign or representation of the thing it considers, should be present to it : and these are ideas. And because the scene of ideas that makes one man's thoughts cannot be laid open to the immediate view of another ... signs of our ideas are also necessary.'[1] Our ideas are signs which represent to us a world which we can never know except indirectly through this medium. And, analogously, words represent to one man the ideas in the mind of another. Unfortunately Locke gives no clear account of what he conceives to be the nature of a sign. We can defer a discussion of Locke's theory of language until we come to deal with Book III of the *Essay*. But 'idea' is the key-word of the *Essay* and it is essential to get a preliminary understanding of the many different uses to which Locke puts it.

'Before I proceed on to what I have thought on this subject I must here in the entrance beg pardon of my reader for the frequent use of the word *idea*, which he will find in the following treatise. It being that term which, I think, serves best to stand for whatsoever is the *object* of the understanding when a man thinks, I have used it to express whatever is meant by *phantasms, notion, species,* or *whatever it is which the mind can be employed about in thinking*.'[2] This wide use of the term 'idea' was common in the philosophy of the seventeenth century. Descartes, who is largely responsible for the usage, had defined the term as 'all that is in our mind when we conceive a thing, in whatsoever manner we may conceive it'.[3] For the present, I am concerned only to point out the chief ambiguities of the word as it occurs in the *Essay*. In discussing these ambiguities it is important to distinguish between the diverse types of ideas and their common *function*. When I say that the word

1. IV.21.4.   2. Intro. 8.
3. Works, ed. Adam and Tannery, Vol. III, pp. 392-3, Letter 245.

'idea' is used ambiguously I mean that ideas may be of widely different kinds. Locke thought, however, that ideas of all these diverse types had a common function, namely, to serve as signs representing to the mind objects with which we can never be directly acquainted. He has consequently to speak, as Descartes did, of ideas being 'in the mind',[1] as well as being objects of the mind. This was a double mistake.

In the first place, a theory of knowledge which asserts that we can know the world only through the medium of certain ideas which have their natural habitat in the mind, as fishes have theirs in water, raises two notoriously awkward questions which have never been satisfactorily answered. (*a*) What does it mean to exist *in the mind*? (*b*) If we can never directly know anything but ideas, how can we ever come to know anything about the world, or its relation to our ideas? Of the second difficulty at least, Locke was aware, and tried, as we shall see, to find an answer for it. But the difficulty of finding in Locke's writings an unequivocal answer to the first question seriously tarnishes the clarity of his 'new way of ideas'. Descartes, from whom Locke inherited this unfortunate theory, had given a more explicit account. 'I hold that there is no more difference between the mind and its ideas than between a piece of wax and the diverse figures of which it is capable.'[2] Just as every piece of wax has always to have some shape or other, so no mind can ever be without an idea. Locke could not accept this account of the way ideas are in the mind as he did not believe, as Descartes did, that the notion of a mind without ideas is self-contradictory. Locke himself does not say anything more positive on the point than that he regards the phrase 'to be in the understanding' and 'to be understood' as equivalent.[3]

In the second place, some sorts of ideas are of a kind which are fitted to 'represent' the world to us and others are not. Locke does not make a clear catalogue of the different senses

1. II.8.7; II.13.1; II.2.2., etc.
2. Works, ed. Adam and Tannery, Vol. IV, p. 115, Letter 347.
3. I.1.5.

in which he uses the word 'idea' but the following are the most important.

(i) 'Idea' is used to mean what we should nowadays call *sense-datum* or *sensum*, or the contents of our sense experience. 'Whenever we see a colour we have a sensation of the colour, but the colour itself is a sense datum, not a sensation.'[1] Sense data are such objects of immediate awareness as coloured patches, noises, odours, feelings of heat or cold, twinges of pain, and so on.

(ii) If I look at and touch a table, I have ideas in sense (i) of brown, square, hard, smooth, and so on; these Locke would call 'simple ideas of sense'. But I have also a sense presentation of a physical object, viz. the table. And this too would be an idea, in another sense, which Locke would call a complex idea of a particular substance.

(iii) Images whether they occur in memory or in imagination, are a third kind of 'idea'. Locke's use of the word in this sense is confined chiefly to his discussion of memory and imagination.

(iv) He also uses the word to refer to characteristics or properties in a general sense which is not restricted to sense-qualities. He instances thinking, motion, gratitude, as examples of ideas in this sense as well as general sense properties like sweetness and hardness. (These must, of course, be carefully distinguished from ideas in sense (i).) In this usage 'idea' means 'general property', 'concept' or even 'meaning'.

(v) Locke has been accused by some of his critics of using the word in a further sense to mean not, as in the previous senses, the *object* of an act of knowledge but the act of knowing itself. I have been unable to find any unequivocal examples of this use of the word with the exception of what Locke calls ideas of reflection. But in these cases the act of perceiving something, for example, is itself supposed to be the object of a simultaneous act of introspection. It is called an idea in virtue of being an *object* of this further act of knowing and not because it is in itself such an act. It was a principle of Locke's

1. Bertrand Russell, *Problems of Philosophy*, p. 17.

theory of knowledge that we cannot know anything without being conscious that we do so; and since anything of which we are conscious is an idea, it would follow that all our acts of knowing of whatever kind are ideas. But they are ideas only because they are objects of our knowledge *as well as* acts of knowing. It is important to notice, however, that to use 'idea' to refer to an *act* of knowing of which we were *not* conscious would conflict with Locke's presuppositions. And anything, whether act or object, of which we are conscious is, by definition, an idea. Thus in a sense, Locke does hold that acts of cognition are ideas, but this sense does not involve the misleading confusion of the act of knowing with its object to which his critics have objected. This usage is, in fact, only a consequence of his presuppositions. (Of course, the analysis of cognition into acts and objects or contents is a controversial one and I shall discuss it more fully later.)

If we now return to the function of these different types of idea, it is easy to see that they cannot all represent the world to us in the same way. We shall see that Locke himself recognizes this to some extent in his doctrine of primary and secondary qualities. He says, for example, that ideas of colour are only the *effects* on our minds of certain physical properties of material things while ideas of shape or number really *resemble* the corresponding property in the material world. But there are differences which he does not notice. Images, for instance, represent to us not things but other ideas. A memory image is a more or less imperfect reinstatement in consciousness of *ideas* which we have previously experienced. Thus images, like words, are second-order signs; they represent other ideas which in turn represent things or properties in the world. Again, general concepts do not represent things in the same way as particular ideas. The relation between my visual image of a table and the table itself is intended by Locke to be a one-one relation like the relation between husbands and wives in a society where monogamy is practised. But my concept of dog, for instance, stands for all members of the class of dogs and the relation between the sign and what it refers to is, therefore, one-many, like the relations between a king and his subjects.

There is a further ambiguity which is of great importance, though it may seem at first sight to be a pedantic subtlety. Suppose someone holds out a book to you and says 'Have you seen this book?' He might mean 'have you seen this particular volume?' but he will more probably mean 'have you seen some copy or other of this book?' Thus a phrase like 'this book' or 'this map' may refer to a particular object, for example, the book I am now holding, or to the content or pattern common to a large number of books or maps. In ordinary conversational language such ambiguities hardly ever mislead us, but in philosophy where we are talking of ideas or signs and not of books or maps, they can give rise to serious mistakes. Philosophers have therefore invented special technical terms to mark the distinction. The particular individual object, word, sign, or idea is called a *token*; the pattern common to the tokens is called a *type*.[1] For example, there are three token-words 'the' in the preceding sentence, but only one type-word 'the'.

The word 'idea', as Locke uses it, is ambiguous in exactly the same way. An idea can either be a particular mental event like a twinge of toothache, a particular image, or the occurrence of a given concept, or it can be the content common to several such particular occurrences of sense data, images, or concepts. In the first sense of the word, one person cannot have the same idea in his mind on more than one occasion nor can two or more people ever have the same idea. In the second sense of the word, both of these things are possible.

Locke does not draw attention to this very important distinction or even appear to recognize it. Sometimes he talks of ideas in the sense of idea-tokens and sometimes in the sense of idea-types. When he talks of ideas as 'nothing but actual perceptions in the mind, which cease to be anything when there is no perception of them'[2] he is using the word in the first

1. 'Token' and 'type' were invented by the American philosopher, C. S. Peirce.   2. II.10.2.

sense. But when he speaks of 'names being supposed to stand *perpetually*[1] for the same ideas and the same ideas having *immutably*[1] the same habitudes one to another'[2] or recommends his readers to 'apply their words as near as may be to such ideas as common use has annexed them to'[3] he is clearly using the word in the second sense.

This is indeed the more crucial of the two senses. The possibility of memory and, with it, the possibility of any sort of coherent experience and knowledge depends on the existence of ideas in the sense of idea-types. But Locke's actual usage in this matter is variable and careless and we have to be careful not to be misled by it. We have to remember that there is still another sense in which ideas have a representative function; every idea-token represents its idea-type in a way analogous to the way in which any individual dog can represent to my mind the class of dogs. But for this function, ideas in their character of mental occurrents could not perform the other functions we have discussed. Locke does not make this point, but it is quite essential for his theory.

There is one other general property of ideas which we have still to note. This is that it is not possible to draw a distinction between ideas as they appear to us and as they really are. The importance of this property will be seen later when we come to discuss Locke's theory of sense perception. 'Let any idea be as it will,' says Locke, 'it can be no other but such as the mind perceives it to be.'[4] This presumably means that ideas have all the properties which they appear to have *and no others*. It follows, though Locke does not draw this consequence, that certain ideas, sense data and images, for example, may have *indeterminate* properties. A coloured patch seen in a brief glance or out of the corner of the eye may appear of uncertain shape or colour, a spotted surface may seem to have a large but indeterminate number of spots. This seemingly paradoxical consequence of Locke's theory has to be accepted. It would of course be contrary to ordinary usage to talk of physical

1. My italics.　　　　　　　2. IV.11.14.
3. III.11.11.　　　　　　　4. II.29.5.

objects having indeterminate properties; but when philosophers introduce a new terminology they are entitled to
prescribe the conventions of language which shall be followed
in making use of it. We may agree to say that ideas are always
as they appear to be and may therefore often have indeterminate properties.

Innate Knowledge

Book I of the *Essay* is an attack on the theory that certain sorts
of human knowledge, are innate or, in other words, not
acquired by the mind after it begins to exist or to be conscious,
but part of its initial endowment. This attack is a preliminary
to a statement of Locke's own theory that all the materials of
knowledge are derived from *experience*, and that though, at
birth, we all have certain *powers* of acquiring knowledge, our
minds are then 'white paper, void of all characters, without
any ideas'.[1] That this theory of innate ideas and principles
seems to us at the present day grotesque and absurd is due to
the fact that Locke's empirical outlook has become part of an
intellectual background which we tend to accept without
reflection. Whether the theory of innate knowledge was ever
held by a respectable thinker in quite the crude form in which
Locke attacks it, is an historical matter, and for our purposes
unimportant. He does not name any of his opponents except
Lord Herbert of Cherbury, and he is mentioned, as Locke
makes clear, as an afterthought and in order to provide some
specific examples of alleged innate principles. Scholars have
disputed whether Locke is here controverting Descartes and
his followers, contemporary scholasticism, or the Cambridge
Platonists. But for the purpose of understanding Locke's own
theory of knowledge we can neglect this historical nicety and
need only attend very briefly to the arguments which he offers
against innate knowledge. He divides these allegedly innate
principles into two classes: (*a*) speculative principles or self-
evident logical propositions. Locke gives as examples the so-

1. II.1.2.

called 'laws of thought', 'Whatever is, is' and 'It is impossible for the same thing to be and not to be'; (*b*) practical principles or rules of morality.

The main argument in favour of innate principles is that they are universally admitted to be valid. Locke has little difficulty in establishing two points. (i) Universal consent to a proposition, if it could be established, would not show that the proposition was innately known unless it could also be shown that the proposition could not come to be known in any other way. (ii) It is not possible to find a single proposition which does command universal assent. Locke points out that speculative principles cannot be grasped by children and feeble-minded persons and that, as regards moral principles, there are enormous divergences between the moral standards accepted in different times and places.

To escape these criticisms it is suggested that the principles are in the mind from birth but that we cannot come to know them until we reach a certain state of mental development. Locke replies that this can mean one of two things. (i) If it means merely that we have innate capacities for knowing certain truths, Locke admits the point but adds that almost any truth, including the most abstruse mathematical theorems, could be reckoned innate by this criterion. (ii) If, however, the doctrine of innate principles is taken to mean that there are certain mental contents present in the mind in embryonic form as part of its native equipment, Locke's reply is that the only evidence of an idea or proposition being in the mind is that it is actually understood. 'If truths can be printed on the understanding without being perceived, I can see no difference there can be between any truths the mind is *capable* of knowing in respect of their original: they must all be innate or all adventitious: in vain shall a man go about to distinguish them.'[1] He himself intends to show that experience is the source of all our knowledge. Book II of the *Essay*, which is the longest and is, historically, the most influential, is occupied with this topic.

1. I.1.5.

CHAPTER THREE

Ideas and Experience

LOCKE is often spoken of, in histories of philosophy, as the founder of the empiricist tradition in British philosophy. The term 'empiricism' has usually been taken to refer to philosophical theories which say that the materials of human knowledge are to be found only in human experience and that, as a consequence of this, we can never have any knowledge of what lies outside the bounds of human experience. It is clear, however, that a definition of this kind is vague until we know how the term 'human experience' is to be interpreted. In Book II of the *Essay* Locke tries to give a systematic account of his own empiricist theory of knowledge.

His arguments in Book I have been designed to prove that none of our ideas are innate. He now brings forward the positive side of his theory and proposes to show 'whence the understanding may get all the ideas it has.'[1] If he can account for all the varieties of human knowledge without appealing to the existence of 'innate ideas' he will clearly deprive the supporters of innate ideas of any excuse for their fantastic theories. 'It is past doubt', he says, 'that men have in their minds several ideas, – such as are those expressed by the words *whiteness, hardness, sweetness, thinking, motion, man, elephant, army, drunkenness* and others. It is in the first place then to be enquired, how he comes by them.'[2] He is asking here how we acquire the ideas which are the materials of our knowledge. 'Let us then suppose the mind to be, as we say, white paper, void of all characters, without any ideas; how comes it to be furnished?'[3]

Locke is asking for the conditions in which one mind, *A*, has a certain idea, *x*, and another mind, *B*, does not have the same idea. And to this question he answers that experience is the source of the materials of our knowledge and that human

1. II.1.1.   2. *Ibid.*   3. II.1.2.

experience is of two kinds. 'Our observation, employed either about external sensible objects, or about the internal operations of our own minds, perceived and reflected on by ourselves, is that which supplies our understandings with all the *materials* of thinking. These two are the fountains of knowledge, from which all the ideas we have, or can naturally have, do spring.'[1] These two sources of the materials of knowledge Locke calls respectively *sensation and reflection*. It should be noted in passing that when Locke says that the mind is 'void of all characters' he means by this phrase 'without any positive content' in the way that a mirror might be said to be 'void of all characters' when it is in the dark and reflecting nothing. The phrases 'void of all characters' and 'without any ideas' should be taken as equivalent and not as supplementary. He does not want to assert that the mind has no positive characters in the sense of having no characteristic functions or activities. On the contrary, such mental activities take an important place in the development of his theory.

Locke does not have a great deal to say about the nature of the two sources of our ideas, sensation and reflection, and in the light of modern psychological knowledge it is easy to point out defects in his account. But these defects of detail do not invalidate the general theory. He wished to maintain that what we might call the 'raw materials' of knowledge can only come from one or other of these two sources. He would admit that these raw materials, the ideas which we get through our senses and through introspecting our own mental happenings, may be worked up by the mind into many complex forms. It may be that the final products of experience when worked on by a developed human mind will no more resemble the ideas of sensation and reflection from which they originated than a motor car will resemble the original steel, copper, rubber, cellulose, etc., from which it was constructed. But in the one case, as in the other, the process of manufacture, so to speak, has not created any new materials: it has merely taken the original materials and given them a new shape and order. As

1. II.1.2.

a matter of fact, Locke did not, as we shall see, give sufficient attention to these 'processes of manufacture' by which the original raw materials of knowledge are worked on by the mind. This has led some of his critics to suggest that he believed that human experience was a sort of mosaic in which the individual pieces were ideas of sensation or reflection or that our experience was built up out of ideas of sensation and reflection as a wall is built up out of bricks and mortar. These critics have pointed out that the findings of psychology (or even of commonsense) give no warrant for such a description of experience. The truth is quite different. Instead of the human mind being presented piecemeal with single ideas which it then works up into a pattern, it is actually presented with what the American psychologist, William James, called a 'blooming, buzzing confusion' which it then proceeds to analyse and reduce to order.

All this is true but it is not a criticism of Locke. He certainly talks of the materials of our knowledge being given to us in sensation and reflection and tries to give a catalogue of those materials and show how they can both account for all the varieties of human knowledge and prescribe its limits. But in doing all this he is talking not as a psychologist but as a philosopher. He is not trying to describe the actual processes by which knowledge originates and develops in human minds. He is merely trying to give a rational reconstruction of the process of knowing, to distinguish the various elements involved in it and to trace them to their origins in experience. And when he insists on experience as the sole source of the materials of knowledge, he is drawing our attention to a fact that many philosophers have overlooked, namely, that the mind may analyse, mix, break down, build up, sort, and order the materials given in sensation and reflection, *but cannot add any new materials*. 'All those sublime thoughts which tower above the clouds and reach as high as heaven itself, take their rise and footing here: in all that great extent wherein the mind wanders, in those remote speculations it may seem to be elevated with, it stirs not one jot beyond those ideas which *sense* or *reflection* have offered for its contemplation.'[1] This statement can be taken as a summary of Locke's empiricism. Let us see how he elaborates it.

As to *sensation*, Locke explains that external objects affect our sense organs in various ways and our senses thereupon 'convey into the mind' what produces the perceptions there. In this way 'we come by those *ideas* we have of *yellow, white, heat, cold, soft, hard, bitter, sweet* and all those which we call sensible qualities'.[2]

Locke does not claim that his catalogue of ideas of sensation is complete. It includes among 'ideas' of sensation only those which are occasioned by the operation of external physical objects on our sense organs. Sensations of movement of joints or tensions of muscles and tendons, organic sensations like nausea, vertigo, etc., are quite ignored. And yet these are by no means unimportant sources of 'ideas'.

The inadequacy of Locke's account of sensation and the vagueness with which he phrases it are no doubt due largely to the deficiencies of seventeenth-century psychology. He has already excused himself in the introduction to the *Essay* from considering what we should nowadays call the physiology of the senses. 'I shall not at present meddle with the physical consideration of the mind; or trouble myself to examine wherein its essence consists; or by what motions of our spirits or alterations of our bodies we come to have any *sensation* by our organs or any *ideas* in our understandings.'[3] This caution is in keeping with his usual good sense. No physiology at all is better than bad physiology, especially as a prelude to a theory of knowledge. Moreover he did not suppose that his knowledge of physiology, such as it was, could throw any light on the process of sensation, in so far as it interests philosophers. 'Impressions made on the retina by rays of light, I think I understand; and motions from thence continued to the brain may be conceived; and that these produce ideas in our mind I am persuaded but in a manner to me incomprehensible. This I can resolve only into the good pleasure of God whose

1. II.1.24.   2. II.1.3.   3. Intro. 2.

44

ways are past finding out.'[1] Nevertheless he cannot abstain from vague talk of our senses (*i.e.* our sense organs) 'conveying into the mind' from external objects the causes of our sensations. Phrases of this type may be regarded either as a loose way of referring to the physiological mechanism of sensation or else as implying that our ideas are to be regarded as the mental effects of unknown physical causes. And as we shall see, this was indeed a part of Locke's theory. Nevertheless, in spite of some obvious omissions, his main contention is clear enough. We can receive information about the world outside us only by means of our senses.

The other of the two sources of our simple ideas Locke calls 'reflection'. We should nowadays call it 'introspection'. He defines reflection as 'the perception of the operations of our own mind within us as it is employed about the ideas it has got', or 'that notice which the mind takes of its own operations and the manner of them'.[2] Examples of the ideas furnished by reflection are 'perception, doubting, believing, reasoning, knowing, willing and all the different actings of our own minds'. And he explains that 'operations' and 'actings' should be taken in a wide sense to include not only *actions* of the mind but also 'some sort of passions arising sometimes from them, such as the satisfaction or uneasiness arising from any thought.'[3] Though Locke thinks it is very like sensation and might properly be called 'internal sense', this mode of cognition differs from sensation in two ways: (i) it is not directly stimulated by objects external to us; (ii) it is a secondary mode of cognition in so far as it cannot occur except as an accessory to other mental activities. It should also be noticed that while the only function of sensation is to provide the mind with material, the materials of reflection are not our acts of sense perception alone but all mental states and operations, cognitive, volitional, and emotional alike. And it follows, I think, that since we can become aware that we are reflecting, just as we can become aware that we are seeing a blue patch or feeling a pain, the act of reflection can become

1. *Examination of Malebranche* 10.   2. II.1.4.   3. *Ibid.*

its own content. But Locke does not comment on this point.

So far then Locke sums up his position as follows: 'The understanding seems to me not to have the least glimmering of any ideas which it doth not receive from one of these two. *External objects* furnish the mind with the ideas of sensible qualities, which are all those different perceptions they produce in us; and the *mind* furnishes the understanding with ideas of its own operations.'[1] He goes on to add that anyone who examines his own mental furniture will find that all his ideas can be traced back to their origins in these two sources, 'though perhaps, with infinite variety compounded and enlarged by the understanding as we shall see hereafter.'[2] This qualification seems to indicate that Locke was aware that his empiricism needed certain further refinements to make it entirely plausible. Nevertheless, given those refinements, Locke is sure of his conclusion.

So far Locke's account of the origins of human knowledge has introduced two factors: (*a*) the mind or 'understanding' and (*b*) the mind's objects, contents, or material which he calls 'ideas'. The rest of Book II of the *Essay* is devoted to expanding and clarifying this preliminary account. By far the greater part of the book is spent in analysing and classifying 'ideas'. In spite of the title of the *Essay*, the nature and operations of the mind or understanding are given rather a cursory and incidental treatment. I shall first of all follow Locke's account of 'ideas' and then examine his views on the nature and function of the understanding.

In discussing the concept of 'idea' in the previous chapter, we saw that there are two main questions which we may reasonably expect Locke to answer for us. (i) How many different *kinds* of ideas do we find in experience and how are these different kinds related to one another? (ii) What is the *function* of these ideas? Let us consider Locke's answer to these two questions in order.

1. II.1.5.   2. *Ibid.*

The Classification of Ideas

We saw above that Locke's appeal to introspection in support of his theory has to be made more plausible by showing in detail how the more esoteric of our mental contents can be shown to take their rise from sensation and reflection alone. He therefore proceeds to analyse and classify ideas, and to show how the different classes are related. The first distinction he makes is between *simple* and *complex* ideas.

The criterion of the simplicity of an idea is that it is uncompounded, of one uniform character 'and is not distinguishable into different ideas'.[1] It is not at all clear how this criterion is to be applied in individual cases. The examples Locke offers here of simple ideas of sensation are the coldness and hardness of a piece of ice, the whiteness of a lily, the smell of a lily, the smell of a rose, or the taste of sugar. But even simple sense data such as these, as they occur in every-day experience, rarely present one uniform character indistinguishable into parts which differ sensibly one from another, be it ever so slightly. And even if we take a coloured patch in which no part is sensibly different in hue from any other part, such a sense datum is clearly not 'uncompounded' in an unqualified sense. It is, for example, made up of smaller patches, *i.e.* it is spatially compounded. Moreover, in order to be sensed at all, it must be temporally extended for a small, but measurable minimum period. Would those conditions disqualify sense data from being 'simple ideas' in Locke's sense? If so, this would mean that the only simple ideas, in a strict sense, would be, for example, the smallest uniform colour patch which is visible and others of this kind. But it is fairly certain that Locke never considered this question.

In fact, he invokes elsewhere quite a different test for the 'simplicity' of an idea. Ideas are simple in whose reception 'the understanding is merely passive; and whether or no it will have these beginnings and, as it were, materials of knowledge, is not in its own power'.[2] Indeed, the phrase 'simple idea' is used in

1. II.2.1.   2. II.1.25.

the *Essay* in no less than four quite different senses: (i) the smallest unit or 'atom' of experience; (ii) a single sense quality like blue, square or sweet; (iii) what is given to the mind in experience, in contrast to what is constructed by the mind from the material provided by sensation and reflection; (iv) it sometimes means a *determinable* quality like 'coloured' or 'shaped' in contrast to a *determinate* quality like 'this precise shade of crimson' or 'circular'. (This last meaning is chiefly obvious in his account of ideas of reflection.) Such an ambiguity is not, of course, fatal to his account of simple and complex ideas although the fact that he was not clear that the phrase 'simple idea' was ambiguous does make his account difficult to follow.

In practice, it is easier not to try to extract a perfectly clear description of simple ideas from Locke's account. Instead, we can characterize them negatively as ideas which are not complex. As we shall see, he gives a much more useful account of complex ideas.

Before he goes on to classify simple ideas and examine them in some detail, he adds that the understanding 'has the power to repeat, compare and unite them, even to an almost infinite variety, and so can make at pleasure new complex ideas. But it is not in the power of the most exalted wit or enlarged understanding by any quickness or variety of thought to *invent* or *frame* one new simple idea in the mind not taken in by the ways before mentioned'.[1] He supports this contention by challenging anyone who disagrees with him to frame such a new simple idea for himself. 'When he can do this, I will also conclude that a blind man hath ideas of colours and a deaf man true distinct notions of sounds.'[2] It is difficult to be sure whether Locke is making a factual assertion here or merely making an analytic statement which cannot be disputed on the basis of the definitions he has laid down. If he is denying that we can ever have a sensory image involving some simple sense quality unless we have previously experienced an instance of the quality, he is making a factual assertion. But

1. II.2.2.   2. *Ibid.*

the assertion is one which it would clearly be very difficult in practice ever to verify. When Hume dealt with the same question some years later, he was forced to admit that there might be some exceptions to the rule. Suppose, he says, a man who has become acquainted with every shade of blue but one; and suppose specimens of all the shades he has met with to be placed before him ranged in order from the deepest to the lightest. Then (*a*) the man 'will perceive a blank where that shade is wanting'; and (*b*) 'he will be able from his own imagination to supply this deficiency'.[1] However this concession of Hume's is nothing more than a plausible conjecture. What we need is some reliable evidence from the psychologist, and this is not available.

Clearly it is not self-contradictory to say that I have visual images of colours I have never seen, auditory images of sounds I have never heard and so on, unless I were to allege that such images were memory-images. And then of course the contention would be true but trivial, for a memory-image is defined in terms of a previous experience. I cannot have a true memory of something I have never experienced. It is improbable that Locke meant no more than this. However, we may come by a qualitatively fresh sense datum in many ways, and not only by the effect of physical objects acting on our sense organs. I might have a certain sensation for the first time in a dream or through some unusual condition of the central nervous system; and in fact I can myself recall a peculiar sensation which I experience only during a certain type of nightmare. What would have been Locke's reply if an opponent had offered him cases of this sort in reply to his challenge? He could hardly have refused to accept such evidence. Yet if he were willing to widen his definition of sensation to include these cases, his contention would then become trivial. The difference between sensation and imagination becomes so tenuous and ill-defined in such borderline cases that Locke would in fact come near to asserting no more than the truism that I cannot experience an idea a

1. Hume, *Treatise*, I.i.i.

second time unless I have also experienced it for the first time.

He goes on to discuss the varieties of simple ideas in more detail and arranges them according to their origins in four classes: (1) The first includes those we acquire through one sense only like colours, sounds, smells, etc.; (2) the second class consists of those we acquire through more than one sense such as space or extension, shape and motion which come to us through both sight and touch; (3) ideas arising from reflection only form the third class. Simple ideas of reflection 'are the operations of the mind about its other ideas.'[1] Locke here divides the actions of the mind under two main heads, perception or thinking and volition or willing. 'The power of thinking is called the *Understanding* and the power of volition is called the *Will* and these two powers or abilities in the mind; are denominated faculties.'[2] These two ideas, then, thinking and willing, are the simple ideas of reflection and all the other ideas of reflection are complex, being modes of these. For the present Locke defers discussion of these modes. (4) The fourth class of simple ideas 'convey themselves into the mind by all the ways of sensation and reflection: viz., pleasure or delight, and its opposite, pain or uneasiness; power; existence; unity.'[3] To these he added the idea of succession. This fourth class is a surprisingly heterogeneous collection of concepts and it is difficult to believe that Locke considered that these were all simple ideas, even in the ambiguous sense in which he used the phrase. He explains that we do not get these ideas by themselves but, as it were, annexed to the other ideas which we receive by sensation or reflection. Existence and unity, for example, are 'suggested to the understanding by every object without and every idea within'.[4] The idea of succession arises from observation of what passes in our own minds and the idea of power from the effects of our volitions or from observation of cause and effect in nature. Pleasure and pain or 'delight and uneasiness' are said to 'join themselves to almost all our ideas both of sensation and reflection'.[5]

1. II.6.1.   2. II.6.   3. II.7.1
4. II.7.7.   5. II.7.2.

By pleasure and pain Locke is here referring not to physically pleasurable or painful sensations like the taste of chocolate or a twinge of toothache. Aches and pains were among the organic sensations which, as we have seen, Locke took no explicit account of. He is referring to what the psychologists nowadays call the hedonic tone of our experiences which can be roughly measured on a scale ranging from very pleasant through mildly pleasant, neutral, mildly unpleasant to very unpleasant. Locke considers that it is a biological necessity that our experiences should be accompanied by some degree of hedonic tone. Man would be otherwise 'a very idle unactive creature and pass his time only in a lazy, lethargic dream'.[1] Pleasure and pain are contrivances of the Deity to keep men both alert and pious; 'that we, finding imperfection, dissatisfaction and want of complete happiness in all the enjoyments which the creatures can afford us might be led to seek it in the enjoyment of Him with whom there is fullness of joy and at whose right hand are pleasures for evermore.'[2]

Complex Ideas

We are now in a position to examine Locke's doctrine of complex ideas of sensation. Ideas of reflection are best considered in discussing his theory of the understanding. 'We have hitherto considered those ideas in the reception whereof the mind is only passive.'[3] We now go on to consider those ideas which are compounded by the mind from this elementary material. In the chapter[4] in which he introduces this distinction he offers what is, in effect, a double classification of complex ideas. The original classification set out in the first edition of the *Essay* is made in terms of the various types of *object* for which the ideas stand. Complex ideas can be exhaustively divided into modes, substances, and relations. Substances are 'such combinations of simple ideas as are taken to represent distinct *particular* things subsisting by themselves'[5] such as

1. II.7.3.   2. II.7.5.   3. II.12.1.
4 II.12.   5. II.12.6.

man or lead. Modes, on the other hand, are 'complex ideas which, however compounded, contain not in them the supposition of subsisting by themselves but are considered as dependences on, or affections of substances; such as are the ideas signified by the words triangle, gratitude, murder, etc.'[1] This distinction, so far, is merely a variation of the uncritical commonsense distinction between things and their properties. As to relations, he merely says vaguely that the idea of relation 'consists in the consideration and comparing one idea with another',[2] and gives no examples.

But in the fourth edition of the *Essay* he added, without amending his previous remarks, a classification based on the activities of our minds. Here he says that complex ideas result from the mental operation of *combining* several simple ideas into one; ideas of relation are the product of the mind's power of *comparing* our ideas, simple or complex, with one another; while general ideas are the product of the operation of *abstraction* in which the mind separates ideas from all other ideas that accompany them in their real existence.[3]

Here he seems to be revising his classification of complex ideas to exclude relations and to add a new class of ideas, general ideas or universals. Clearly these two accounts are incompatible as they stand. The second represents his later opinions on the matter, but, of course, the rest of the *Essay* is written largely in terms of the account given in the first edition. Nevertheless in examining the remainder of Book II we should bear in mind his second thoughts on the matter. It will help to explain some of the inconsistencies which occur in working out the consequences of his empiricism. These consequences will become clearer as we consider his account of complex ideas in detail.

Modes

Modes are sub-divided into simple and complex. 'First. There are some which are only variations or different combinations

1. II.12.4.　　　　2. II.12.7.　　　　3. II.12.1.

of the same simple idea, without the mixture of any other ; – as a dozen or score; which are nothing but the ideas of so many distinct units added together, and these I call *simple modes* as being contained within the bounds of one simple idea. Secondly. There are others compounded of simple ideas, of several kinds, put together to make one complex one; v.g., beauty, consisting of a certain composition of colour and figure, causing delight to the beholder; theft, which being the concealed change of the possession of anything, without the consent of the proprietor, contains, as is visible, a combination of several ideas of several kinds: and those I call *mixed modes*.'[1]

Locke's discussion of simple modes is important because the ideas of space, time, number, and infinity are all classed as simple modes. He conceives these modes as originating from their corresponding simple ideas through the mental operation of 'enlarging', *i.e.* putting together several ideas *of the same kind* and describing them as one idea. What does Locke mean here by the phrase 'ideas of the same kind' ? The answer to this question is best given by examining the examples he offers.

We can see the main trend of his theory by examining the account he gives of the origins of our ideas of space, time, number, and infinity. It is not difficult to find objections to the details of his account, but the main point of it is as follows. We all become acquainted in the ordinary ways of sensation and reflection with small bits of space and with small bits of time. Our visual and tactual sense data, for example, are extended in space and they endure for short periods of time. Once a human mind has had this experience, it can, in Locke's phrase, 'enlarge' it or mentally add together the individual extensions and durations we meet with, and thus build up in imagination a space extending indefinitely beyond that which we experience and a time extending indefinitely before and after the time we experience. Locke calls this idea of one common space in which the whole universe is extended 'expansion' and he reserves the word 'space' for the simple ideas given to us in sense experience from which our complex idea of 'expansion'

1. II.12.5.

is built up. He adds that the other simple modes of space such as 'place' and 'distance' are built up in a similar way and that modes of duration such as 'time' and 'eternity' are constructed likewise from the simple ideas of succession and duration. Ideas of number, both finite and infinite, are acquired by the same process. The idea of unity or 'one' is one of the simple ideas which are suggested to the mind 'by all the ways of sensation and reflection'. And once the mind is familiar with the idea 'by repeating this idea in our minds and adding the repetitions together, we come by the *complex* ideas of the *modes* of it. Thus by adding one to one, we have the complex idea of a couple; by putting twelve units together we have the complex idea of a dozen; and so of a score or a million or any other number'.[1]

An important part of Locke's task in attempting to justify his empirical principles is to show how ideas which are, at first sight, not derived from sensation and reflection can be proved to be so. Of these the idea of infinity is one of the most important. Locke does not consider here the infinity of God, who is 'incomprehensibly infinite'. Since the matter is admitted by the pious and orthodox to be incomprehensible, he is excused from debating this troublesome question.

Infinity, so far as it can be intelligibly discussed, is for him a quantitative matter. 'Finite and infinite seem to me to be looked upon by the mind as the modes of quantity and to be attributed primarily in their first designation only to those things which have parts and are capable of increase or diminution by the addition or subtraction of any the least part; and such are the ideas of space, duration and number.'[2] He points out that qualitative concepts like colour cannot be classified as either finite or infinite, because the mental operation of 'enlarging' or indefinitely repeating ideas in imagination cannot be applied to such concepts to produce new complex ideas. But he does not discuss the important question of the relevant differences between quantitative and qualitative concepts in virtue of which only quantitative concepts possess

1. II.16.2.   2. II.17.1.

these additive properties. What Locke is really concerned with here is the notion of infinite numbers, for space and time are infinite, if at all, only in a derivative sense; viz. they are measurable in terms of numbered units. Thus our idea of infinity 'is nothing but the infinity of number applied to determinate parts of which we have in our minds the distinct ideas'.[1]

Locke did not succeed in giving a correct definition of the phrase 'infinite number'. This was a mathematical discovery which was not made until the nineteenth century. But we can put to his credit (a) that he saw that the word 'infinite' has no meaning except as applied to numbers or to what can be numerically measured like space and time; (b) that the idea of infinity is not non-empirical merely because we can never actually experience an infinite manifold as infinite, or count an infinite number. The definition of an infinite number which is current in modern mathematics confirms Locke's insight on this point.

The main defect of his account of simple modes when we examine it in detail is that the mental operations of 'compounding' and 'enlarging' the simple ideas given in experience are not adequate to explain the origin of the complex ideas of space, time, and number which we actually possess. He gives no more than the vaguest description of these mental processes. From what he does say, it appears that to 'compound' or 'enlarge' our simple ideas is to repeat and extend them in imagination. But it is clear that the formation of complex ideas is a much more subtle and intricate affair than this and calls for other processes: for example, the power to analyse our concepts, to abstract, to unify several ideas into one, to apprehend a complex idea as a unity and so on. But this is an example rather of the defects of Locke's psychology than of his theory of knowledge. He is, in general, much better in his critical analysis of knowledge than in his descriptions of actual mental processes.

1. II.17.10.

JOHN LOCKE

Mixed Modes

The chapter on 'mixed modes' in Book II is only a preliminary
account and Locke reserves most of the important things he
has to say about them for his discussion of the relation
between ideas and language in Book III. Mixed modes are
complex ideas consisting of more than one idea not 'of the
same kind'. They are distinguished from ideas of substance
in that it is a necessary condition for an idea of substance that
it should have a prototype in nature. Mixed modes, on the
other hand, are 'such combinations of simple ideas as are not
looked upon to be characteristical marks of any real beings
that have a steady existence but scattered and independent
ideas put together by the mind'.[1] His ordinary examples of
mixed modes are moral or legal terms: 'obligation', 'drunkenness', 'a lie', 'murder', etc. Unlike simple modes, they are the
result of mental *activity*. Any group of simple ideas of different
kinds, provided that they are mutually compatible, can be a
mixed mode. It may happen that it has a counterpart in nature
or it may not. The unity of the idea is purely artificial and,
indeed, arbitrary. 'It has its unity from an act of the mind,
combining those several simple ideas together and considering
them as one complex one, consisting of those parts; and the
mark of this union or that which is looked on generally to
complete it, is one *name* given to that combination.'[2] There is
thus an unlimited possible number of mixed modes consisting
of all the possible combinations of simple ideas which are not
'of the same kind'. Which of these possibilities we select for
notice and mark with a name depends on our interests and
what we desire to communicate to our fellows. There are
three sources of our ideas of mixed modes: (1) observation
and experience; (2) the voluntary putting together of simple
ideas; (3) verbal explication of our concepts. This is, Locke
thinks, the most usual way. But we can defer a closer examination of this doctrine until we consider Locke's theory of
language.

1. II.22.1.   2. II.22.4.

Relations

What is a relation? At the level of commonsense we can best answer this question by giving examples. If I look at my table with a book lying on it, I see two things or substances, a book and a table, related by the spatial relation 'on'. 'To the left of', 'between', 'to the north of' are all spatial relations; 'before' and 'after' are relations of time; 'greater than' and 'less than' are relations of quantity. And we could go on taking examples endlessly. Perhaps the best way of getting a rough general idea of the concept of relation is by considering relations as adjectives or predicates which qualify more than one subject. I can say 'this book is blue' because 'blue' is an adjective referring to a property which is capable of qualifying one thing without reference to any other thing. But it would not make sense to say 'this book is between' because the word 'between' needs at least *three* nouns to give it sense: 'the *book* is between the *pen* and the *ashtray*'. Relations are features of the world which are very easily neglected by commonsense, perhaps because the words which usually express them, prepositions and transitive verbs, are not such obviously important and interesting words as the nouns and adjectives which, in general, refer to things and their qualities. But, for philosophy, they are very important features of the world indeed and no philosopher can afford to neglect them. No adequate philosophical account of relations was given until they became a topic of importance in symbolic logic within the last hundred years. We cannot therefore expect that Locke's account of relations will be entirely satisfactory; we can however reasonably ask that he shall show how our ideas of relation can be derived from sensation and reflection.

Locke gives his general account of ideas of relation in chapters 25–8 of Book II after he has dealt with our ideas of substances. It is however convenient to consider his doctrine of relations before we examine his views on substance as his doctrine of relations throws some light on this important question. His views of relations were, in fact, in a great muddle, but it is important, nevertheless, to disentangle them as far as possible as the concept of relation is the key-concept of the last book of the *Essay* where he tries to account for knowledge in terms of relations between ideas.

It was pointed out in discussing Locke's classification of ideas that there is an important inconsistency between the first and the fourth editions of the *Essay*. In the first edition where ideas are considered without reference to their psychological origins, relations are classified as one of the three varieties of complex ideas co-ordinate with modes and substances. In the fourth edition where he is considering ideas with reference to the mental operations by which they are generated, relations form a class by themselves and are said to be causally dependent on the mental operation of 'comparing'. And it is more charitable and more just to Locke to treat what he has to say about relations as far as possible in the light of his second thoughts on the subject. The implausibility of treating relations as complex ideas is only too patent. The difficulty is then to preserve Locke's consistency as an empiricist. Is it possible to derive ideas of relation from our experiences in sensation or reflection?

It is clear, I think, that Locke was himself worried on this point, but thought that he was able to meet the difficulty: 'I shall now proceed to show, in some instances, how all the ideas we have of relation are made up as the others are only of simple ideas; and that they all, how refined or remote from sense soever they seem, terminate at last in simple ideas.'[1] But it is not difficult to notice the ambiguity in the phrases Locke uses here. The way in which relations 'terminate in' simple ideas is entirely different from the way in which other complex ideas do so. Modes and substances 'terminate in' simple ideas in the sense that they can be *analysed into* such simple ideas. Similarly modes and substances are 'made up out of', are 'derived from' or 'take their beginning from' simple ideas in the straightforward sense that they are *constructed out* of them. But it is quite obvious from Locke's analysis that these phrases

1. II.25.11.

have a new meaning when he applies them to relations. They have in fact *two* new meanings, one direct and one indirect. To say that relations 'terminate in' simple ideas may mean (*a*) merely that the related terms *are* simple ideas or (*b*) that the related terms are complex ideas which themselves 'terminate in' simple ideas in the first sense of the phrase. An example of (*a*) might be two twinges of toothache related by the relation of 'earlier than' or 'more intense than' or something of the sort. Examples of (*b*) are much more common: 'father of', 'older than', 'north of' or any relation which can hold between two or more modes or substances.

The main instance of relation which Locke takes for analysis is the relation of cause and effect. But this relation is important in its own right and I shall defer discussion of it to another occasion. He also lists a number of other sorts of relation: (1) 'proportional' relations of degree, 'like to', 'bigger than'; (2) 'natural' relations of consanguinity like 'father of', etc.; (3) 'instituted' or 'voluntary' relations like that of a general to his army; and (4) 'moral' relations of human actions to a rule or standard. But here Locke is merely drawing attention to some of the more important types of relation and this is not a complete classification. It is, he thinks, not possible to make such a classification of the varieties of relation 'which is so various and the occasions of it so many (as many as there can be of comparing things one to another) that it is not very easy to reduce it to rules or under just heads'.[1] Moreover he cannot find any way of classifying his notions of relation by analysis and ends by confessing that 'we have for the most part, if not always, as clear a notion of the relation as we have of those simple ideas wherein it is founded'.[2]

The upshot of Locke's account of ideas of relation is no more than this: We derive our ideas of relation from the mental act of comparing other ideas, simple or complex. It is natural to the understanding to 'look beyond' its immediate object 'to see how it stands in conformity to any other'.[3] Any comparison of two ideas in this way can give rise to the idea

1. II.28.17.   2. II.28.19.   3. II.25.1.

of a relation. Nevertheless this idea is not 'contained in the real existence of things, but something extraneous and super-induced'.[1]

There are three obvious and important questions we would like to ask about this account. (1) Does the mind come to know relations between ideas in the way that it comes to know general principles, viz.: by observing instances and grasping the principle which the instances exemplify?[2] If so, how is this process to be accounted for in terms of Locke's psychology? (2) Does Locke mean by the phrase 'extraneous and super-induced' that relations have a mental existence only with no objective counterpart in the things related? (He does talk, perhaps in an unguarded moment, of relations 'having no other reality but what they have in the minds of men'.[3]) (3) If this is so, are we to draw any distinction between 'relations' and 'ideas of relation'? And if not, is there not a radical difference between relations and other sorts of ideas? The answers to these questions are not easy and in any case it is best to postpone further discussion until we consider Locke's account of the nature of knowledge.

There are, moreover, certain relations, those of identity and causality, which raise important philosophical problems and I shall therefore discuss them separately in the following chapters. It is convenient to discuss causality in connexion with the concept of ideas of substances. Locke's treatment of substance is one of the most important and influential parts of the *Essay* and it must be deferred to the next chapter.

The Functions of Ideas

We have already seen that Locke regards ideas as *signs* which represent to us something other than themselves. This representative function of ideas is one of the most characteristic features of his theory of knowledge and also one of its weaknesses. He was himself aware of some of the weaknesses and, as we shall see, tried to make them good. For the present, it is

1. II.25.8. 2. See Chapter 8 below. 3. II.30.4.

important to make clear the essential features of his 'representative' theory of knowledge. The main point of the theory may be expressed by saying that the process of knowing involves not *two* factors, a mind and the object known by the mind, but *three*, a mind, the object, and the idea of the object. Such a theory is clearly more complicated and less obvious to commonsense than the theories which say that knowing consists in a relationship between two factors only, the mind and the object which the mind knows. The first step in understanding the theory is therefore to grasp the reasons which have led many philosophers to adopt it. (It is not without defenders even at the present day.)

Locke himself did not originate the theory and the fact that he does not give any detailed defence of it seems to indicate that he considered it to be sufficiently obvious to be accepted without much proof. It was, in fact, implicit in the philosophical assumptions of the physicists of his day. Descartes had adopted it and Galileo, the great founder of modern physical science, had stated it quite explicitly. It had moreover a long history. Versions of the theory were current in the Middle Ages and St Augustine, writing in the fifth century, took over a variant of it from the Greek philosopher, Plotinus.[1] And going back still further in the history of philosophy, we can find the origins of the theory in the teachings of the Greek atomists in the fifth century B.C.

A little critical reflection on the facts of our sense experience will immediately provide reasons in favour of the representative theory of sense perception, which is a special case of the representative theory of knowledge. I look at a penny from several different points of view. From one it appears circular, from others elliptical. Held close to my eye, it will appear larger than the door of my room; held at arm's length, it occupies not a hundredth part of the apparent area of the door. Now I have good reason for believing that the penny itself does not in fact change so drastically in size and shape from one moment to another. But its sensible appearances do. I

1. Ennead IV.4.23.

therefore have to distinguish between the *real* penny and its
sensible appearances, or, in Locke's terminology, the sensible
ideas of the penny. To make such a distinction at once raises
the question: how is the real penny related to its sensible
appearances? To say that the sensible appearances *represent* the
real physical penny to us is a vague way of indicating this
relation.

Again if I look at the sun, I see a bright circular patch of
light a little smaller than a shilling held at arm's length. But
we have good evidence from physics and astronomy that the
real sun is an enormous globe of incandescent matter many
times larger than the earth and over 90,000,000 miles away.
Now the sun cannot be simultaneously many times larger than
the earth and also smaller than a shilling. Moreover, we learn
from physics that light from the sun takes over eight minutes
to reach our eyes, so that when I look at the sun I have, in
Locke's phrase, an idea of the sun which represents not its
state contemporary with my act of looking but its state of over
eight minutes ago. If the sun had been annihilated or had
exploded five minutes ago, I should not know about it until
over three minutes from now. Locke himself draws attention
to this example in the course of his criticism of the French
philosopher, Malebranche.

It is considerations of this kind, and they can be multiplied
indefinitely, which have led philosophers to adopt a representative theory of perception and say that when we are in touch
with the external world through our sense organs, the *immediate* objects of our perception are ideas of sensation or, in
modern terminology, sense data, which stand for or represent
material objects to us perhaps in something like the way a
portrait represents its original or a map represents the country
or district which it maps.

The theory has commonly been presented in a special form
which depends for its premises on the findings of empirical
science. Locke states the theory in an important chapter
entitled 'Some further considerations concerning our simple
ideas'. Here he makes a distinction between 'idea' and

'quality'. 'Whatsoever the mind perceives in itself or is the immediate object of perception, thought or understanding, that I call *idea*; and the power to produce any idea in our mind, I call *quality* of the subject wherein that power is.'[1] He then considers qualities and divides them into three classes: (i) the *primary* qualities of bodies are those which are 'utterly inseparable from the body in what state soever it be'.[2] He lists these qualities as solidity, extension, shape, motion or rest, and number. He explains (*a*) that no mechanical deformation or subdivision of a body can deprive it of these properties; (*b*) the ideas we have of these primary qualities really resemble them.

(ii) Colours, sounds, tastes, etc., are ideas of *secondary* qualities of bodies and the qualities themselves 'in truth are nothing in the objects themselves but powers to produce the various sensations in us by their primary qualities'.[3] He adds that the ideas of secondary qualities are produced in us 'by the operation of insensible particles on our senses',[4] or, as we should now say, through the operation of light rays on our eyes, sound waves on our ears, chemical effluences on our nose, and so on. The secondary qualities of bodies differ from the primary in that they do not in any way *resemble* the ideas they occasion in us.

(iii) The third class of qualities are powers of bodies by the operation of their primary qualities 'to make such a change in the bulk, figure, texture and motion of *another body* as to make it operate on our senses differently from what it did before. Thus the sun has a power to make wax white and fire to make lead fluid.'[5] Thus secondary qualities and powers are both capacities or dispositions, in the one case of a material thing to affect our minds, and in the other of one material thing to affect another.

This well-known doctrine did not originate with Locke. It can be traced back as far as the Greek atomists and in the seventeenth century the rapid growth of physical science

1. II.8.8.   2. II.8.9.   3. II.8.10.
4. II.8.13.   5. II.8.23.

gave it a new plausibility. It is, however, very difficult to present it in a form which will stand criticism, and in the vague form in which Locke presents it, it is particularly easy to attack.

Most people are aware nowadays that the sciences of physics and physiology seem to offer strong support to this theory. We know, for example, that sensations of light, sound, and heat are due to waves of various kinds which are emitted from material objects and which stimulate the sense organs of human beings and animals causing them to see light and colours, to hear sounds and to feel heat. Thus we are familiar with the idea that sensations of colour, sound, temperature, taste, smell and so on are effects, occurring in our consciousness, of causes which are very different in nature from the actual sensations themselves. And it follows as a corollary of this theory that the world apart from minds is a world of microscopic particles in motion and nothing else.

A modern philosopher has parodied the theory thus: 'The bodies are perceived as with qualities which in reality do not belong to them, qualities which are in fact purely the offspring of the mind. Thus nature gets the credit for what should in truth be reserved for ourselves: the rose for its scent: the nightingale for his song: and the sun for his radiance. The poets are entirely mistaken. They should address their lyrics to themselves and turn them into odes of self-congratulation on the excellency of the human mind. Nature is a dull affair, soundless, scentless, colourless; merely the hurrying of material, endlessly, meaninglessly.'[1]

It is important to distinguish the philosophical theory of primary and secondary qualities, which is a special form of the representative theory of perception, from the perfectly respectable scientific theory about the physical and physiological causes of our sensations. It is only too easy to assume that because the latter is true, the former is true also. But this is by no means the case. In so far as Locke means merely that physics is right in asserting that our various colour sensations

1. A. N. Whitehead, *Science and the Modern World*, Chapter III.

depend on differences in the wavelengths of the light rays which stimulate our eyes, that various sounds are correlated with differences in the length and amplitude of waves in the air and so on, he is talking science and not philosophy. And there is no doubt that he is substantially correct. But if he means to assume the existence of causes, the hypothetical secondary qualities which on his own theory can never be experienced, he is involving himself in serious difficulties. For we have only to ask: if all we can ever experience directly are ideas and if we can never look behind the curtain of ideas to observe the physical objects which cause our ideas, how can we ever know anything about the 'qualities' of such objects or even know that they exist at all? Locke was himself aware of this difficulty but thought, as we shall see, that it could be evaded.

Twenty years after the publication of the *Essay*, Berkeley exposed some of the cardinal defects of Locke's account of primary and secondary qualities in his *Principles of Human Knowledge*. His two main criticisms were as follows: (*a*) We have no more reason for supposing that the primary qualities of shape and extension can qualify bodies which are not present to our senses than we have for supposing that such bodies can be literally coloured, noisy, or fragrant. For we can no more talk of things being *merely* extended without having some extensible quality such as redness, smoothness, etc., than we can talk of a non-extended colour or tactual property. (*b*) The argument that ideas of secondary qualities cannot be genuine properties of the objects they seem to qualify because they change with the position of the observer and with his physical and mental state applies equally to ideas of primary qualities. Size, shape, and motion, as we perceive them, are all relative to the conditions under which they are perceived, no less than colour, taste, temperature and the other ideas of secondary qualities.

These objections are fatal to the theory of primary and secondary qualities in so far as it is more than merely a restatement of the scientific theory about the physical causes of our

65

sensations. But there are special difficulties which arise from Locke's own way of presenting the theory.

Primary Qualities

It should be noticed first of all that Locke does not make it clear if the word 'quality' is here to be taken in the sense of *determinable* quality, like coloured, shaped, etc., or in the sense of *determinate* quality, like crimson, triangular, etc. Presumably he intends the first alternative when he says they are 'utterly inseparable from the body in what state soever it be'. That is to say, he means to point out that if I break up one piece of chalk in three, the chalk still has solidity, shape, number, etc., although the determinate forms taken by some of these general properties will now be different. We can still count the pieces but they are now three instead of one; the shapes and sizes are now different, though the pieces still have some shape and size; and so on. But when he asserts that the ideas we have of these primary qualities really resemble them, it looks as though he is using 'quality' in the sense of 'determinate quality'. It would be both trivial and misleading to assert that our ideas of primary qualities resemble the qualities and that 'their patterns do really exist in the bodies themselves',[1] if he meant, for example, merely that what we sense as circular has some sort of shape. Locke does in fact assert that 'the *particular*[2] bulk, number, figure and motion of the parts of fire or snow are really in them'.[3]

The second point to note is that not all the primary qualities listed by Locke are, in fact, simple ideas. Now it is clearly necessary that they should be so if the ideas of primary qualities are exact resemblances of the determinate primary qualities of the object. Complex ideas are mental constructions; primary qualities, on the other hand, really are in bodies 'whether anyone's senses perceive them or no'.[4] Moreover

---

1. II.8.15.   2. My italics.   3. II.8.17.
4. *Ibid.*

Locke says that we 'observe' these primary qualities to produce simple ideas in us.[1]

Now he does not claim that his previous catalogue of simple ideas is complete. 'These, if they are not all, are at least (as I think) the most considerable of those simple ideas which the mind has.'[2] Thus we cannot object merely on the ground that his list of simple ideas does not include all the primary qualities. Nevertheless the list of primary qualities he gives plainly needs drastic revision.

In the first place, motion and rest cannot qualify as primary qualities. Locke admits that motions which are very swift or very slow are often unperceived;[3] thus he cannot consistently maintain that our ideas of rest and motion are resemblances whose 'patterns do really exist in the bodies themselves'.[4] The same may be said of texture, *i.e.* the microscopic arrangement of the particles of bodies (crystalline structure, for example) which helps to determine the ideas of secondary qualities which the bodies arouse in us. Our beliefs about the 'texture' of bodies are often mistaken; and our knowledge, such as it is, is not direct but the result of long and complex processes of scientific inference.

We are left with solidity, extension, and shape. The first is defined as that property of a body in virtue of which it fills space and 'excludes all other solid substances'.[5] Now if solidity is a property of *solid* substances only, where 'solid' has its ordinary meaning, then it is not a primary quality of bodies. For primary qualities are characteristic of a body 'in what state soever it be' and bodies lose their solidity in the liquid or gaseous states to which they can always be reduced by suitable alterations of temperature. And solidity, as Locke describes it, is not a property of liquids or gases. With extension and shape, of course, the case is different. No material body, whether in the solid, liquid or gaseous state, can fail to fill *some* determinate volume. It is true then that material things can be said to have the primary qualities of shape and

1. II.8.9.   2. II.7.10.   3. II.14.7.
4. II.8.15.   5. II.4.2.

bulk, *i.e.* their dimensional extension. But the reason for this is not a contingent fact, viz., that the primary qualities of bulk and figure always do, in practice, qualify material objects. Rather it is the case that material objects are *defined* in terms of these properties so that Locke's assertion that material things always have the primary qualities of bulk and figure is no more than an analytic triviality, exemplifying the ways in which these English terms are used. Thus Locke's doctrine of the primary qualities of material things will not bear examination. The only primary qualities of bodies which accord with his definition are their defining properties. And in this case, of course, it is not surprising that they are inseparable from bodies 'in what state soever they be', nor that our ideas of them 'resemble' their prototypes.

Secondary Qualities

Locke's doctrine of secondary qualities says that these qualities are dispositional causal properties of bodies in the sense that they tend to excite in us sense data of colour, taste, sound, etc., whenever the bodies are brought into appropriate spatio-temporal relations with our sense organs. The doctrine says, in other words, (1) that ideas of secondary qualities are *events* which are caused; (2) that they are not properties which qualify material bodies in the way in which primary qualities do qualify such bodies. The second part of the doctrine is independent of the first. There is no reason why an effect should not be a property in the way that the colour of red hot iron is normally spoken of as the effect of its being heated.

Locke's proof of the first proposition is as follows: Let us assume that every material body has its own microscopic structure due to the arrangement of its primary particles. Now we know that we can change the sensible qualities of an object by mechanical means. We can change the appearance and taste of an almond, for instance, by pounding it with a pestle. Now clearly such mechanical deformation can produce no change in the body other than changes in the arrangement and pattern of its primary particles. Therefore, such changes in the arrangement of the primary particles of a body are the causes of the changes in the sensible appearances of the body.

He supplements this argument with the following. A piece of porphyry is red and white when light strikes it but has no colour in the dark. The presence or absence of light cannot change the 'configuration of particles' in the porphyry. Therefore the light merely provides the occasion for the porphyry to exercise its dispositional property of causing red and white sense data in an observer.

These look like straightforward inductive arguments designed to identify the causal elements in a complex situation by varying certain conditions and keeping others constant. Such arguments are commonplaces both in science and in everyday experience and are often dissected in text-books on logic to show the operation of Mill's 'methods of experimental enquiry'. But there is a very important difference. between the use of these methods by the laboratory scientist and their use by the philosopher.

Such methods of argument are used to elucidate and identify uniformities in the observable world. As they are used in scientific enquiry, there is no appeal to any hypothetical entities which not only can never be directly experienced but whose existence can never be rendered probable or improbable by any observable evidence whatever. And Locke's secondary qualities are in just this position. Scientists do, of course, rely on hypothetical entities like genes, molecules, and electrons for the development of their theories. But the point is that these entities do not perform the same logical function as Locke's secondary qualities. Electrons are postulated to explain certain observable events which occur in physical laboratories. The supposition that they 'exist' can be justified by observable results and could conceivably be refuted if the expected results were not forthcoming. But Locke's theory of secondary qualities could not be proved false by any evidence whatever: it is compatible with *all* our experience and therefore explains nothing.

For a secondary quality is not anything observable. It is merely the disposition of a piece of matter to cause certain experiences in an observer under suitable conditions. And so long as we have the experiences, the physical object in question is said to have the secondary quality. But the statement that a cause is capable of producing the effects which it actually does produce and that, therefore, it has the 'quality' of being capable of producing them is a trivial and uninformative statement. It may, indeed, masquerade as something more important by being set out in pretentious language: but however it is expressed it tells us nothing about the world, any more than a statement like 'all black cats are cats'.

But the doctrine of secondary qualities is open to a more serious objection than this. For a secondary quality is held to be something which is not only a *cause* but an *unobservable* cause. It can be said, in general, that it is a necessary condition for the validity of any causal argument that both the cause and the effect referred to should be events which are, in principle at any rate, capable of being directly experienced. The apparent exceptions to this rule such as arguments which attribute causal properties to hypothetical entities like genes and electrons can all be explained by the fact that such hypothetical entities are merely a convenient and economical way of referring to certain rather complex sets of phenomena, for example, those photographs, pointer readings, etc., which would normally be said to be the 'evidence for' the electron. But any argument which postulates causes which are not only unknown but are, in principle, *unknowable*, is merely misusing the word 'cause' and invoking its prestige to hide a fallacy.

The second part of Locke's doctrine of secondary qualities and their ideas asserts that these ideas are not properties of things in the straightforward sense of the word 'property'. If we observe an orange, for example, we normally say that it has the properties of being roughly spherical, yellow, acid-tasting, having a certain characteristic texture and so on. But according to Locke, the only one of these properties which is a property *of the orange* is the primary quality of shape of which the idea in our minds is a counterpart of the quality in the body. We have already considered the difficulties in this part of his theory. What are we to say of the suggestion that its qualities of colour, smell, taste, etc., are not properties of the thing at all; and that 'what is sweet, blue or warm in idea is but the certain bulk, figure and motion of the insensible parts in the bodies themselves which we call so'?[1] His argument for this position is as follows: There are certain sensible properties which we have good reason for supposing to occur only as part of the experience of some mind. If a sword cuts a man's flesh, no one would suppose the pain which the man experiences to be a property of the metal. Similarly the same water will feel cool to a hand that has been heated and warm to a hand that has been cooled and no one supposes that those temperature sensations are literally properties of the water.

Now we know what it means to say, *e.g.*, 'I thought that cloth was green but now I see it's blue.' In other words, we have accepted ways of determining the occasions on which we make mistakes about the qualities of sensible objects. But two things should be noticed. (i) We always replace our erroneous judgement by another of the same sensory type. We never say, for example, 'I thought it was green but now I see it has no colour at all'. (ii) Our criteria for judging when these errors occur are normally our own experiences, previous or subsequent. Sometimes, though less commonly, we accept the experiences of others. But in all cases, we correct our empirical judgements *by experience*.

I think it will be obvious from these considerations that Locke is here using the language of everyday experience in a most misleading way. In saying that the ideas of secondary qualities are not, after all, properties of material objects, he is offering to us no new and surprising *factual* discovery like that of a scientist who makes a new discovery about the structure of matter. He is rather making clear a philosophical problem by bringing out certain logical difficulties into which we are led by our ordinary ways of talking about our sensory know-

1. II.8.15.

ledge of physical objects. His proposal for the solution of these difficulties involves using words like 'quality' and 'property' in ways rather different from those in which we normally use them. But we must remember that Locke himself did not make this distinction between factual discovery and linguistic proposal which is nowadays familiar to philosophers. He probably did regard his doctrine as very similar in logical character to a scientific theory. And we must remember also that before we accept his proposal, we have to ask ourselves if it might not involve us in bigger difficulties than those it purports to solve.

CHAPTER FOUR

Substance and Causality

THE philosophical problem of substance arises out of the commonsense distinction between things and their qualities. Leaves are green; diamonds are hard; ice is cold; and so on. The distinction seems obvious. Things or substances are the real and important features of the world while the qualities of things and the relations between things seem in some way derivative and therefore less real and important. A quality like green or sweet can exist only as the property of some substance. And a relation like 'to the north of' cannot exist except as relating two positions in space. And though it is also true that things cannot exist without having some properties and relations, the same thing can exist at different times with many different properties and stand in many different relations. In other words, a thing can change without ceasing to be the same thing but a quality or relation cannot change without ceasing to be the same quality or relation. All this seems clear enough, but as soon as we try to scrutinize this commonsense distinction a little more closely, difficulties begin to be seen. And the various philosophical theories of substance are attempts to explain these difficulties.

Locke's theory of substance and the criticism of the traditional concept of substance which his theory embodied was one of the most important parts of the *Essay*. In Berkeley's words, he 'bantered the idea of substance' and though he himself did no more than point the way to his successors, the traditional theory never recovered from the attack which he led. The concept of substance had acquired a peculiar prestige in scholastic philosophy for a number of reasons but it had received hardly any serious criticism. This was not entirely due to a superstitious reverence for the logic and metaphysics of Aristotle from which the traditional concept was derived. The fact was that medieval philosophers were at their best in trying

73

to rationalize their religious beliefs and make them intellectually respectable. Now the idea of substance as developed by the scholastic philosophers was of first-rate importance in theology. In so far as the dogmas of the Eucharist, Incarnation and Trinity could be rendered at all plausible or even meaningful, they rested on an elaborate and subtle theory of substance as a philosophical underpinning. It followed that the concept of substance could not be seriously analysed or criticized without endangering the associated theological dogmas. It thus acquired a diplomatic immunity from criticism as long as religious absolutism made philosophy the servant of theology.

Although Locke was writing in the comparatively civilized England of the seventeenth century, his theory of substance was considered by the orthodox to be theologically obnoxious and Locke's controversy with Dr Stillingfleet, Bishop of Worcester, turned largely on this point. But Stillingfleet's criticism was fortunate in that it stimulated Locke into restating his position with more clarity than he stated it in the *Essay*.

Before examining his position in detail, there are one or two preliminary remarks to be made. The traditional theory, from which Locke in spite of his criticism never dissociated himself, was a compound of three independent and not entirely compatible elements.

(*a*) Substance was *ens per se stans* [1] or that which had a capacity for independent existence and was the genuinely real feature of the universe. All other features, qualities, relations, events, or facts had a reality merely derivative from that of substance. This concept of substance was emphasized by Descartes and was developed by Spinoza into pantheism.

(*b*) Substance was also *quod substat accidentibus*, the substratum in which qualities must inhere.

(*c*) Substance was that which could be subject but not predicate of a proposition in logical form. [2] This subject-predicate

1. To be distinguished from God who is *ens a se stans*.
2. We must say, in logic, 'the leaves are green' and not 'green are the

analysis of propositions was one of the unfortunate Aristotelian doctrines which had, long before Locke's time, reached the status of an unquestioned presupposition of all philosophical thinking. It is impossible at this date to decide whether Aristotle's subject-predicate logic was a formative influence on his substance-accident metaphysics or merely a consequence of it. Certainly they were not developed independently. Many medieval philosophers, at any rate, did not distinguish clearly between logical and metaphysical questions and Locke, writing in the seventeenth century, is hardly to be blamed if the limitations and confusions of the traditional logic served to blunt his criticism of the concept of substance.

For Locke, however, it was the notion of substance as the substratum necessary for the existence of qualities which is the important sense of the word, and Locke points out that we find in nature certain groups of simple ideas in constant and uniform conjunction, 'which being presumed to belong to one thing, and words being suited to common apprehensions, and made use of for quick dispatch, are called, so united in one subject, by one name; which, by inadvertency, we are apt afterward to talk of and consider as one simple idea, which indeed is a complication of many ideas together: because, as I have said, not imagining how these simple ideas *can* subsist by themselves, we accustom ourselves to suppose some *substratum* wherein they do subsist, and from which they do result, which therefore we call *substance*.'[1]

It follows that anyone's idea of 'pure substance in general' is not a clear idea with any positive content but 'only a supposition of he knows not what *support* of such qualities which are capable of producing simple ideas in us'.[2] We naturally ask, Locke says, what is the subject in which a given quality inheres. Colour and weight, for example, would be said to inhere in the solid extended parts of a body. But where do

leaves'. The latter phrase is merely a poetic inversion and does not alter the logical and grammatical fact that 'leaves' is subject and 'green' is predicate.　　　　1. II.23.1.　　　　2. II.23.2.

solidity and extension inhere? We can only reply, 'In something, we know not what.' But to say this is to talk like children who use this sort of answer to disguise their ignorance. Our idea of substance, such as it is, is 'obscure and relative', 'being nothing but the supposed but unknown, support of those qualities we find existing, which we imagine cannot subsist *sine re substante*, without something to support them'.[1]

Locke now passes from our idea of substance in general to our ideas of particular substances. This is, at first sight, surprising. On empiricist principles he should surely demonstrate how our idea of substance arises in particular cases and then go on to derive the general idea from the particular by abstraction in the usual way. This would be a reasonable objection if Locke had thought that the idea of substance was derived from sensation or reflection. But already in Book I, during his discussion of innate ideas he had admitted that the idea of substance could not be derived in that way. 'I confess there is another general idea which would be of general use for mankind to have, as it is of general talk as if they had it; and that is the idea of *substance* which we neither have nor can have by sensation or reflection.'[2]

I think that this unusual order of exposition is merely a sacrifice of consistency to convenience. He thinks that he can explain his position most clearly if he starts with a rough outline of the topic and proceeds to fill in the details by reference to concrete examples. But when we turn to concrete examples, we find that they give us no clear ideas other than of a certain set of co-existing sensible qualities. The co-existence of properties like gold colour, a certain density, malleability, etc., in gold, for example, is a matter of experience. And in this way, by ordinary observation 'we come to have the ideas of a man, horse, gold, water, etc.; of which substances, whether anyone has any other *clear* idea, further than of certain simple ideas co-existent together, I appeal to everyone's own experience. It is the ordinary qualities observable in iron, or in a diamond, put

1. II.23.2.   2. I.3.19.

together, that make the true complex idea of those substances, which a smith or jeweller commonly knows better than a philosopher'.[1] And he found that a similar conclusion was necessary in the case of immaterial substances or selves.

So far then Locke has done nothing more than point out that the concept of substance cannot be justified on his empirical premises. But he was too deeply committed to traditional ways of thinking to draw all the conclusions which his assumptions permitted him. And when Dr Stillingfleet accused him of having 'almost discarded substance out of the reasonable part of the world', Locke tried to amplify his doctrine to avoid the theological odium which a rejection of the concept of substance would incur.

In his first letter to Stillingfleet he explains that his arguments concern the *idea* alone and not the *being* of substance, and that to show that we have no clear idea of substance is not to deny that substances exist. Nevertheless, he tries to find a better foundation for our ideas of substance, as follows: 'All the ideas of all the sensible qualities of a cherry come into my mind by sensation; the ideas of perceiving, thinking, reasoning, knowing, etc., come into my mind by reflection. The ideas of these qualities and actions or powers are perceived by the mind to be of themselves inconsistent with existence ... Hence the mind perceives their necessary connexion with inherence or being supported; which being a relative idea superadded to the red colour in a cherry or to thinking in a man, the mind frames the correlative idea of a support. For I never denied that the mind could frame to itself ideas of relation but have showed the quite contrary in my chapters about relation.'

This passage is important for two reasons: (*a*) He states here more clearly than he does in the *Essay* why he was unable to discard the notion of substance completely. (*b*) He attempts to provide a justification for ideas of substance by an appeal to ideas of reason. It is important to examine these two points with some care. I will take the second first.

1. II.23.3.

Locke is referring here to certain features of relational thinking which have been emphasized by modern psychologists. Spearman[1] expresses these features in the form of psychological laws as follows:

'(i) The mentally presenting of any two or more characters (simple or complex) tends to evoke immediately a knowing of relation between them.

'(ii) The presenting of any character together with any relation tends to evoke immediately a knowing of the correlative character.'

The first is the principle of 'eduction of relations' and the second the principle of 'eduction of correlates'. Instances of the operation of these mental tendencies are common in the performance of verbal intelligence tasks. Analogy tests, where children are confronted with examples of the following kind, '"Book" is to "page" as "forest" is to " . . ."', are an exercise in the eduction of correlates. Now Locke is suggesting that we obtain our idea of substance as a result of this sort of mental process. We are given in experience the idea of red colour and the relation of 'inherence' is logically connected with the idea. We then educe the appropriate correlate, 'substance'. But it is clear that there is a big difference between ordinary relational thinking and hypothetical thought processes of the sort Locke is trying to describe. Not everyone would subscribe to Spearman's way of talking about the matter, but few would deny that he was substantially right in claiming that we can educe relations between things or properties *given in experience* or that we can educe a correlate if we are *presented* with a term and a relation. It will be remembered that Hume admitted that if we were given in experience shades of blue ordered by the relation 'darker than' we could use this material to evoke an image of a shade of blue which we had never experienced. This would be a case of eduction of a correlate which had not previously occurred in experience. But Locke is suggesting that we can use this type of thinking to establish the existence of entities which not only never have

1. *Nature of Intelligence*, Ch. V. and VII.

been experienced but which *ex hypothesi*, *never can* be experienced. And this is quite another matter.

Moreover, in his discussion of relations he has given no indication that they could provide such a bridge between what is experienced and what exists but is unknowable. On the contrary, he emphasizes that relations are 'not contained in the real existence of things, but something extraneous and super-induced'.[1] Admittedly his discussion of relations is too confused and sketchy to enable much detailed criticism to be offered. It is obvious, nevertheless, that neither his theory of relations nor any other, however clear, consistent, and satisfactory, could justify him in passing from empirical premises to a metaphysical conclusion of this sort. Nor could he reply that this criticism is irrelevant on the ground that the argument concerns not the *existence* of substance but merely the *idea* of substance. It is not the existential character of his conclusion that is at issue here but its non-empirical character. The idea of substance is 'obscure' and 'confused' because it is not given to us in sensation or reflection and never could be.

We can now discuss, in the light of the passage quoted above, why it was that Locke could not dissociate himself from a view of substance which was so much at variance with his empirical outlook. 'The ideas of these qualities and actions or powers are perceived by the mind to be of themselves inconsistent with existence ... thence the mind perceives their necessary connexion with inherence or being supported.'[2] And this is a reaffirmation in stronger terms of what he had already said in the *Essay*. 'Hence when we talk or think of any particular sort of corporeal substances, as horse, stone, etc., though the idea we have of either of them be but the complication or collection of those several simple ideas of sensible qualities, which we used to find united in the thing called horse or stone; yet *because we cannot conceive how they should subsist alone, nor in one another*, we suppose them existing in and supported by some common subject; which support we denote

1. II.25.8.　　　　　2. First letter to Stillingfleet.

by the name substance, though it be certain we have no clear or distinct idea of that thing we suppose a support.'[1] In other words, he says in the *Essay* that we cannot imagine how simple ideas can exist without a substratum in which they inhere; and he adds in the first letter to Stillingfleet that we see it to be logically self-contradictory that they should exist in their own right without a substance to support and unify them.

The question we have to consider, therefore, is: is it logically self-contradictory to suppose that ideas of 'qualities and actions or powers' should exist without a substance? And if not, what is the source of the psychological difficulty which according to Locke we find in supposing that they do so? We can start by admitting two facts: (i) With the vast majority of the sense data which occur in our experience we have no difficulty in identifying them as 'belonging to' some substance or other. The phrase 'belonging to' is ambiguous and is notoriously difficult to analyse. But in saying this, we are admitting no more than that as a matter of fact *most* sense data can be referred to semi-permanent groups or families which we call physical objects or material things. (ii) There are certain events or operations which it is analytically necessary to refer to substances in whose history the events or operations occur. For example, it would be nonsense to talk of a sneeze or a cough occurring except as an event in the history of an animal with a respiratory system of a certain character and complexity. And this is not owing to any mysterious ontological necessity but merely because sneezing and coughing are *defined* as certain types of convulsion occurring in such respiratory systems. And for similar reasons, running or walking cannot occur except as events in the history of animals with legs. In such cases, there is a trivial and prosaic reason for the conclusion that accidents cannot exist apart from their substances. But these two concessions are all we need make to Locke's preconceptions.

It is certainly not logically necessary, or even true, that colours, for instance, cannot occur except as properties of a

1. II.23.4.

coloured something. If I stare at a light for a few seconds and then turn my gaze away, I shall see an 'after-image' in the form of a coloured patch which certainly does not inhere in any substance. The supporter of the substratum theory of substance has either to claim that (i) the after-image is itself a substance or (ii) that it inheres in my visual field. (i) is a *reductio ad absurdum* of the substratum theory, though a sense datum would qualify as a substance in the *logical* sense of the word: it has properties without being itself a property of anything. (ii) uses the word 'inhere' in the sense of 'forms a part of' which is a new (and quite misleading) sense of the word, which could not be applied to other alleged cases of inherence without destroying the substratum theory altogether. The only other course open to him is to claim that such sense-data are events in the history of a continuing self. And apart from the fact that this suggestion, as we shall see later, raises difficulties of its own, it cannot be said that a red after-sensation, for example, is a property of the self who perceives it in the same sense as the red colour of a cherry is a property of the cherry. And similar exceptions can be found in all other types of sense data. Abnormal psychology can provide plenty of instances of 'detached' or 'wild' sense data which cannot be said to inhere in any substance. It is a purely contingent fact that sense data are normally found in the stably constituted groups which we call material things. There is no necessity that they should be found so and often they are not.

It seems probable that the concept of substance as an unknown substratum with no positive qualities of its own other than the relational properties of 'supporting' or 'uniting' its qualities arises from two sources. (i) Our ordinary language distinguishes between 'nouns' on the one hand and 'verbs' and 'adjectives' on the other. It is a rule of syntax that adjectives should qualify nouns and that verbs should express the states or actions of the referent of the noun which is their subject. This convenient syntactical device was fossilized in the traditional subject-predicate logic. Moreover, because we cannot think except in a symbolic medium and because ordinary language is the medium in which most of our thinking is carried on, we come to regard the noun-adjective or noun-verb patterns as pictures of the way in which the world is constructed.

To a certain extent, of course, this tendency is justifiable and even useful. But it is easy to imagine that because the substances which the nouns stand for have properties and undergo processes without themselves being properties or processes of anything else, their essential character consists in being a subject of attributes and that they have no positive, non-relational character at all.

(ii) The 'unknown substratum' theory of substance ostensibly offers an answer to the question: 'What is it that supports qualities and unites them into stable individual things?' This question is of a type very common in popular philosophizing, like 'what caused the universe?' or 'what is the meaning of life?' They arise from an illegitimate extension or generalization of a perfectly genuine type of query. Some questions about uniform conjunctions of characteristics are quite proper and understandable. 'Why are cacti always found in dry conditions?' is an example of this sort. 'Why do yellow-skinned men tend to have straight hair and narrow eyes?' is also a question of this sort, since, although it might be difficult to answer, we do know roughly the *sort* of answer which we should accept. But 'why are qualities found in stable inter-relations?' is only superficially similar to questions of this type. In this case, we do not even know what sort of answer we should find acceptable. All we can say is that if qualities did not occur in such stable groupings, the universe would be an unknowable chaos. To suppose that coloured and tangible surfaces must be supported by a substance as a tablecloth has to be supported by a table is to manufacture problems. In Berkeley's phrase, 'We have first raised a dust and then complain we cannot see.' And it is equally silly to suggest that the unity of qualities in one subject has to be 'explained' in the way that the unity of sticks in a bundle is explained by the string that binds them. To reply that the qualities of a body must be united and supported by a sort of transcendental glue in which they inhere does not solve any problem, because there is no problem to solve. In changing the form of the question from 'Why is property p found in conjunction with property q?' to 'Why is *any* property found in conjunction with certain other properties?' we have destroyed the possibility of an answer; for we have destroyed the ground of our legitimate puzzlement and with it the problem.

I conclude then that Locke had no good reasons for concern over the problem of substance as he conceived it. However, by emphasizing that there are no empirical grounds for the substratum theory, he gave it a blow from which it never recovered. And largely on account of his criticism it has not been taken seriously by philosophers for many years.[1] Nevertheless, there is a problem connected with substance which we might have expected Locke to discuss, namely: 'What are the factors in experience which enable individual substances to be recognized as such?' As we have seen, Locke denied that the idea of substance could be derived from sensation and reflexion, but he could not, of course, deny that we do recognize complex ideas of substances. And it is a fair question to ask how, from his empirical standpoint, Locke can account for the origin of our ideas of individual substances. For that we possess such ideas is an indubitable fact of experience.

This question is in part a question of psychology. We want to know what are the features of our experience which enable us to class together certain properties as 'belonging to one thing'. It is perhaps not such an easy question to answer as it appears at first sight. We are asking, in effect, for an account of the genesis and development of our conception of the external world. And the evidence we should want to decide the matter would have to be taken largely from the experience of young children which is, in the nature of the case, not available. Nevertheless, we can ask the question also at the

1. One important exception should be mentioned. The modern scholastic philosophers are compelled by the demands of their theology to defend the traditional concept of substance.

level of our developed experience. The answer cannot, of course, be quite clear-cut and definite because the concept of material things is not free from vagueness. Men and animals, books and tables are clearly things. But it would be difficult to decide, for instance, if a cloud is a 'thing' or if a piece of coal is one thing when it is in one piece and three separate things when it is broken into three. Again, a copper vase is clearly one thing. If we melt it into an amorphous lump of metal we should still be inclined to say that it was one substance. But if we raise the temperature of the metal until it becomes liquid and then gaseous we should be more inclined to say that the volume of liquid or gas was a *collection* of things, viz., the molecules making up the volume, than itself one thing. There could, of course, be no conclusively right or wrong answer to such a question. The position is that our linguistic conventions governing the use of the phrases, 'material thing', 'physical object', 'substance', etc., are not sufficiently well established to govern these borderline cases.

Nevertheless, it is possible to determine to a useful degree of accuracy what the main conditions are which do determine our use of these phrases.

(i) The first condition to which instances of qualities must conform in order that they may be grouped together as one substance is that they should be manifested in the same spatio-temporal neighbourhood. When we eat an apple, for example, we find instances of the qualities red, smooth, round, sweet, juicy, etc., occurring in one locality at one time.

(ii) We normally require also that the members of such groups should be associated in this way during a certain minimum period of time. What this minimum period is will, of course, have to be determined separately for each substance or type of substance. If an object appears in my room answering in all respects to the description of a chair and vanishes utterly after a minute, we should naturally be inclined to say that it was an hallucination and thereby implicitly deny that it was a substance. For similar reasons, we should normally call a flash of lightning an event rather than a thing and a star a thing rather than an event. And we should no doubt find it difficult to decide if a candle flame should be called a thing or an event.

(iii) The third condition is that the members of such groups should change, when they do so, jointly and in co-ordination. If the form of change in question is local change or movement, it is not sufficient that when one part of a thing moves, other parts should move also. The movement must preserve the relative positions of the parts of the thing. And, of course, there must be certain regular connexions between the movements of the visual sense data and those of the tactual sense data; and there will be corresponding changes in the centre from which the auditory, olfactory, thermal, etc., data emanate. And if the form of change is qualitative change, the changes are concomitant. 'Changes which affect a group of qualities together, either as regards their spatial relations or otherwise, tend to be regarded as changes in the qualities of the same thing. When a piece of paper comes into contact with a flame and burns, the resulting changes affect permanently its appearances to all our senses.'[1]

(iv) Physical objects must be what has been called 'public and neutral'. That is to say, they must be accessible to all observers on equal terms. A man may have an hallucination which conforms to all the other criteria for an independent substance and be brought to admit his mistake by the lack of corroboration by other observers. And other non-standard sensory presentations such as those received during dreams, hypnosis or mirror gazing, are in the same class.

(v) The last condition to which groups of sense data must conform to merit the title of 'material substance' is that they should contain both visual and tactual components. Of these two the second is the more important. Unless we are blind, we do not, as a matter of fact, meet with objects which are tangible though invisible. However, such a hypothetical object would have a better claim to the title of substance than one which was visible but intangible. But, of course, whether or not we were

1. Stout, *Manual of Psychology*, p. 445.

to stretch our use of the phrases 'material substance' and 'physical object' to cover such cases is purely a matter of convention. *The idea of substance, in Locke's terminology, is itself a mixed mode.*

I have been concerned here only with those conditions to which groups of our sensory presentations have to conform if they are to be called collectively 'substance' or 'thing'. A description of these conditions is, in effect, a description of the conventional rules which govern our use of the phrases 'physical object', 'material substance', and their synonyms.

There are other conditions which are, perhaps, important psychologically in drawing our attention to the existence of material objects. They are therefore treated in text-books of psychology in discussions about the growth of our knowledge of the external world. For example, the extent to which the sensory pattern presented by the thing conforms to what the Gestalt school of psychology calls the 'law of Prägnanz',[1] *i.e.* is simple, regular, stable, and symmetrical, is certainly a factor in the genesis of our recognition of objects as substances. But it is hardly a *condition* for the correct use of the phrases we are considering, that objects should conform to the 'law of Prägnanz'. Similarly, the fact that a thing is useful or otherwise interesting to us tends to give it a special claim to the status of 'thinghood', without being a necessary condition of the status.

The point of this discussion is to show that Locke could very well have accounted for our ideas of substance, such as they are, without appeal to any awkward 'something-I-know-not-what'. The determination of the proper conditions for the application of the term 'substance' is purely a matter of descriptive psychology and not in any way outside the limits set by Locke's empirical premises.

However, Locke's intuitions were often more valuable than the reasoned conclusions drawn from his premises and pre-conceptions. It would not be fair to him to leave the subject of substance without quoting a famous passage from Book IV of

1. Koffka, *Principles of Gestalt Psychology*, p. 108.

the *Essay* in which he sketches an entirely new approach to the problem:

'We are wont to consider the substances we meet with, each of them, as an entire thing by itself, having all its qualities in itself, and independent of other things; overlooking for the most part, the operations of those invisible fluids they are encompassed with, and upon whose motions and operations depend the greatest part of those qualities which are taken notice of in them, and are made by us the inherent marks of distinction whereby we know and denominate them. Put a piece of gold anywhere by itself, separate from the reach and influence of all other bodies, it will immediately lose all its colour and weight, and perhaps malleableness too; which, for aught I know, would be changed into a perfect friability ... This is certain: things, however absolute and entire they seem in themselves, are but retainers to other parts of nature, for that which they are most taken notice of by us.'[1] Locke is here pointing out that if to be a substance means, as it did for the scholastics, to have a capacity for independent existence, then substantiality is a matter of *degree*. The universe, in the sense of the sum total of everything that exists, would then be the only instance of substance in the absolute and unqualified sense of the word. And this was, indeed, the conclusion that Spinoza drew from this aspect of the scholastic theory. It would follow that large and systematic portions of the universe like the solar system would be more substantial than a single organism, for example, whose continued existence and efficient functioning is dependent on association with food, water, oxygen, a a certain narrow range of temperature, and other such conditions.

It would follow also from this line of argument that relatively unorganized individual things like stones or pieces of metal would, in so far as they would be more independent of changes in their environment, have a *higher* degree of substantiality than highly complex organisms like human beings. Presumably the things with the greatest capacity for indepen-

1. IV.6.11.

dent existence in utter isolation from everything else would be
single atoms or even sub-atomic particles. But this, of course,
is a matter of physical science and not a philosophical question.

Locke did not develop this line of thought and left nothing
on the subject but the passage quoted, in part, above. But just
as his criticism of substance as an unknown substratum indicated to his successors the bankruptcy of one part of the
scholastic theory, so his observations on substances as independent existents showed that the logical development of this
other scholastic dogma led to conclusions which even its
supporters could not accept. It was only the logical element in
the scholastic theory which Locke accepted uncritically and
left unscathed. And this has been disposed of, in recent years,
by modern developments in logic.

Causality

In this discussion of Locke's views on substance, I have not
considered either his theory of the self or his views on our
knowledge of substances. These matters will be discussed in
more appropriate contexts. But it would be in place here to
say something about Locke's theory of causality. There is
commonly supposed to be a close connexion between the
notions of 'thing' and 'cause'. Not all philosophers would
endorse this point of view but at least Locke did not dissent
from it.

In his chapter on our complex ideas of substances, he
emphasized the importance of the causal properties of individual things. 'For he has the perfectest idea of any of the particular sorts of substances, who has gathered, and put together,
most of those simple ideas which do exist in it; among which
are to be reckoned its active powers, and passive capacities,
which, though not simple ideas, yet in this respect, for
brevity's sake, may conveniently enough be reckoned amongst
them. Thus the power of drawing iron is one of the ideas of
the complex one of that substance we call a loadstone; and a
power to be so drawn is a part of the complex one we call iron:

which powers pass for inherent qualities in those subjects.'[1]
His main reason for stressing the fact that powers make 'a
great part of our complex ideas of substances'[2] is, of course,
the fact that secondary qualities themselves are 'nothing but
bare powers' and our ideas of its secondary qualities are the
chief features by which we commonly distinguish one substance from another. But he also recognizes that the causal
relations between substances are the expression of the powers
making up their nature.

His doctrine of power is one aspect of his general theory of
causality. But he gives separate treatment to 'the most comprehensive relation' of causality. Thus causality is a relation;
but the idea of power, strangely enough, is treated as a simple
idea. We need not pay much attention to this peculiar classification; Locke himself recognized that it was not really defensible. He wished to treat ideas of powers as simple ideas on
the ground that instances of causal succession, both in mental
and physical events and in the psycho-physical relation, are
directly given to us in our experience of change. But he knew
very well that this was to admit to the class of simple ideas
members which were not covered by his original definition.
'I confess', he added, 'power includes in it some kind of
relation.'[3]

What, then, is Locke's theory of causality as set out in his
chapters on cause and effect and on power? Chapter 26 ('Of
cause and effect, and other relations') treats causality rather
summarily in two short sections in which he says nothing
more than: (*a*) Anything which 'produces' any '(simple or
complex) idea we call a cause and any idea which is 'produced'
we call an effect. (*b*) Various kinds of 'production' are: creation, 'generation', 'making' and 'alteration'.

But he does not attempt to analyse the notion of 'production' or show how it is derived from experience.

The chapter on power[4] is a long chapter of seventy-two
sections nearly all of which concern questions of volition.
Locke starts by observing that the idea of change is a con-

1. II.23.7.　　2. II.23.10.　　3. II.21.3.　　4. II.21.

89

comitant of all our experience, sensory and introspective. 'The mind being every day informed, by the senses, of the alteration of those simple ideas it observes in things without; and taking notice how one comes to an end, and ceases to be, and another begins to exist which was not before; reflecting also on what passes within itself, and observing a constant change of its ideas, sometimes by the impression of outward objects on the senses and sometimes by the determination of its own choice; and concluding from what it has so constantly observed to have been, that the like changes will for the future be made in the same things, by like agents, and by the like ways – considers in one thing the possibility of having any of its simple ideas changed, and in another the possibility of making that change; and so comes by that idea which we call *power.*'[1]

Locke explains that he is concerned only to show how we come by the idea of power, and this limitation accounts for the rather naïve transition from our observation of change to the presumption of causal connexion between the changing ideas. He does not try to give an analysis of the causal relation. The farthest he went in this direction was to take over from the prevailing scholasticism the distinction between active and passive powers, *i.e.* between a capacity for producing change and a capacity for receiving change. Fire has an active power to melt gold and gold a passive power to be melted by fire. He admitted that 'active power' was 'the more proper signification of the word', but apparently did not see that the notion of 'passive power' was a verbal triviality. If we know that A affects B, it is an analytic and uninformative statement that B is affected by A. Whenever we observe any change 'the mind must collect a power somewhere, able to make that change, as well as a possibility in the thing itself to receive it'.[2] Locke seems to have thought that this statement was more than the mere tautology: whenever x occurs it must have been possible for it to occur. In his proof of the existence of God in Book IV he uses as a premise 'what had a beginning must be produced by something else'. And in his first letter to Stillingfleet he

1. II.21.1.　　　　2. II.21.4.

states his position on this point quite explicitly: '*Everything that has a beginning must have a cause* is a true principle of reason or a proposition certainly true.' He regarded this as a general proposition of fact which is nevertheless self-evident and indubitable. And his acceptance of this general proposition would account for his conviction that we have to look for a cause to explain or account for every change.

Nevertheless, although this proposition is, according to Locke, applicable to experience, it is clearly not established by experience. All we ever know directly when we observe instances of physical causation is a succession of changing ideas. That such changes must have causes we know *a priori*, but we do not directly experience the manner of their operation. 'A body at rest affords us no idea of any active power to move; and when it is set in motion itself, that motion is rather a passion than an action in it. For, when the ball obeys the stroke of a billiard stick, it is not any action of the ball but bare passion. Also when by impulse it sets another ball in motion that lay in its way, it only communicates the motion it had received from another, and loses in itself so much as the other received; which gives us but a very obscure idea of an *active* power moving in a body, whilst we observe it only to *transfer* but not *produce* any motion.'[1] Locke is here stating, rather vaguely and clumsily, the point which Hume afterwards made with such effect: we never *experience* the operation of causes, only the temporal sequence of cause and effect. If then we confine ourselves to physical causation we could know, Locke is saying, that changes must be caused, but we could not know how the causes operate. And although he insists that we conclude from what we have constantly observed, 'that the like changes will for the future be made in the same things by like agents',[2] he gives us no grounds whatever for *identifying* the cause of any given effect.

But if we turn to the evidence of introspection, Locke thinks that we are on surer ground. 'The idea of the *beginning* of motion we have only from reflection on what passes in our-

1. II.21.4.   2. II.21.1.

selves; where we find by experience, that, barely by willing it, barely by a thought of the mind, we can move the parts of our bodies, which were before at rest.'[1] In our experience of volition, we are directly conscious of the operation of a cause and its connexion with its effect. When Hume later discussed this question, he tried to show that the evidence of introspection was no more valuable than the evidence of ordinary observation in this respect. 'The motion of our body follows upon the command of our will. Of this we are every moment conscious. But the means by which this is effected; the energy by which the will performs so extraordinary an operation; of this we are so far from being immediately conscious, that it must for ever escape our most diligent enquiry.'[2] Part of Hume's evidence for this conclusion is that there is no more obvious connexion between a volition and its corresponding bodily movement than there is between a physical cause and its effect. But this overlooks the fact that a volition is a complex mental event of which the intention to produce the willed action is an essential part. He also points out that the connexions between volitions and their results have to be learned by experience like any other regular causal sequences. Moreover the facts of neurology and the experience of paralytics show that, at best, volitions cannot be more than a partial cause of bodily movement. He might have added that they are not even *necessary* conditions of bodily movements which can just as well be brought about by discharges of nervous energy not associated with volitions.

But it is doubtful whether Hume's arguments disprove the contention that it is at least *sometimes* possible to know that a volition is a causal condition of a certain movement and if we do not look too closely at the notion of 'volition', this will suffice for Locke's purpose. All he wants to show is that it is possible to have an immediate experience of the causal connexion, and so prove that our ideas of cause have an empirical foundation. Nevertheless, the most that this example enables him to say is that psycho-physical interaction is a type of

1. II.21.4.   2. *Enquiry, Sect.* VII.1.52.

causation whose operation is directly known to us in experience. But this experience in no way enlightens us about the mode of operation of mind on matter or of one physical object on another.

Locke's views on causality may be summarized as follows: (i) Causality is a relation which holds between ideas of substances or their modes. In so far as it is a relation holding between ideas, it is a mental construction.

(ii) The physical or real foundation of the relation of causality is the various 'powers' of substances. These powers are dispositional properties of bodies. They may be powers to operate on our sense organs ('secondary qualities') or powers to operate on and produce effects in each other.

(iii) The empirical basis for our ideas of causality is (a) our experience of change and succession; (b) our alleged direct experience of causal operation in volition.

(iv) The element of necessary connexion between cause and effect is not provided by experience but by our intuition of the *a priori* proposition, 'Everything which has a beginning must have a cause'.

It will be seen that the only interesting or constructive suggestions are (iii) (b) and (iv). And these are just the points which are most difficult to accept and difficult to establish, though Locke himself did not seem to think that they needed elaborating or defending. I shall defer for the present a critical examination of these suggestions as it will be more convenient to deal with them in discussing Locke's psychology and theology. The most surprising omission from his account is any treatment of the notion of causal law. That this seems to us nowadays a cardinal notion in any discussion of causality is due to the success of natural scientists in mapping the universe according to systems of causal law. But in the seventeenth century, natural science, in spite of its impressive achievements, did not enjoy the prestige it has to-day. Locke pointed out that our experience of regularities of causal sequence leads us to express these regularities in the form of causal laws, but, as we shall see, he did not consider that they gave us knowledge in any important sense of the word. 'The things that, as far as our observation reaches, we constantly find to proceed regularly, we may conclude do act by a law set them; but yet by a law that we know not: whereby, though causes work steadily and effects constantly flow from them, yet their connexions and dependencies being not discoverable in our ideas, we can have but an experimental knowledge of them. From all which it is easy to perceive what a darkness we are involved in, how little is of Being and the things that are that we are capable to know.'[1] Thus Locke's doctrine of causality is one of the least satisfactory features of the *Essay*. It is true that in Book IV of the *Essay* he fills out the doctrine a little with a discussion of our knowledge of causes but he nowhere tries to show how the empirical basis of our thinking about causality is related to the *a priori* element embodied in the principle that every change has to be explained by a cause. And, as we shall see, this lack of connexion between reason and experience is one of the basic defects of his theory of knowledge.

1. IV.3.29.

CHAPTER FIVE

The Nature of the Understanding

WE shall be largely concerned in this chapter with questions which would nowadays be called questions of psychology. I do not mean that the questions to be discussed are properly questions of fact which can be decided by the sort of evidence produced by laboratory or clinical psychologists. But it has become customary to call questions about the nature and activities of mind psychological questions, even where empirical findings are not directly relevant to their solution. They should perhaps be called, less misleadingly, philosophical problems of psychology. Every science has, of course, its associated philosophical problems. But because psychology is the science which has most recently advanced from the status of a branch of philosophy to that of an independent science and because the subject-matter of psychology has had, traditionally, a greater intrinsic interest for the philosopher than those of the other sciences, the philosophical problems of psychology form a specially large and important group.

The main questions to be discussed are those which arise out of Locke's doctrines of 'ideas of reflection' and of mental activities in general. But there are also questions about the nature of the self which he raises in his discussion of the relation of 'identity', and questions about the nature of volition which he discusses at length in his chapter on the simple ideas of power. These psychological questions are not all treated together in the *Essay* but we shall not do any violence to Locke's thought if we group them together here.

Reflection

Reflection, or as we should nowadays call it, introspection, is one of the two sources from which, according to Locke, we obtain all our simple data of experience. 'The other fountain from which experience furnisheth the understanding with ideas is, – the perception of the operations of our own minds within us, as it is employed about the ideas it has got; – which operations, when the soul comes to reflect on and consider, do furnish the understanding with another set of ideas, which could not be had from things without. And such are *perception, thinking, doubting, believing, reasoning, knowing, willing*, and all the different actings of our own minds; – which we being conscious of, and observing in ourselves, do from these receive into our understandings as distinct ideas as we do from bodies affecting our senses.'[1]

Locke regards our 'perception' of our own mental operations as analogous to our perception of sensible objects and thinks that this similarity justifies us calling it 'internal sense'.[2] But he does not elaborate the comparison between sensation and reflection. It appears from his account that the similarities between them are: (i) both provide us with a direct, intuitive acquaintance with the materials of knowledge; (ii) both acquaint us with *ideas*, in the one case of sensible objects and in the other of mental operations. They do *not* acquaint us with sensible objects or mental operations themselves. 'By reflection then, in the following part of this discourse, I would be understood to mean, that notice which the mind takes of its own operations, and the manner of them, by reason whereof there come to be ideas of these operations in the understanding.'[3]

The chief defect of Locke's account of reflection is the uncritical manner in which he treats the subject. He does not hesitate to talk as if it were a mode of experience analogous to sensation and even talks occasionally as if it were co-ordinate with sensation; he certainly believed that the evidence of introspection may be accepted with no more criticism than the deliverances of our sense organs. In this belief he was seriously mistaken. In the first place there are three important points of difference between sensation and reflection which Locke tacitly recognized, but did not seem to think important.

1. II.1.4.   2. *Ibid.*   3. *Ibid.*

(*a*) Reflection is not co-ordinate with sensation, but is, as it were, parasitic upon it. The mental operations which are the contents of the introspective activity of mind are 'employed about the ideas it has got'. And in Locke's view there cannot be either primary mental activities, still less a reflective activity of mind which is directed to such primary activities until sensation has first provided some material. 'In time the mind comes to reflect on its own operations about the ideas got by sensation and thereby stores itself with a new set of ideas which I call ideas of reflection.'[1] (*b*) Reflection is a voluntary activity; sensation is not. In other words we cannot help having sense experiences, whenever our sense organs are subjected to the appropriate stimuli, but whether we 'take notice of' our perceiving is, to a large extent at least, within our power. That this is so is, of course, confirmed by everyone's experience. Locke makes the point indirectly. It follows from his statements (i) that we 'cannot *think* at any time, waking or sleeping, without being sensible of it;'[2] and (ii) that the mind comes *in time* to reflect on its own operations. Thus introspection is something quite distinct from the reflex awareness which, Locke thinks, accompanies all mental activity. (*c*) It will be remembered that the ideas with which sensation directly acquaints us all function as 'signs' of a reality with which we are not directly acquainted. This is Locke's version of the notorious 'representative theory of knowledge'. Reflection likewise acquaints us only with 'ideas' of our mental activities; we have no direct and immediate awareness of them. But the mind itself is said to be 'present to the understanding' so that it itself can be directly known.[3] Two questions are naturally suggested by this account. (i) What does it mean to say that we are directly acquainted with the ideas of mental operations and not with the operations themselves? (ii) What does it mean to say that the mind can be known directly and immediately, apart from its contents and activities? A consideration of these two questions will bring out some of the difficulties in Locke's account of reflection.

1. II.1.24.   2. II.1.10.   3. IV.21.4.

The first defect of the doctrine of reflection is, then, a failure to develop the implications of the very sketchy outline which Locke provides. A second defect has become apparent only since the development of psychology as an independent science. Locke holds that we can observe our own mental activities and that observation of this kind is an important and reliable source of the materials of knowledge. Modern psychologists and philosophers would be inclined to raise doubts about this statement. They have expressed their doubts in questions of the following kind: Is introspection even possible? If so, can it give us reliable information? Are there mental processes which can be properly referred to as *activities* or *operations* of the mind? The answers to questions of this sort are by no means so obvious and easy as Locke's rather artless account would suggest. And I think it will be worthwhile considering what some of the difficulties are.

But before going into this question it is worth mentioning one important difference between 'introspection' in the sense in which the word is used by psychologists and 'reflection' in Locke's sense. The term 'introspection' is often loosely applied to our observations of our own mental *states* as well as of our mental *acts*. It is distinguished from other cognitive activities more by its purpose than by its mode of operation or the nature of the objects observed. When we introspect we try to determine and describe the detailed characters of our immediate experience without any sort of interpretation or extrapolation. Acts of introspection are a sub-class of acts of attention. 'Introspection is in fact merely experiencing our mental state.'[1] For Locke, however, reflection was nothing more than a way of accounting for the origin of our concepts of our mental activities like thinking and willing. It comprised only the observation of our own mental *operations* together with the concomitant experiences of pleasure or unpleasure, succession and the other ideas which come to us 'by all the ways of sensation and reflection'. Thus for Locke's doctrine of reflection to be justified we have to justify not only the possi-

1. Alexander, *Space, Time and Deity*, Book I, Chap. 18.

bility and reliability of introspection but also the notion of mental *acts* or *operations*.

Moreover, Locke apparently failed to realize that he could not make a distinction between reflection and the ordinary reflex awareness which he alleged to accompany every mental state without having to amend his doctrine of sensation. If the awareness is sufficient to account for the fact that we come by ideas of sensation, there seems no reason why it should not account for the origin of ideas of reflection also. But if the mind cannot acquire ideas of reflection without a special mental activity of 'taking notice of' its own operations, how can it acquire ideas of sensation without an analogous process of 'taking notice of' those ideas?

Locke divides mental activities into perception or thinking and volition or willing. And it might perhaps be suggested that though thinking and its modes should not, for the reason given above, need to be supplemented with a special activity of 'reflection' before the mind can have its ideas of them, the same cannot be said of volition and its modes. He does indeed admit that 'some degree of voluntary attention' must be an ingredient of a mental state before we can properly speak of the mind being active.[1] I think the answer to this suggestion will be clear when we consider Locke's account of volition and its modes. But for the present I conclude that Locke had no reason to introduce the notion of reflection as a unique and necessary source of cognitive material; or, alternatively, he should have provided a corresponding reflex activity to account for the genesis of our ideas of sensation. But the absurdity of the second alternative is sufficiently obvious without comment. If, however, he had taken the trouble to work out a theory of attention, he would have clarified this confusion and rendered his theory of reflection superfluous.

The question as to whether introspection is à reliable method of obtaining information for the psychologist or even a possible method is still a controversial one. Most psychologists in their experiments avoid introspective methods. But

1. II.9.1.

psychology, like most subjects, is influenced by fashion and it may be that introspection will one day come to be accepted again as a respectable laboratory method just as it was in the laboratories of Külpe and Titchener some fifty years ago. But even if we accept the criticisms which have been made of alleged introspective methods in scientific psychology, there is a sense of the word 'introspection' in which no one but the most dogmatic behaviourist would hesitate to use it. We can *attend to* what we are momentarily aware of even when the object to which we are attending is something as indubitably private as a twinge of toothache, a mental image or an emotional condition. Professor Broad has suggested that we should refer to this sort of attention as 'inspection'. 'Inspection' in this sense would not, of course, be identical with the reflex awareness which, as Locke admits, accompanies our sense experience. When we *inspect*, no less than when we *introspect*, we attend to an object; but the object, in the case of inspection, is the characteristics of our immediate experience. By adopting this suggestion we shall avoid confusing a recognizable and respectable mental state with a far more dubious and debatable process for which Professor Broad reserves the word 'introspection', viz. the process of attending to *other mental acts* or *events* such as perceiving, remembering, desiring, willing and so on. In calling the process dubious and debatable, I intend to suggest that it is very doubtful (i) if such alleged acts of introspection ever occur, and (ii) whether, if they did occur, they could be introspected.

Suggestions of this sort are, of course, a matter of debate among contemporary philosophers. It is therefore important to understand the points I am considering here. Two questions are involved: (i) Are there mental acts at all? (ii) Is there a special kind of mental act satisfying two conditions: (*a*) it is itself an act of *attention*; (*b*) its object is another mental act of such a kind as to have an object of its own. Unless we can answer 'Yes' to *both* these questions, we shall have to deny that introspection, in the sense required by Locke's account of reflection, ever occurs.

The word 'act' when it occurs in phrases like 'mental act', 'act of volition', and similar contexts is an unfortunate one. It is used by analogy with moral or legal phrases like 'a good act', 'an act of murder', etc., where 'act' means 'deed' and we can identify the *agent* to whom we refer the act in question. But when we talk of mental acts there is no observable agent; there is only a hypothetical entity, a mind, self, or soul to which, by analogy, we refer the act. To avoid begging such important questions, let us rather talk of mental *processes* or *events*. If we carefully limit the reference of these substitute phrases they need cause no difficulty. It is easy to define the notion of a mental *state*. Let us say that a mental state is a short slice of the history of a mind in which there is no discernible change. A mental event or process can then be defined as a set of successive mental states in which later members of the set are discernibly different from earlier members. But it is clear that some mental events or processes in the sense defined differ from others in important ways which are relevant to the controversy about mental activity. When we are trying hard to remember someone's name or working out a difficult problem in mathematics, we seem to ourselves to be mentally active in a way analogous to the way in which we are said to be physically active when we are executing a physical task which calls for energy, persistence, and concentration. No one can doubt that mental processes do often manifest these properties. It is mental events of this type, together with choices and the assents of a non-volitional kind, which take place when we are said to 'see the point' of a problem, that some philosophers would like to call mental acts. It should be remembered, however, that the distinction between active and passive mental processes is entirely a matter of degree. Psychologists can provide good empirical evidence to show that the most barely 'passive' of our perceptions is infected with an active element of mental construction or interpretation. And we could, in theory at least, arrange our mental processes in an order according to the degree of 'activity' which is manifested in them. If we decide, on surveying this series, that it is conve-

nient to have a special name for its later members and that the
word 'act' would usefully fill the bill, no great harm is done.
We should, however, bear in mind the question-begging
associations of the word which I have already mentioned. It
would be more prudent, in view of those associations, to talk
of mental events or processes as exemplifying or being accompanied by greater or lesser degrees of attention. It may indeed
be objected that it is not a *sufficient* description of so-called acts
to say that their status in the scale of activity is proportional
to the degree of attention which accompanies them. Nevertheless it is, I think, in accordance with ordinary usage to talk
of *acts* of attention. And if anyone wishes to talk of mental
acts, he can hardly refuse to admit that complex mental processes of which attention is a prominent ingredient are
correctly spoken of as 'mental acts' in accordance with the
convention he is adopting. It would not be proper, for
instance, to talk of 'unconscious mental acts', though we
might speak of 'unconscious mental processes'.

In answer to my first question, then, 'Are there mental
acts?', I shall say that this is not a question of fact but one
concerning a linguistic convention. In so far as the word 'act'
is not used merely to give colour to a theory of a hypothetical
self or soul to which the acts are referred as an agent, its use
seems to be occasioned by the prominence of 'attention' as an
ingredient of mental processes. And this will give a clue to the
answer to the second question. For this will now be expressed
as follows: Can we attend to x and simultaneously attend to
our attending to x?

'Let us call the totality of objects which are present to the
mind at any one moment the "field of consciousness". Only
part of this field is attended to; with the remainder we are not
actively occupied. Thus the total field of consciousness is
broadly divisible into two parts, the field of attention and the
field of inattention. This is frequently illustrated by comparison with the field of view presented to the eye. At any moment
only those features of the field of view are clearly and distinctly
seen on which we fix our eyes, so that impressions coming

from them reach a certain circumscribed portion of the retina called the yellow spot. The other parts of the visual field, seen, as we say, "from the corner of the eye", are, in a peculiar way, blurred and dim.'[1]

This is a purely descriptive account of everyday experience. I do not think that the defender of introspection would refuse to accept it, though he might wish to add to it. But if it is a correct description of the effects of attention, it throws some light on the question: can we attend to x and simultaneously attend to our attending? It is a *necessary* condition of attention (even if it is not a *sufficient* condition) that it increases the clarity and distinctness of certain parts of our field of consciousness. In general, the greater the degree of attention, the greater is the clarity and distinctness of the objects attended to and the smaller the part of our field of consciousness which is thus, as it were, brought into focus.

Now it is true that I can attend to x and say to myself at the same time, 'I am now attending to x'. It is true also that I cannot attend to x without knowing that I am doing so. And if to introspect my acts of attention means merely to do either or both of these things, then obviously I can introspect in this sense. But such a claim would be trivial. What I cannot do is to make my attending to x the object of a second and *contemporary* act of attention. I cannot do this for the simple reason that my acts of attention have no content or positive character other than (*a*) the character of the object to which I am attending, and (*b*) such concomitant organic and muscular sensations (feelings of eyestrain, muscular tensions, etc.) as may accompany my attending. There is thus nothing relevant which I can make clear and bring, as it were, into focus, by my act of introspection. This is admitted by all defenders of mental acts and of introspection. They commonly [2] express their recognition of the fact by saying that consciousness is 'diaphanous' or 'transparent'. And to say this is merely to say, in a metaphorical way, that mental acts have no positive

1. Stout, *Manual of Psychology* (Fourth Edn.), p. 161.
2. Cf. Moore, *Philosophical Studies*, p. 20.

character of their own. And if this is so, it follows, *a fortiori*, that their content cannot be rendered more clear and distinct by attention.

Ideas of Reflection

So far I have been trying to make clear what can and what cannot justifiably be said about 'reflection' in the sense in which Locke uses the word. Had he restricted himself to the modest claim that when we think, choose, believe, etc., we can be aware that we are doing so, he would have been on perfectly safe ground. Moreover, this would have enabled him to demonstrate the empirical origin of our ideas of mental process, just as he could guarantee the empirical origin of our ideas of sensation by referring to the reflex awareness which accompanies sensation. The statement that men 'cannot *think* at any time waking or sleeping without being sensible of it'[1] was sufficient for his purposes in both cases. He introduced unnecessary complications and difficulties by defining reflection as 'inner sense' or 'the perception of the operation of our own mind' or 'the notice which the mind takes of its own operations'. Two of these phrases beg important questions about mental acts, introspection, and the self, and Locke's account of the nature of reflection is not clear or full enough to enable us to know whether or not these phrases are innocently used. And when he states that ideas of reflection are 'as capable to be the objects of (the mind's) contemplation as any of those it received from foreign things',[2] he claims more for reflection than the most conservative psychologist would claim for introspection.

What then, are the ideas which we acquire by reflection? One group of these ideas, those which 'convey themselves into the mind by all the ways of sensation and reflection' has already been examined and I shall not discuss them any further here. The remainder of the ideas of reflection are divided, like other ideas, into simple and complex. We have already seen that Locke did not make clear the basis of this

1. II.1.10   2. II.6.1.

division, even when he used it to classify ideas of sensation. And its application to ideas of reflection seems to have been little more than a superficial show of consistency. He starts with a distinction between two mental 'powers' or 'faculties', the understanding and the will; later he adds a warning about the sense in which the word 'faculty' is to be taken. Faculties must not be supposed 'to stand for some real beings in the soul that performed those actions of understanding and volition'.[1] He does not add a positive explanation of the sense in which he uses the term, but we may conclude from this warning that he is referring by the words 'power' and 'faculty' to dispositional properties of the mind. That we think proves we have a power or faculty of thinking. This is a trivial and uninformative use of the words, but perhaps a harmless one. The simple ideas of reflection are our ideas of these actions of perceiving and willing. And Locke implies, though he does not say so explicitly, that these are the only simple ideas which we receive from reflection alone. The modes of these simple ideas are remembering, reasoning, discerning, abstracting, knowing, judging, believing, and all other mental activities.

Locke starts his account of perception by equating it with *thinking*, but when in Book II.9 he comes to give an exposition of the nature of perception he refers to sense-perception only. And since sensing is later described as a *mode* of thinking and therefore of perceiving,[2] Locke's readers are very naturally confused. The explanation seems to be as follows: 'Thinking' or 'perceiving' are generic terms or rather determinables which refer to a process which can take various determinate forms. The modes of thinking are the relatively determinate ideas which we have of these various determinate processes. It must be remembered that we do not know mental processes directly, but only our ideas of these processes. Thus, in this case also, the relation of simple to complex ideas seems to be the relation of determinables to determinates.

'Perception' is used by Locke generally to refer to processes of an intuitive character and 'thinking' to refer to those of a

1. II.21.6.   2. II.19.1.

discursive character. For example, he has, in another context, a threefold classification of acts of perception. 'Perception, which we make the act of the understanding, is of three sorts: (1) The perception of ideas in our minds. (2) The perception of the signification of signs. (3) The perception of the connexion or repugnancy, agreement or disagreement, that there is between any of our ideas. All these are attributed to the understanding, or perceptive power, though it be the two latter only that use allows us to say we understand.'[1] As Fraser points out,[2] Locke is concerned with the first of these senses in Book II, the second in Book III and the last in Book IV. (This would account for the misleading account of perception he gives in Book II.9.)

If we now enquire about the complex ideas of reflection which are the determinate forms of thinking we meet with a further ambiguity in Locke's exposition. He has a short chapter (Book II.19) entitled *Of the Modes of Thinking*, in which he refers to various modes of which, he says, we have as distinct ideas as we have 'of red and white, a square or a circle'. He lists, as examples of such modes, sensation, remembrance, contemplation, attention, as well as more important modes like judging, reasoning, and knowing, which he promises to treat in more detail elsewhere. (This treatment is given in Book IV.) But there is nothing in the chapter to explain the exact sense in which these mental processes are modes of thinking. There are, however, two previous chapters (Book II.10 and 11) in which he deals with ideas of reflection. These follow his chapter on perception but precede his general discussion of complex ideas in Book II.12. He starts the chapter on complex ideas by remarking that he has previously been discussing simple ideas. This means that the ideas of reflection discussed in Book II.10 and 11 are simple ideas. Unfortunately some of them, like contemplation and remembering, are also classified as complex ideas in Book II.19. Others, such as discerning and comparing, are mental processes which must have attention as

1. II.21.5.
2. Locke's *Essay Concerning Human Understanding*, Vol. I, p. 314, n. 5.

an ingredient, and attention is likewise classed as a *mode* of thinking in II.19.

These confusions alone are sufficient to indicate the absurdity of trying to treat sensation and reflection analogously as though they were independent but co-ordinate sources of ideas. Locke himself seems to have realized the impossibility of pressing the analogy too closely. He makes no attempt to parallel the division of ideas of sensation into simple and complex modes or to find analogies in the field of reflection for ideas of relations. These distinctions are unclear when he applies them to ideas of sensation and they are, of course, quite unfitted to describe ideas of reflection.

Locke's account of ideas of reflection is thus confused and unsatisfactory. But there are two sides to this account. Ideas of reflection are part of the material of our knowledge, it is true. But we can also extract from Locke's account a description of the nature of the understanding (in the wide sense of the word 'understanding' which he uses in the title of the *Essay* where it means 'mind'). The mind, like any other natural object, is known to us through the ideas we have of its operations; and these operations are the activation of the dispositional properties which Locke calls 'powers' or 'faculties'. Both minds and material things are substances. 'Besides the complex ideas we have of material sensible substances, of which I have last spoken, – by the simple ideas we have taken from those operations of our own minds, which we experiment daily in ourselves, as thinking, understanding, willing, knowing and power of beginning motion, etc., co-existing in some substance, we are able to frame the *complex idea of an immaterial spirit*. And thus by putting together the ideas of thinking, perceiving, liberty and power of moving themselves and other things, we have as clear a perception and notion of immaterial substances as we have of material ... The one is as clear and distinct an idea as the other: the idea of thinking and moving a body being as clear and distinct ideas as the ideas of extension, solidity and being moved. For our idea of substance is equally obscure, or none at all, in both; it is but a supposed

I know not what, to support those ideas we call accidents.'[1] The rather exact parallel between minds and material substances which Locke draws here is a little misleading, as there are two important ways in which he modifies it elsewhere.

(i) In accordance with the scholastic tradition, he regards minds as simple substances, *i.e.* as not being made up of parts. He gives this as a reason for the difficulty of explaining mental operations. 'No man can give any account of any alteration made in any simple substance whatsoever.'[2] And this is, of course, an important point of difference between minds and material substances. For the latter are defined as possessing 'solid, and consequently separable, parts.'[3] It must be admitted however that Locke does not keep to the traditional scholastic tradition on this point. He admits that minds may have certain spatial properties. ' *When* and *where*' are questions belonging to all finite existences.'[4] Minds are thus *located* at definite points in space and *mobile*, for they can be at different points in space at different times. So much might have been admitted by the scholastics. But are they also *extended* in space? Clearly, they can hardly be so if they are simple substances. Yet Locke wavers on this point. He does not, indeed, suggest that minds are extended but he is prepared to say that it is not a self-contradictory hypothesis that 'the first Eternal thinking Being or Omnipotent Spirit, should, if he pleased, give to certain systems of created senseless matter, put together as he thinks fit, some degrees of sense, perception, and thought'.[5] We cannot know that such an action on God's part is impossible 'since we know not wherein thinking consists'.[6] Locke is not suggesting here that a materialist philosophy is tenable, for he insists that whether or not our minds are simple and immaterial, we must derive our powers of thinking and willing from God. For he believed, with Descartes and the scholastics, that there could be no more positive qualities in any effect than

1. II.23.15.   2. *Remarks upon Mr Norris' Books, Section* 2.
3. II.23.17.   4. II.15.8.   5. IV.3.6.
6. *Ibid.*

were in its cause. Consequently a thinking being could be explained only by a thinking cause.[1] However the suggestion that God could, if he wished, give matter the power of thinking, was attacked by Dr Stillingfleet because it rendered invalid the premises of the traditional proof of the immortality of the soul.

It had been supposed by the scholastics that if the soul was a simple substance it could not be destroyed. For material substances can be destroyed only by breaking them down in their component parts and as the soul has no such parts, it is indestructible. But it is, of course, clearly sophistical to argue that the soul must be *both* so unlike a material substance that it cannot have parts *and* at the same time so like a material substance that it can be destroyed only by dissolution into parts. If the phrase 'immaterial substance' can be supposed to have any meaning at all, it must at least refer to things which do not have the defining properties of material substances. We cannot therefore assert without self-contradiction: 'x is immaterial *and* x is not destructible unless decomposed'. For the second predicate is an essential property of material substance. The point of the argument, if it can be called such, can be made more obvious by the following example: Living substances can be destroyed only by preventing the oxidation of their tissues. Therefore motor cars can never be destroyed for they have no tissues which require oxygen. That no one would put forward so preposterous an argument is due to the fact that the terms 'living substance' and 'motor car' are fairly well defined and have a fairly definite positive content of their own. The phrases 'immaterial substance' and 'simple substance' have no such positive content and can be defined only in negative terms.

Locke had the good sense not to rest what was to him an important dogma of religion on metaphysical arguments of so dubious a character. He does not positively reject the argument although in his controversy on this matter with the Bishop of Worcester he points out some serious ambiguities

1. IV.10.5.

of the phrase 'immaterial substance'. And in the *Essay* he expresses his doubts about the concept as follows: 'He who will give himself leave to consider freely, and look into the dark and intricate part of each hypothesis, will scarce find his reason able to determine him fixedly for or against the soul's materiality. Since, on which side soever he views it, either as an *unextended substance* or as a *thinking extended matter*, the difficulty to conceive either will, whilst either alone is in his thoughts, still drive him to the contrary side.'[1] He is himself content to rest the certainty of immortality on religious grounds, and thinks that 'all the great ends of morality and religion are well enough secured, without philosophical proofs of the soul's immateriality'.[2] But he doubts whether mind should be thought of as an immaterial substance or as a function of a material substance and this doubt clearly modifies his original statement at Book II.23.15, that our ideas, of mind are as 'clear and distinct' as our ideas of matter.

(ii) The second point on which Locke modifies this original statement is important but puzzling. In the last chapter of the *Essay* where he is referring to the way in which ideas function as 'signs' of things, he says that we have to make use of such signs since the things the mind contemplates are none of them, · *'besides itself*, present to the understanding'. (The italics are mine.) This presumably means that we know the mind directly and not through the medium of representative ideas. He does not explicitly confirm this position anywhere else in the *Essay*. The passage in Book II.23, which I have quoted above, certainly seems to contradict it and in the *Examination of Malebranche*[3] he says that we know only the operations of the mind in reflection and not the mind itself. We can, of course, regard this exception to the representative theory merely as a careless inconsistency. It should be remembered that the scholastics had usually regarded the power of direct self-knowledge as a characteristic of mind and, indeed, as a proof of the immateriality of the soul.[4] It may well be that

1. IV.3.6.   2. *Ibid.*   3. Para. 46.
4. St Thomas Aquinas, *II Contra Gentiles*, 49 and 66.

this is merely another of the unassimilated remnants of Locke's scholastic training.

Yet there are reasons for regarding it as something more. Locke was perfectly well aware of the difficulties of the representative theory of knowledge, as we shall see, and was anxious to avoid certain absurd consequences which might follow from the theory expressed in an injudicious form. He did not wish to deny, for example, that we are certain that we ourselves exist. 'As for *our own existence*, we perceive it so plainly and so certainly, that it neither needs nor is capable of any proof. For nothing can be more evident to us than our own existence. I think, I reason, I feel pleasure and pain; can any of these be more evident to me than my own existence? If I doubt of all other things, that very doubt makes me perceive my own existence and will not suffer me to doubt of that. For if I know I feel pain, it is evident I have as certain perception of my own existence, as of the existence of the pain I feel; or if I know I doubt, I have as certain perception of the existence of the thing doubting, as of that thought which I call *doubt*. Experience then convinces us, that we have an *intuitive knowledge* of our own existence, and an internal infallible perception that we are. In every act of sensation, reasoning, or thinking, we are conscious to ourselves of our own being; and in this matter, come not short of the highest degree of certainty'.[1]

This passage can certainly be read as supporting the statement that we have a direct and immediate knowledge of our own minds. But, such is the looseness and ambiguity of Locke's expression, it can also be read as meaning no more than: (*a*) when we think, we are always aware of the fact, (*b*) 'I think' logically entails 'I exist'. But (*b*), Descartes' famous *cogito, ergo sum*, is merely an analytic triviality. For the word 'I', like all personal pronouns and proper names,[2] is an index-sign

1. IV.9.3.
2. By a 'proper name', I mean a verbal label attached by convention to an actually existing thing or person. Grammatical proper names referring to mythical personages are not proper names in this sense.

which cannot be meaningfully used except to refer to an existent particular. And to say 'this existent particular thinks, therefore it exists' conveys no more new information in the conclusion than does 'this is a black cat, therefore it is a cat'. (Of course, if 'I think' means merely 'thinking is going on' it does not, of itself, form an adequate logical basis for a proof that there is a mind or self which is doing the thinking.)

There are, therefore, two important ambiguities in Locke's views on the nature of the self. (i) It is not clear whether he thought (a) that minds are immaterial substances which we know only through their operations in the same way as we know material substances; or (b) that mind is a function of matter. (ii) We do not know whether he thought (a) that we have the same direct intuitive knowledge of mind that we have of ideas; or (b) that we have a certain belief in our existence but the belief can be logically justified only as a conclusion inferred from the premiss 'I think' which is given to us in experience. It is clear that (i) and (ii) are not logically independent of one another. For example (ii) (a) is incompatible both with (i) (a) and (i) (b). As (ii) (b) is compatible with both (i) (a) and (i) (b) we can save Locke's consistency by assuming that this was his meaning. We do so, however, at the cost of concluding that he mistook a tautology for a factual argument.

There is one further problem which arises out of Locke's discussion of the nature of the mind. The ideas of reflection, like those of sensation, are signs of mental events or processes with which we are never directly acquainted. But if what we become aware of in reflection are only *ideas* of our mental operations, what can we say about the operations themselves? There is, of course, an analogous question about material objects which Locke answers, in part, by his distinction between primary and secondary qualities. But it is obvious that this distinction cannot helpfully be applied to mental operations.[1] We might, indeed, postulate for every deter-

1. In II.21.75 he classifies 'perceptivity or the power of perception or thinking' and 'motivity or the power of moving' as ideas of primary qualities which we receive from reflection. The other primary qualities of

minate idea of reflection a corresponding physical process in the cells of the brain and nervous system. But it would be misleading to describe the physical process as a mental operation and our corresponding idea of reflection, as the idea of a mental operation. If Locke had intended this it would follow (*a*) that minds have secondary qualities only, since it is clear that none of our ideas of reflection can resemble a physical process; (*b*) the concept of mind as an immaterial substance would be superfluous as it could be more simply explained as a by-product of physiological processes. But as we have already seen, Locke explicitly disclaimed any intention of 'meddling with the physical consideration of the mind'.[1] We are therefore left to make what sense we can of the following statements. (i) We know the mind directly. (ii) We do not know its operations directly but mediately through our ideas of reflection. But how we can have a direct acquaintance with a thing without being directly acquainted with any of its properties, Locke does not explain. It is clear that this position is unsatisfactory and that he has failed to work out a clear and consistent account of the nature of mind.

Volition and Freedom

Locke discusses the will and its operations in his chapter *Of Power*.[2] The chapter is the longest in the *Essay*, but unfortunately is by no means the clearest. Yet Locke spent a great deal of trouble on it and introduced extensive and important amendments in the second edition. Nevertheless, as one of his critics has remarked, it is 'a chapter which, notwithstanding all Locke's painful labour, is perhaps the least satisfactory in the *Essay*'. Of the seventy-five sections comprising the chapter, all but six are concerned not with the idea of power, but with the question of freedom of choice. This arises naturally enough from a discussion of volition.

minds, common also to bodies, are listed as existence, duration and number. But this is an exceptional classification and does not correspond with what he has previously written.

1. Intro. 2.   2. II.21.

Locke is concerned at first with making some preliminary distinctions and clarifying his terminology. In the first place he insists that the will and the understanding are *powers* of the mind and *separate* powers. The understanding is the power of 'perceiving', which we have already discussed, and the will is 'this power which the mind has thus to order the consideration of any idea, or the forbearing to consider it, or to prefer the motion of any part of the body to its rest, and *vice versa*, in any particular instance'.[1] The will is thus the mind's capacity for determining what particular thoughts and bodily movements shall occur and at what time. The mind cannot, of course, determine whether or not a waking man shall think or not, for such a man is 'under the necessity of having some ideas constantly in his mind';[2] but it can determine to some extent, at least, *what* he shall think at a given time. Similarly we cannot determine whether or not our bodies shall be in some state of motion or rest for that they shall be so is an essential property of a material body. But we can determine, within certain limits, the determinate manner in which our bodies are to move.

This, then, is Locke's account of the will and the exercise of the will which we call 'volition'. How does he develop this account to meet what has been traditionally known as the problem of free will? He starts with an energetic protest against the propriety of the phrase 'free will'. He thinks that the question 'Whether man's will be free or no?' is 'altogether improper'. 'Liberty, which is but a power, belongs only to *agents*, and cannot be an attribute or modification of the will, which is also but a power.'[3] The misleading implications of the phrase 'free will' have been a source of great confusion in discussions of human freedom. Even in quite recent years philosophers have had to remind us that it is persons who can be said to be free and not their acts or their faculties.[4] Locke did philosophers a valuable service in pointing to this source of confusion, but the rest of his discussion is not so happy.

1. II.21.5.   2. II.21.12.
3. II.21.14.
4. Susan Stebbing, *Philosophy and the Physicists*, ch. X.

Liberty, which, like will, is a power, *i.e.* a dispositional property of agents, is defined as 'a power to think or not to think, to move or not to move according to the preference or direction of (a man's) own mind'.[1] This definition is so similar to the definition of 'will' given above that it is easy to wonder why Locke insists that my will and my freedom are entirely separate powers. The relation between them seems to be as follows. Both understanding and will are necessary conditions of freedom, but they are not sufficient conditions. 'Agents that have no thought, no volition at all, are in everything *necessary agents.*'[2] Locke explains that will is a kind of preference, although a preference of things within our power. A man might prefer flying to walking but he could not be said to will or choose to fly. Our will is, according to Locke, the power of deciding or setting the course of our actions and liberty is our power of putting into effect the decisions we have made. Thus although they can be said to be distinct powers, liberty presupposes will.

It looks from this account as though it can never be said with propriety that we choose freely, although we can freely carry out the choices we have made. This would surely be a paradoxical conclusion; yet it seems to be implied by much of what Locke has to say. '*Liberty*, on the other side, is the power a *man* has to do or forbear doing any particular action according as its doing or forbearance has the actual preference in the mind; which is the same thing as to say, according as he himself wills it.'[3] But it is obvious that if our choices are necessitated, it is little use to add that we are free in putting them into effect. Our freedom would then be something purely negative and consist merely in a capacity to defer the execution of what we have ourselves chosen.

On the definition I have just quoted it would not indeed be even so much, as my action or forbearance from action are said to be determined by my actual preferences. But elsewhere Locke is more generous. He grants that the will is determined though he thinks that the determining factor is not what we

1. II.21.8.   2. II.21.13.   3. II.21.15.

think good or even necessarily what we desire. The constant and natural tendency of the individual is to remove present pain or 'uneasiness' and the desire which the will must accept as dominant is the desire to be rid of the greatest of our present pains. Locke seems to regard this statement as a law of psychology based on empirical generalization and even attempts to support it with factual evidence. It is, however, clearly no more than an analytic circularity akin to the well-known sophism: the strongest motive always prevails; and it is proved to be strongest by the fact that it prevails.

Locke then admits what looks like an exception to the determinism he has so far outlined. 'There being in us a great many uneasinesses, always soliciting and ready to determine the will, it is natural, as I have said, that the greatest and most pressing should determine the will to the next action; and so it does for the most part, but not always. For, the mind having in most cases, as is evident in experience, a power to *suspend* the execution and satisfaction of any of its desires; and so all, one after another; is at liberty to consider the objects of them, examine them on all sides and weigh them with others. ... This seems to me the source of all liberty; in this seems to consist that which is (as I think improperly) called *free will*.'[1] His conclusion is that when we desire, will and act according to the last result of a fair examination, our freedom consists in the fact that we can defer action to ensure that the examination is a fair one.

This alters our situation from being determined by a desire to remove our greatest present uneasiness to being determined by our judgement as to what will best further our ultimate happiness. But Locke considers that this is no abrogation of our freedom. If our actions were in no way determined, they would be merely random and capricious and as little a proper subject of a moral judgement as any involuntary action. No doubt there is a good deal of truth in this contention. But his whole account is not the smallest use in enabling us to answer the question: is it ever true to say of a man who does action *A*

1. II.21.48.

in a given situation, that he *could have done* action B without any change at all in the antecedent circumstances, mental and physical? For unless we can answer this question in the affirmative it is misleading, to say the least, to talk of moral freedom. It may be, of course, that the question cannot be answered because it is based on a confusion. But in that case, we solve the difficulty by showing how the confusion has arisen. And Locke's account gives us no help in this direction.

It should be noted, in conclusion, that Locke's doctrine of human freedom is not original. It is a rather weak and muddled version of the theory expounded by St Thomas Aquinas. Aquinas sets it out with his usual lucidity but even in his hands it is not very satisfactory. When Locke took it over, he had, of course, to divorce it completely from the psychological and metaphysical presuppositions from which, in its scholastic context, it derived much of its plausibility. This is an example of the unfortunate effect on Locke's thinking of the unassimilated residue of his early scholasticism.

The Unity of the Mind and Personal Identity

The discussion of this important question arises, like Locke's discussion of volition and freedom, indirectly from his treatment of ideas of relation. He devoted a chapter[1] to the subject *Of Identity and Diversity* and discusses in this chapter four different senses in which we may use the word 'identity'.

(1) The identity of inorganic material bodies consists in the fact that they can be uniquely described and identified in terms of space-time co-ordinates. 'Could two bodies be in the same place at the same time; then those two parcels of matter must be one and the same, take them great or little.'[2] This example makes clear at once what Locke is doing in this discussion of identity. He is not making any metaphysical discoveries or proposals as to what identity *really consists in*, though he may well have thought that he was doing so. He is, for the most part, merely describing the linguistic rules we follow when we

1. II.27.   2. II.27.2.

use the words 'identity' and 'identical', and, to some extent also, he is making proposals as to how the word should be used when the rules of usage are not perfectly clear or sufficient. We cannot imagine a state of affairs which would verify the statement that the same thing was in two places at the same time; the reason is that if two discontinuous portions of space are simultaneously occupied, it is one of our linguistic conventions to call the occupants 'different things', whatever their origins may be and however closely they may resemble one another.

It seems to me, however, that Locke's account of this type of identity is incomplete. For it is surely also a criterion of identity, in this sense of the word, that at least in the case of ordinary macroscopic bodies, a thing's space-time history should be continuous. By this I mean that one and the same thing cannot exist at two different times, without having continuously existed through the period separating the two times. Nor can it exist first in one place and then later in another without having moved continuously through the region separating the first place from the second.

(2) In the case of compound bodies, like a cube of sugar made up of a number of crystals or a crystal of salt made up of a number of molecules, there is a further condition which he thinks must be satisfied before we can speak, for example, of an object as identical with the one I saw five minutes ago. This condition is that there should be the same number of parts and that each part should be identical, in sense (1), throughout the period concerned. Locke adds that as long as this condition is satisfied the configuration of the particles may be changed without prejudice to the identity of the whole. He is here recommending a new usage rather than describing one which is established. The word 'identical' is not always used in this strict way.

(3) This case leads on to a third: 'In the state of living creatures, their identity depends not on a mass of the same particles, but on something else. For in them the variation of great parcels of matter alters not the identity: an oak growing

from a plant to a great tree, and then lopped, is still the same oak.... The reason whereof is, that in these two cases, a *mass of matter* and a *living body*, identity is not applied to the same thing.'[1] In general, the identity of an organism consists in the fact that the organism 'partakes of the same life, though that life be communicated to new particles of matter vitally united to the living plant, in a like continued organization conformable to that sort of plants'.[2] Identity depends in such cases on the organization of the parts and Locke recognizes that machines as well as organisms have identity in that sense. He believes that the only difference between them is as follows. A machine may be in working order without actually working because the organization is a necessary but not a sufficient condition for the machine to work; the appropriate force must be applied from outside. In the organism, however, the appropriate configuration of parts is both a necessary and a sufficient condition of life. 'The fitness of the organization and the motion wherein life consists, begin together, the motion coming from within.'[3] Locke is here making a factual statement but it is doubtful if a modern biologist would accept it.

(4) When we talk of the identity of a man, we may use the word in two quite different senses. In one ordinary use, we may be referring to his identity as a living body (and therefore, too, as a physical object). If a man were completely to lose his memory through mental disease and to have his temperament and character transformed beyond recognition, we should still say, in this sense, that he was the same man. This use is covered by what has been said above. But the other sense is important too. In one of Kafka's stories[4] the hero wakes up one morning to find himself transformed into an enormous insect. But his mental life, his memory, character, tastes, ambitions, etc., remain as before. He can still say to himself, 'I am the same person who went to sleep here last night.' And so he is, of course, *in a sense* the same person. But what is this sense?

Locke's answer to this question occasioned a great deal of

1. II.27.4.   2. II.27.5.
3. II.27.6.   4. *The Metamorphosis.*

controversy, for here, of course he was trespassing on theological preserves. It had been traditional to regard the identity of the self as the identity of an immaterial substance, the soul. Locke was sufficiently critical of the concept of substance and, in particular, of immaterial substance, to be aware of the difficulties of this view. 'If the identity of soul alone makes the same man and there be nothing in the nature of matter why the same individual spirit may not be united to different bodies, it will be possible that those men living in different ages and of different tempers may have been the same man: which way of speaking must be from a very strange use of the word "man". . . . But yet, I think, nobody could he be sure that the soul of Heliogabalus were in one of his hogs, would yet say that hog were a man or Heliogabalus.'[1] In other words, the supporters of this view propose that we should use the phrase 'the same man' in an entirely new way, without being able to offer any empirical criterion for the correctness of the proposed usage.

Locke sees quite clearly that the answer to the question does not depend on a matter of non-linguistic fact but entirely on the established usage of the phrase 'the same person'. 'To conceive and judge of it aright, we must consider what idea the word it is applied to stands for.'[2] His own view is that personal identity consists in consciousness. This statement is extremely vague and it is important to decide just what he means by it. By 'consciousness' Locke appears to mean (a) the awareness I have of my present experiences, (b) the awareness I have that my past experiences were once present to me. I have tried to condense Locke's theory into ordinary language and it will readily be seen that there seem to be at least two serious objections to it as it is expressed. (i) It is tautologous and therefore uninformative to say that my past experiences were once present to me. (ii) The explication of 'consciousness' contains personal pronouns and adjectives. Such words are significant only if they refer to individual persons and an analysis of 'personal identity' which contains such words is

1. II.27.7.   2. II.27.8.

therefore circular. (The same objection can be made if we substitute 'anyone' or '*x*' for '*I*'.) It is however possible to rephrase Locke's account without using personal pronouns. For such pronouns are only a convenient shorthand for referring to certain sets of experiences or mental states. The empirical facts on which the notion of personal identity is based are the substantial continuity of consciousness[1] and the possibility of a later state in the continuous series being (or containing) a memory that an earlier state was in fact a member of the series. In other words, we can just as easily explain the notion of personal identity by referring to the relations between the mental states themselves as we can by referring to the relations between a hypothetical substantial self, on the one hand, and the mental states on the other. And our explanation will not be at variance with any of the facts of common experience on which the conventional usage of terms like 'personal identity', 'self' and their synonyms depend.

I shall now state what seems to me to be the point of Locke's theory. It is true that his own statement of the theory is incomplete and not too clear. And his defence of it, in his controversy with the Bishop of Worcester, is concerned only with entertaining but undecidable theological niceties such as the nature of the bodies in which we must appear at the judgement seat. I think however that Locke's view can be defended on the following lines, without departing too far from the spirit of his argument. Questions about the nature of personal identity are questions about the meaning of the phrase 'personal identity'. And these questions can be decided in one way only, namely, by ascertaining the way in which the phrase is used by English-speaking people. When we have ascertained the conventional usage, we have done all we can. There is no secret 'real meaning' to discover, though to suppose that words have such real meanings, distinct from their usage, is a common superstition.

1. Consciousness can be said to be continuous when two adjacent mental states have the same sort of similarity as two adjacent frames in a cinematograph film, *i.e.*, there is a minimal discriminable difference between them.

What Locke has done is to point out that people do normally use the phrase 'personal identity' in the way he suggests. For instance, it is the criterion used in diagnosing cases of 'multiple personality'. Evidence of this kind is all he needs to prove his case. For 'personal identity' is for Locke the name not of a substance but of a mixed mode. And ideas of mixed modes are made by the mind, as Locke says, arbitrarily and without any necessary reference to real existence, 'wherein they differ from those of substances, which carry with them the supposition of some real being, from which they are taken, and to which they are conformable'.[1] On the other hand, we demonstrate the meaning of the name of a substance by showing (a) that a substance of a certain kind actually exists and (b) that people do use the name to refer to things of that kind.

The scholastic metaphysicians who believed that the word 'person' referred to an immaterial substance failed on both counts. For they could never prove (a) to the satisfaction of anyone but themselves and in consequence the usage they recommended could never be widely adopted. And if it were adopted, that fact would not, of itself, have any weight at all in proving the existence of the alleged immaterial substances.

1. III.5.3.

CHAPTER SIX

Language and Thinking

IN Book II, Locke has analysed, classified, and traced the origins of what he calls the 'instruments or materials of our knowledge'. And as he explains in the concluding section of the book, he had intended to proceed immediately to discuss the nature of knowing. 'This was that which, in the first general view I had of this subject, was all that I thought I should have to do: but upon a nearer approach, I find that there is so close a connexion between ideas and words, and our abstract ideas and general words have so constant a relation one to another, that it is impossible to speak clearly and distinctly of our knowledge, which all consists in propositions, without considering, first, the nature, use, and signification of language; which, therefore, must be the business of the next book.'[1] He returns to this topic in the final chapter of the *Essay*. 'The consideration, then, of *ideas* and *words* as the great instruments of knowledge, makes no despicable part of their contemplation who would take a view of human knowledge in the whole extent of it. And perhaps, if they were distinctly weighed and duly considered, they would afford us another sort of logic and critic, than that we have been hitherto acquainted with.'[2]

Nowadays philosophers do not need to be reminded of the importance of linguistic questions for philosophy, but in the seventeenth century it was unusual to pay them any special attention. Thus though Book III was not the most influential part of the *Essay*, it is in some ways the most original. Locke makes a serious attempt to demonstrate the relations, as he conceived them, between thinking, the signs which we use in thinking, and the referents of these signs. And though he makes some serious mistakes, the mistakes are instructive.

Locke starts by observing that language is necessary for man

1. II.33.19.   2. IV.21.4.

in his capacity of social animal. In order that he shall be able
to use language, three things are necessary: (1) he must be
able to frame articulate sounds or words; (2) he must be able
to use these sounds as marks of *ideas*; (3) he must be able, if
necessary, to use words generally so that one word can 'mark
a multitude of particular existences'.[1] (All words, except proper names, are, in fact, general.) (2) is one of Locke's major
errors. And (3) raises the traditional problem of universals.
I shall, first of all, discuss these two points in order.

Words and their Referents

'Thus we may conceive how *words*, which were by nature so
well adapted to that purpose, came to be made use of by men
as the signs of their ideas; not by any natural connexion that
there is between particular articulate sounds and certain ideas,
for then there would be but one language amongst all men;
but by a voluntary imposition, whereby such a word is made
arbitrarily the mark of such an idea. The use, then, of words is
to be sensible marks of ideas; and the ideas they stand for are
their proper and immediate signification.'[2] Locke's proof of
his assertion that words signify ideas directly and not things is
based on his representative theory of knowledge. As words
are sounds arbitrarily selected to stand for certain *designata*,
the things, qualities or relations which they designate, the
designata in question must be things with which we are directly
acquainted. And the only things we know directly in this way
are our own ideas. 'A man cannot make his words the signs
either of qualities in things, or of conceptions in the mind of
another, whereof he has none in his own (mind).'[3] Nevertheless our words do, of course, refer indirectly both to ideas in
the minds of other people and to things and their properties.
This is shown by (*a*) the fact that men speaking the same language can make themselves mutually understood and (*b*) the
fact that 'men would not be thought to talk barely of their
own imagination but of things as they really are'.[4] Neverthe-

1. III.1.3.   2. III.2.1.   3. III.2 2.   4. III.2.5.

less Locke insists that it is 'perverting the use of words' if we suppose them to stand for anything but our own ideas.

The defects of this theory are, in part, the defects of the representative theory of knowledge. And in so far as this is so, I shall consider them later. But there is a certain corollary of this view which is very widely held both by philosophers and the ordinary man, quite independently of any particular theory of knowledge. Generally it can be expressed in outline in the following terms. When we are considering human thinking, we have to distinguish between the thoughts and the vehicle or medium in which the thoughts are expressed. We all know what it means to be able to say the same thing in different words or to be at a loss how to express our thoughts correctly. It is alleged that facts like these show quite clearly that a judgement expressed in the English language, for example, is a complex entity consisting of at least two separate components, a material component, the thought, and a structural component, the language in which the thought is expressed. Further, we may encounter words with, as we say, no thought behind them and also thoughts which are not expressed in words or, indeed, in any symbolic medium. When we are talking or reading or listening to a lecture there are two simultaneous and parallel mental processes going on in our heads. When we are talking ourselves, for example, we are thinking and at the same time translating our thoughts into language which our listeners will understand. Our listeners, on the other hand, are decoding or translating our language into their own thoughts. The whole procedure, in fact, is very like what happens at an international conference where the speeches have to be interpreted before they are universally intelligible. I shall call this the 'translation theory of meaning'.

It may be objected that metaphorical expressions like 'translating' or 'decoding' are misleading because there is a big difference between expressing our thoughts in language or understanding what another person is saying and translating a passage from English into French. This is true, no doubt. But such metaphors, which admittedly show the absurdity of the theory, are suggested by the language in which this point of view is usually propounded by its supporters. There seem to be obvious analogies between expressing our thoughts in words and translating, between mistranslating and misunderstanding, between being unable to express one's meaning and being at a loss for the right word or phrase in a foreign language, and so on. What the differences are is for the supporters of the theory to point out, not for its opponents.

And here they are in a difficulty. For in order to be able to give an account of the relevant differences between these processes, they must be able to say what thinking is like. They have, in other words, to give an empirical account of the thought process before it is expressed in any symbolic medium. And nobody has ever been able to do this. If we carefully introspect what is happening when, for example, we are listening to someone talking, we shall not find anything except the words we are listening to, *so long as we understand them*. If I am talking myself, I shall not be able to introspect any separate process of thinking which is mirrored by my words, *so long as I am not at a loss for a word*. But these phrases I have italicized do not indicate exceptions which support Locke's theory. For what takes place when there is a momentary hitch in our understanding or expression is not a flow of words without any thoughts to give them meaning in the one case or a flow of thoughts without any words to express them in the other. It is just that our mental contents, words, images, bodily tensions, and feelings, etc., no longer seem appropriate or fitting to the context. When we are at a loss for a word or phrase, it is not like trying on gloves in a shop to find a pair which fits us. It is not, in other words, that we know what we want to say but cannot express it. Rather it is that we do not know exactly what we want to say until we say it. The process of trying to remember a name is very similar. Here also we do not know just what it is we are trying to find until we have found it.

There is a well-known controversy in psychology about the occurrence of 'imageless' or non-symbolic thinking which is relevant to this question. If the theory we are considering is correct, then not only does imageless thinking sometimes occur, but it must occur *whenever* symbolic thinking occurs. For to say that we are thinking in words or other signs would mean that we were translating our pure non-symbolic thinking into an appropriate symbolic medium. But it would not, of course, be sufficient to prove the 'translation' theory, if it could be proved that imageless thinking *sometimes* occurs.

Now the question about the occurrence of imageless thinking is a question of fact which can be established, if at all, by the methods of the experimental psychologist. During the first decade of the present century when introspective methods were still fashionable among psychologists, a great deal of work was done on this topic.[1] The results were inconclusive. Anything which was affirmed on experimental evidence in support of the thesis that non-symbolic thinking occurs was denied with equal authority on the basis of other experiments. We can say that at present there are no well-established empirical findings to support the suggestion that a thought process can occur in the absence of some form of symbolic expression.

It is possible, of course, that future work may alter this position. For example, a careful study of thought processes in patients whose powers of symbolic expression have been disordered by brain injuries could throw new light on the question. But whatever the outcome of such further enquiries, it is very improbable that the 'translation' theory could ever be rendered plausible. For the available experimental evidence has at least made it clear that if non-symbolic thinking does occur, it is an extraordinarily rare and elusive kind of happening. But the theory asks us to believe that such pure thinking continuously accompanies and mirrors all our symbolic thinking, and all our talking and listening, and that without it no symbols could have meaning. And it is surely impossible to believe that so universal and important a feature of our mental life could escape the most cursory inspection.

1. For an account of this work see E. G. Boring, *A History of Experimental Psychology*, pp. 393–411.

It is not difficult to see the mistake which has been responsible for this popular philosophical myth. It has been also a contributory cause of a number of metaphysical muddles, including some of the more extravagant theories about universals and objective values. The mistake lies in a tendency to hypostatize features of our experience. We tend to suppose that because some of these features are especially pervasive or important, they can or must exist in a pure form either in our experience or beyond it. Aristotle, for example, pointed out that we can distinguish in every material object a formal element, its shape or organization, and a material element, that which is shaped or organized. He thus provided two useful correlative concepts, matter and form, which have sometimes been valuable in philosophical analysis. But he went on to suppose that it was significant to talk of *pure form*, which is not the shape or organization of anything, and of *prime matter* which is totally devoid of shape or organization of any kind. But matter and form are useful concepts only because they are *correlative features of experience*. As soon as the concepts are generalized so that they lose their mutual reference they become mere empty terms. For their significance lies in their relational character and it would be as absurd to talk of form without matter as of an owner who possessed no property or a husband who had no wife. A similar fallacy is responsible for the view we are considering. We can, indeed, distinguish in every meaningful sentence two essential components, the meaning and the verbal expression which conveys it. But the fact that this is a distinction which we find necessary does not entail that it is helpful or even significant to suppose that these correlative components ever exist in isolation.

What I have said above relates to the general objections to this point of view. But we must now consider more closely the difficulties of the special form in which Locke held it. He believes that words refer directly to ideas and an idea is 'whatsoever is the object of the understanding when a man thinks';[1] whether it is sense-datum, image, or concept. Think-

1. Intro. 8.

ing is a mental process or activity which is directed to ideas which form, as it were, the material of our thinking. Individual words stand for, or are signs of, individual ideas, simple or complex, and sentences are presumably to be regarded, though Locke does not say so explicitly, as signs of propositions, questions, or imperatives. He does distinguish, however, between two kinds of words out of which we build our sentences. Words are either 'names of ideas in the mind' or signs of the relations between ideas or between propositions. The latter class he calls 'particles', a word which covers prepositions, conjunctions, and the logical copula. Such words are 'not truly by themselves the names of any ideas'[1] but are 'all marks of some action or intimation of the mind'.[2]

Locke probably means that if I say, for example, 'my dog is black', the logical copula 'is' *expresses* the fact that I am asserting a proposition but does not *refer* to my assertion or denial. But though this may be true in some cases it cannot account for all the uses of particles. Prepositions, for example, often refer to spatial or temporal relations between ideas. It has been seen that Locke gives an ambiguous and unsatisfactory account of relations. On the whole he tends to emphasize the mental character of relations and the fact that they are a product of the mental activity of comparing ideas. But even he can hardly suppose that the fact that St Paul's Cathedral is *in* the city of London and not *outside* it is due to our mental activity in comparing the ideas of St Paul's and the City of London. However, he is insistent on the principle that relations being known as the result of a mental process, must hold between ideas,[3] and this makes him neglect the foundation for the relation which exists in the things themselves. I think therefore we shall have to amplify Locke's account of the symbolic function of particles by saying that they can either *express* mental attitudes or activities or *refer* to relations between ideas.

So far then we may say that Locke recognizes two functions of signs, the *referential* and the *expressive* functions. For ex-

1. III.7.2.   2. III.7.4.   3. II.25.9.

ample, when I say 'it is raining' my statement refers or points to the state of the weather and also *expresses* my belief that it is raining just as if I say 'ow' when I cut myself, the exclamation expresses my feeling of pain. But unfortunately he does not go much further than this, in analysing the functions of language. We have seen that he regards the task he sets himself in the *Essay* as being a part of the 'doctrine of signs' but he does not explain how it is that certain sounds or marks come to function as signs or in what that function consists. All we have to go on is the fact that he believes both that ideas are signs of things and their properties and that words are signs of ideas.

But is the sense in which the idea is a sign of a property, for instance, the same as the sense in which a word is the sign of an idea? Locke does not consider this question explicitly, but there are some obvious differences between the two cases. (i) We are directly acquainted with both words and ideas; we are not directly acquainted with both ideas and the things they represent except, of course, in the case of images. (ii) Words signify ideas 'by a perfect arbitrary imposition'.[1] In other words, the connexion between words and their referents is purely conventional. The connexion between ideas and what they represent is, on the other hand, a part of nature and unalterable by human decisions. (iii) The mode of representation is different in the two cases. Ideas of primary qualities and images at least are iconic; that is, they resemble the qualities they represent. Words, with a few onomatopoeic exceptions like 'boom' and 'bow-wow', are never iconic. Some nonverbal signs, of course, do picture what they signify, but Locke is considering here verbal signs alone. It is therefore clear that Locke is using the word 'sign' in two very different senses. When he talks of an idea as a sign he is using the word in an extended or metaphorical sense. The way in which a word functions as a sign is the primary sense in which a sign serves as a substitute for what it signifies. 'There comes, by constant use, to be such a connexion between certain sounds and the

1. III.2.8.

ideas they stand for, that the names heard, almost as readily excite certain ideas as if the objects themselves, which are apt to produce them, did actually affect the senses.'[1]

Language, then, in Locke's view, functions by exciting the ideas to which it has become bound by associative bonds. When we reflect that 'ideas' for Locke consist largely of sensory elements like sense data and images it is not very difficult to see the defects of his view. It is, in fact, a particularly crude form of the 'translation' theory of meaning which I have criticized above. Words refer to ideas. Ideas by definition cannot be known to the mind unless they are actually present to it. Therefore words cannot occur significantly unless they are actually co-present in the mind with the appropriate ideas.

What sort of ideas is Locke referring to? He cannot mean 'sense data' since it is patently false that the hearing or reading of the words evokes any sense data (except of course those actually involved in hearing or reading the words). Nor is it true that understanding or using language is always or even normally accompanied by relevant imagery. The extent to which imagery is a prominent feature of mental life varies enormously from one person to another, as psychological studies have shown. It may be totally absent without in any way affecting understanding or expression, or abundant without facilitating them. The only types of ideas other than sense data or images would be 'imageless thoughts'. Their status and credentials have been sufficiently discussed already.

We should notice, too, that, in his discussion of the relation between words and ideas, Locke seems not to have realized that words themselves *are* ideas as he defines them. Now every occurrence of a word is an idea, in Locke's sense, in the minds of the people who speak, hear, read, or write it. For marks on paper (as seen by us), noises, and kinaesthetic sensations in speech organs are all ideas. Thus in saying that words are signs of ideas in the minds of those who use the words, Locke is doing more than involving himself in the difficulties of the 'translation' theory of the thought process. He is propounding

1. III.2.6.

a theory of language which makes it difficult to understand how communication can ever take place. Certain ideas in the mind of *A* are signs of certain other ideas in the mind of *A*; and similarly for *B*, *C*, and so on. Locke says, indeed, that men 'suppose their words to be marks of the ideas in the minds also of other men, with whom they communicate'.[1] But on Locke's theory we have no reason at all for supposing this, for he gives no grounds whatever for allowing an idea in *A*'s mind to become a 'mark' or sign of an idea in *B*'s mind. Our languages are as private as our worlds. And once the representative theory of knowledge is taken seriously, it is difficult to see how it could be otherwise.

General Ideas and the Problem of Universals

Philosophical problems often take their origin from facts which are so trivial and obvious that they are not ordinarily remarked on in our everyday thinking and talking about the world. One of these facts is that the world is made up of a large number of things – plants, animals, people, houses, stones, stars, planets, and so on – which resemble each other in some respects and differ in others. When two things are alike or different, they are so in virtue of their properties or qualities. Two apples, for example, may be alike in shape, colour or texture but differ in size or taste. Two cubes of metal, one of gold and one of silver, may be alike in size and shape, be alike shiny and malleable, but differ in weight, colour and in their reaction to nitric acid. If we take two new shillings, minted at the same time, we shall find them exactly alike in weight, size, shape, colour, and so on, but even they cannot have *all* their properties in common. For they cannot both occupy exactly the same position in space at the same time. If one of them, *A*, is on top of the other, *B*, 'being on top of *B*' is a property which *B* cannot share with *A* as it can share its size, shape, weight, and so on. (Properties of this kind, like

1. III.2.4.

'being above', 'being larger than', 'being to the left of', and so on are called *relational properties*.)

Thus it seems, at first sight, that the whole universe is divided into entities of two kinds, particular things or substances and their properties, qualities, or attributes, and the relations between them. This apparent division of the world into two radically different kinds of entity is the starting-point for a number of philosophical problems. We have already considered Locke's discussion of one of these, the problem of substance. We have now to consider his treatment of the problem of universals. What is this 'problem'? It is extraordinarily difficult to give a precise answer to this question in spite of all the time and energy which philosophers have spent on it from Plato to the present day. Any answer we give is apt to beg the very question at issue. But the puzzle arises in the following way.

We all do distinguish at a commonsense level between particular things and their properties. We see that a particular thing may share any or all of its properties with another thing *except* the relational properties which give it its position in space and time. No two things can occupy the same place at the same time. Thus the crucial difference is not between things and their properties but between what can be uniquely distinguished and identified by space-time measurements and what can be manifested at the same time in many different places. For example, the pen I am now writing with can be uniquely identified by giving its *exact* latitude, longitude, height above sea level, and date. But its colour, shape, structure, and so on are common to all pens of the same make and pattern. The crucial distinction, in other words, is not that between things and their properties but between *instances* of qualities or relations and the qualities or relations themselves.

But what meaning are we to put on this phrase 'the qualities or relations themselves'? We are used to the particular things and events, and the particular instances of qualities and relations which make up our experience, and there seems nothing in any way mysterious about them. But if we ask ourselves what it means to be *general* or *universal* and so capable of being common to many different instances, it is very difficult indeed to give an answer that will stand up to criticism. The 'problem of universals' is just the problem of giving an answer to this question.

The Greek and medieval philosophers devoted a great deal of acute discussion to this problem and worked out three main types of answer. Subsequent philosophers have elaborated one or other of these types. According to Plato and the Realists, universals are real but immaterial entities existing outside the world of space and time but capable of being manifested in particular things and giving them their characteristic pattern and qualities rather as a die imposes a pattern on the metal when medals or coins are struck from it. (This metaphor is not a very good one as the die is itself a particular thing.) Realism has, however, not always taken the fantastic and unplausible form in which it was formulated by Plato. Later Realists, following suggestions by Aristotle, agreed with Plato in regarding universals as general natures common to individuals of the same kind but differed from him in holding that these general natures existed only in the individual things and could not exist apart from them. The Conceptualists, on the other hand, held that the universal was the *idea* or *concept*, a purely mental entity and that there was no generality in things outside the mind. Lastly, the Nominalists believed that the universal was merely the *word* or *sign* by which things, qualities, or relations are represented to us. The generality of the universal lay for them in the representative function of the word.

Realism, Conceptualism, and Nominalism, described in this summary fashion, are nothing more than rough suggestions for an answer to the problem and as worked out in detail by individual philosophers they can take many different forms.

Locke introduced the problem of universals in the following terms: 'All things that exist being particulars, it may perhaps be thought reasonable that words, which ought to be conformed to things, should be so too, I mean in their signification: but yet we find quite the contrary. The far greatest part of words which make all languages are general terms: which has not been the effect of neglect or chance, but of reason and necessity'.[1] He then goes on to detail the reasons why it is both impossible and undesirable that languages should approximate to the limit at which 'any particular thing should have a distinct peculiar name'.[2]

Thus Locke introduces the question as a puzzle arising out of the nature of language. This is not, of course, the only way in which the problem can arise, but it is an important one. The difficulty arises in the following way. Language can be regarded, for certain limited purposes, as a *map* of the whole universe, physical and mental. (Serious mistakes can result from pressing this metaphor too far and we must be careful not to do so.) Now it is obvious that there is never a perfect similarity of structure between the world and a given language. A natural language, even a highly developed one like English, will be much poorer and much less complex than the world which it maps. To take one obvious example, there are, according to the experimental psychologists, over 30,000 colour differences[3] discriminable by the normal human eye, but few languages would have as many as a hundred words by which to mark these differences. But this lack of isomorphism between language and the world is not necessarily a defect in a language. The scale and detail which we require of a map are always determined by the particular purposes for which we are using it. And there is always a limit to the scale and detail which is useful even for our most exacting requirements. A map of scale 400 yards to the mile would be valueless for any purpose.

Now Locke is well aware of all this though he discusses the matter in different terms. He points out that it is psychologically impossible that every feature of the world should be reflected in a corresponding feature of language. The multitudinous detail of what logicians have called a 'perfect lan-

1. III.3.1.   2. III.3.2.
3. This was Titchener's rather conservative estimate. Other psychologists have put the figure much higher.

guage' which would have a proper name for every particular and for every relation between particulars, would be just as impossible to memorize as the world itself. Thus the first reason why there must be general terms in a language is that no one could ever memorize a language which consisted entirely of proper names. And he adds that, even if it were possible, such a language would be useless for communication. 'This cannot be done by names applied to particular things; whereof I alone having the ideas in my mind, the names of them could not be significant or intelligible to another, who was not acquainted with all those very particular things which had fallen under my notice.'[1] In other words, such a language would not enable us to convey any new information or enable us to refer to anything outside our immediate present experience. It would have a third defect also. Having no general terms, it would afford us no means of recording comparisons, classifications and generalizations and so 'would not be of any great use for the improvement of knowledge'.[2]

For all these reasons, we cannot dispense with general terms. Since this is so, Locke proceeds to the question of the origin of such terms. 'For, since all things that exist are only particulars, how come we by general terms; or where find we those general natures they are supposed to stand for?'[3] Locke's point here is that the word 'blue', for example, written or spoken, on a given occasion is a particular event with a unique set of spatial, temporal, and other relational properties. These properties uniquely identify it and distinguish it from all other events, including all other occurrences of the word 'blue'. Yet this particular event can function so as to call to mind any one of an indefinite large class of shades of colour. How does this sign-relationship arise? It is easy enough to account for the origin of proper names. A man is introduced to us as 'Mr. A.B.' and we thereafter associate the phrase 'Mr. A.B.' with that particular individual. Nothing is involved here but our memory of the fact that a certain label is assigned by custom to a certain individual. But more than this is in-

1. III.3.3.   2. III.3.4.   3. III.3.6.

volved in calling a dog 'dog'. We learn when we are children to assign the name 'dog' to the few dogs we happen to meet and thereafter we find we can apply the word substantially in accordance with custom to a large variety of animals, none of which we have seen before. And in the same way we come to use all the general terms in our vocabulary.

Locke accounts for this process in the following way. All words refer to ideas and general words refer to general ideas. That is to say, a word becomes a general word not by signifying indifferently any one of a given class of things or properties, or even any one of a given class of ideas, but by signifying one general idea. 'Words become general by being made the signs of general *ideas*, and *ideas* become general, by separating from them the circumstances of time and place, and any other ideas that may determine them to this or that particular existence. By this way of abstraction they are made capable of representing more individuals than one; each of which having in it a conformity to that abstract *idea* (as we call it), of that sort.'[1] Ideas become general then in consequence of a mental process which Locke calls 'abstraction'.

He refers first to this process in Book II where he is discussing ideas of reflection but the account he gives there is almost identical with the short description I have quoted above. This is a pity because the notion of abstraction is basic to Locke's theory of universals. He talks of abstraction as an activity or function of the mind in rather the same way as we talk of digestion as a function of the body. In other words, abstraction and digestion are respectively just ways in which the mind and the body work. And universals, for Locke, are *products* of abstraction.

What are we to understand by the word 'abstraction'? Our ordinary use of the word is hopelessly vague and when we are talking philosophy, we have to try to make this ordinary use a little more precise. Psychologically, attention is a precondition of abstraction. We know what it means to attend to a certain feature in a total situation, to the screen, for example, in a

1. III.3.6.

cinema or to the sounds in a concert hall. Abstraction involves much more than this but we have to attend before we can abstract. We have to attend to those features of a situation which are universal or general, to those features which can *recur* in other particular situations. Abstraction may take many different forms on different levels of complexity. The most primitive form occurs when we attend to a property of a particular thing, the colour, say, of a particular flower and recognize that it is capable of occurring as a quality of other particular things. When we do so, we consider the quality *in abstraction from* the concrete circumstances of the time and place in which we observe it. At higher levels of abstraction, we may *compare* several things, say, a cat, a bird, and a fish and recognize that they have several properties in common. We may then mentally group these properties together to form the complex concept of 'vertebrate animal', which represents the common nature of the three things we have been considering. At another level again, suppose we are doing an intelligence test and have to answer the following question: 'What are the next three numbers in the following series: 7, 9, 13, 21, 37, ... ?' To answer this question, we have to understand the general principle on which the series is constructed. Once we see that the differences between successive terms of the series themselves form a series of the integral powers of 2 ($2, 2^2, 2^3, 2^4$, and so on), we have a general rule which enables us to extend the series. And to grasp the general rule in this way is an instance of abstraction. This form of abstraction, which is very important in mathematical and scientific reasoning, is called 'intuitive induction'.

It is hardly possible to give an exhaustive catalogue of the different types of abstraction but the three types I have listed above are probably the most important. Locke understands by 'abstraction' chiefly the formation of general concepts in the manner sketched in the second example above. He believes that an idea produced by this process of abstraction is 'made capable of representing more individuals than one; each of which having in it a conformity to that abstract idea, is (as we call it) of that sort'.[1] It becomes capable of representing more individuals than one by containing no elements but those which are common to all the individuals in question. A general idea, then, becomes a sign or representative of a class of particular ideas. (It cannot, on Locke's theory, *directly* represent a class of particular *things* or *properties*.) When we ask in what the sign-relationship consists, we find that it lies in a 'conformity between the general idea and the members of the class each of which it indifferently represents. And the conformity consists in a partial resemblance, each of the individual ideas containing as components all of the properties making up the general idea. When, for example, children arrive at the general idea of man, 'They make nothing new; but only leave out of the complex idea they had of Peter and James, Mary and Jane, that which is peculiar to each, and retain only what is common to them all'.[2]

He goes on to say that nothing existing in the world is general and universal. These terms are 'the inventions and creatures of the understanding, made by it for its own use, and concern only signs, whether words or ideas'.[3] This follows, of course, from what he has said already. For to call anything general or universal is the same thing as to say that it is a sign standing in a one-many relationship of representation with the members of a certain class. But this does not mean that there is no foundation in fact for the class names which we assign. We sort things under names in virtue of the fact that we find resemblances in nature. For example, we meet with a certain set of animals resembling each other in fairly definite and specifiable ways. We form an abstract idea consisting of a set of properties possessed by all the animals in common and assign an arbitrarily chosen word, say 'cat', to be a sign of the general idea. The general character of such ideas consists in 'the capacity they are put into by the understanding of signifying or representing many particulars'.[4] Thus Locke is not a pure nominalist. He does not say that the *word* is the sign which

1. III.3.6. 2. III.3.7.
3. III.3.11. 4. *Ibid.*

139

stands for or represents the class members. It is the abstract idea which does this. But an abstract idea considered as a particular mental occurrence which happens at a certain time in a certain mind is just as particular as a word. It differs from the word only in being an iconic sign of the class members it represents. And it is very difficult to see what advantage Locke gains from this modification of nominalism.

Nevertheless the defects of the theory lie more in what Locke has omitted to say than in what he has said. The theory is incomplete rather than unworkable. Perhaps this will be more obvious after I have stated what seems to me to be its most serious defects.

(i) He does not explain how we can have general ideas of simple qualities like blue, square, hot, or sweet, or of relations. For the particular instances of sense data or relations which we meet with cannot be compared with one another in terms of a set of *common* properties and another set of properties peculiar to some of the instances in question. There is all the difference in the world between the way in which, for example, two cats resemble one another and the way in which two shades of blue do so.[1] I shall discuss this question more fully below. His omission of relations is especially curious in view of his tendency to exaggerate the mental character of relations and to minimize their function in ordering the world independently of our knowledge.

(ii) The complex general idea which is the product of abstraction is none the less just as much a particular mental event as any other idea. The fact that its components form the highest common factor, as it were, of the various sets of properties which characterize the members of a given class in no way alters its character as a particular idea. And Locke explicitly recognizes this. 'Universality belongs not to things themselves, which are all of them particular in their existence, even those words and ideas which in their signification are

1. In II.11.9, he talks as if resemblance between simple ideas were the same as identity.

general.'[1] The general character of an abstract idea lies only in its *representative* function. But Locke says no more about this function than that abstract ideas 'become general representatives of all of the same kind',[2] and that 'for the signification they have is nothing but a relation that, by the mind of man, is added to them'.[3] He adds nothing that would enable him to meet the usual objection to the nominalist theory that universals are just words or other signs with such a representative function. It is objected that the nominalist can never know what individuals are represented by the class-name without mentally reviewing all the members of the class. And if such a feat were psychologically possible, the theory of representation would be superfluous. It is possible to offer a plausible defence to this objection but Locke has provided no basis for doing so.

(iii) The notion of *representation* is one of the key-concepts of the theory. Yet Locke makes no serious attempt to explain what he means by the word. He uses the same word in other contexts when he talks of ideas being signs or representations of things or their properties and of words being signs of or marks of or standing for their corresponding ideas. Locke uses the phrases, 'sign of', 'mark of', 'standing for', 'representation of', as though they were both synonymous and unambiguous. We have seen already that he gives no general account of the sign-relationship and he has just as little to say about the way in which general abstract ideas function as signs. There is, however, one obvious difference between the two cases. When a word becomes a sign of an idea or an idea is considered as a sign of the thing or property which it represents to us in knowledge, the sign-relationship is a one-one relation. But the relationship of a general idea to its significata seems to be a one-many relation. Yet Locke denies this. 'The next thing therefore to be considered is, what kind of signification it is that general words have. For, as it is evident that they do not signify barely one particular thing; for then they would not be general terms, but proper names, so, on the

1. III.3.11.   2. II.11.9.   3. III.3 11.

other side, it is as evident that they do not signify a plurality; for *man* and *men* would then signify the same; and the distinction of numbers (as grammarians call them) would be superfluous and useless. That then which general words signify is a *sort* of things; and each of them does that, by being a sign of an abstract idea in the mind; to which idea, as things existing are found to agree, so they come to be ranked under that name, or, which is all one, be of that sort.'[1]

The important notion here is that of 'agreement' between things or (as Locke should say, to be consistent) ideas of things and the abstract general idea. And what can 'agree' mean here but 'resemble'?

(iv) A fourth defect of Locke's theory is that he offers no analysis of the notion of resemblance. And this is an essential preliminary to any theory of universals. Whatever the problems may be with which philosophers are concerned when they talk about universals, it is clear that the fact that similarities occur in the world is a necessary condition of these problems. To say that if there were no resemblances, there would be no problem of universals, is indeed, obvious, though perhaps it is unhelpful, since a world in which there are no relations of resemblance is quite unthinkable. Some philosophers (*e.g.* Plato) have talked as if the relation itself were a puzzling one which their own theory of universals attempted, in some sense, to explain. If they thought so, they were badly in error. The fact that resemblances occur is just one brute fact among others and single facts taken by themselves do not call for any explanation nor should they puzzle anyone. It is true that one fact taken in conjunction with others may provide a legitimate demand for explanation; for example, why does a balloon rise when I release it while other bodies fall? But the facts of resemblance do not seem to occasion any questions of this sort.

There is, however, an important question about universals which has not generally been considered by the philosophers, including Locke, who have discussed the problem. The ques-

1. III.3.12.

tion is this: what does it mean to say that two terms (things, qualities, events, relations) resemble each other? There are clearly important differences between the way in which, for example, one man resembles another and the way in which a patch of crimson resembles a patch of scarlet. Yet philosophers have, in general, been quite content to talk about the universals 'redness' and 'humanity' as if they were certain that these differences were totally irrelevant to their problem. The fact that $a_1, a_2, a_3 \ldots$ are similar and $b_1, b_2, b_3 \ldots$ are also mutually similar is commonly thought to demand universals A and B for their explanation. But it seems clear enough that if the word 'resembles' in the case of the a-class means something quite different from 'resembles' in the case of the b-class, the puzzle about the universal A-ness might be quite a different puzzle from the one about the universal B-ness. And it is in fact quite easy to show that resemblance between simple sense qualities is quite a different relation from resemblance between concrete particulars.

If I say, 'John resembles his father', I can specify the *respects* in which the two men are similar. For example, they are both over six feet tall, have red hair, noses of the same shape, and so on. And if I say 'John resembles his father more than James does', one possible analysis of what I mean is equally simple. I make a list of the respects in which John resembles his father and another list of the respects in which James resembles his father and show that the first list is longer than the second. But if I say, 'crimson resembles scarlet' or 'crimson resembles scarlet more than it resembles orange', I cannot explain and justify my judgement in this way.

Those are only two of the several different types of resemblance which can be distinguished, but I think it will be clear from this example how important such distinctions are for a preliminary classification of the problem of universals. Locke recognizes only one sort of resemblance, that namely which is signified by a general idea arrived at by abstraction. And such a general idea is a complex idea composed of the qualities common to all the resembling particulars. It is particularly unfortunate, in view of the important place he gives to simple ideas, that he has given no account whatever of the way in which simple ideas can be similar.

Real and Nominal Essences

So far what Locke has had to say in Book III is either wrong or sketched in such an incomplete form that it is misleading. We come now to a part of his theory of language which is both original and valuable. This is the distinction he makes between real and nominal essences and the use to which he puts this distinction.

He distinguishes between two important meanings of the word 'essence'. In the first sense, 'the real internal, but generally (in substances) unknown constitution of things, whereon their discoverable qualities depend, may be called their essence'.[1] Although Locke finds that this sense of the word is no more useful than the analogous notion of substance as an unknown 'something I-know-not-what', he does not reject it as meaningless. It presupposes the belief in an objective and necessary connexion between properties on which, as we shall see, his theory of knowledge so largely depended. But he does protest strongly against 'those who, using the word essence for they know not what, suppose a certain number of those essences, according to which all natural things are made, and wherein they do exactly every one of them partake, and so become of this or that species'.[2] Nature cannot be exhaustively classified and sorted into a number of neat pigeonholes in this way. He points to the wide divergences from the standard type which occur in every biological species and asks by what criteria it can be decided whether these anomalous cases are to be admitted as members of the species.

The second sense of the word 'essence', and the important one for Locke, is 'abstract idea' as defined above. In that sense, abstract ideas of substances, for example, 'have their foundation in the similitude of things', but there is, nevertheless, an

1. III.3.15.   2. III.3.17.

arbitrary or conventional element in their construction. The work of nature is the production of certain systematic resemblances among natural objects. The work of mind is to abstract the common elements in which the resemblances consist and to assign names to the general ideas so formed. Thus species are established by human decisions and to ask if a given individual, *a*, belongs to species *S*, is the same as to ask if the statement '*a* is an *S*' conforms to our established conventions governing the use of the word *S*.

But there is, obviously, a close relationship between the real essence and the nominal essence. He deals in turn with simple ideas and the various sorts of complex ideas which he has distinguished and discusses in each case how the real essence and the nominal essence are related.

In simple ideas, the real essence and the nominal essence are always identical, and similarly in the case of modes and relations. But in the case of substances, they are 'always quite different'.[1] What Locke means is partly, no doubt, that when we have become aware of something as blue, sweet, or square, our abstract idea of the quality can be nothing else, on his theory of abstract ideas, than an image of the quality. Because simple ideas are uncompounded, abstraction in such cases must mean something other than the selection of a set of qualities common to the class in question. Abstraction here means, in fact, no more than selective attention.

But there is a more important point to notice. We might have expected him to refer here to the distinction between primary and secondary qualities. Since ideas of secondary qualities are only the effects produced in our minds 'by the bulk, figure, texture, and motion' of the insensible parts of bodies, there seems just as good a reason for distinguishing between real and nominal essence here as in the case of substances. The reason for the omission is probably that as long as Locke is talking about *ideas* only, he recognizes that it is irrelevant to discuss the 'real but unknown constitution of bodies'. But when he starts to talk about *ideas of substances*, the

1. III.3.18.

fatal ambiguity of the word 'idea' soon traps him into talking of *substances*. And then it becomes proper and sensible to make the contrast between real and nominal essence. But it is a contrast which is meaningless when we confine ourselves to talking of ideas. Thus when Locke says that in simple ideas and modes, real and nominal essence are the same, he should really say that the distinction between the two kinds of essence is inapplicable here. For a nominal essence is an abstract idea and a real essence is the real but unknown (and, according to Locke, unknowable) constitution of a material body.

In this respect then, simple ideas and modes are grouped together and contrasted with ideas of substances. But there is a further respect in which simple ideas and substances are grouped together and contrasted with mixed modes. 'The names of simple ideas, substances, and mixed modes have also this difference: that those of *mixed modes* stand for ideas perfectly arbitrary; those of substances are not perfectly so, but refer to a pattern, though with some latitude; and those of *simple ideas* are perfectly taken from the existence of things, and are not arbitrary at all.'[1] (In this respect, Locke classes simple modes with simple ideas and relations with mixed modes.)

When Locke says that names of mixed modes and relations stand for perfectly arbitrary ideas and names of other ideas do not, he means something like this. We find in nature an enormous number of qualities related to each other in various ways. The languages we use are rather inefficient inventories of this enormously complex world and contain two classes of words, among others. The words in the first of these two classes reflect features of the world which are forced on our notice by its nature and construction. These are names of ideas of simple qualities like red, square, or sweet, or of substances like apple, dog, gold, or table. But there are other words which name ideas which are not forced on our notice in this way, but are rather constructed from features of the world

1. III.4.17.

selected by us to serve some special interest or purpose. The examples Locke gives are taken largely from moral, theological or legal terms and weights and measures. He cites, as examples, words like obligation, murder, gratitude, resurrection, hour, pound, procession. Indeed the larger part of the words which fill English dictionaries are names of mixed modes.

Locke is here emphasizing a very important point which even at the present day has not been thoroughly assimilated by philosophers. But he makes the point in a misleading way which has led his readers to underestimate its importance. He says that the mind makes mixed modes by a succession of three operations: (*a*) it selects certain ideas, simple or complex, from its field of experience; (*b*) 'it gives them connexion, and makes them into one idea';[1] (*c*) 'it ties them together with a name'.[2] This is clearly a grossly over-simplified account of the formation of such concepts and is an example of Locke's bad habit of trying to deal with complicated questions of empirical psychology by casual untrained introspection and imaginative guessing.

Yet his basic conviction that there is an important difference between ideas which mirror nature and ideas which are constructed for special purposes without natural prototypes is a sound one. Nevertheless his belief that simple ideas and substances fall into the first class and complex modes and relations into the second is true only as a rough generalization. Locke's reason for believing that mixed modes have no natural prototypes is that it is possible to frame certain moral and legal notions prior to meeting with any instances of them. But this can happen also with ideas of substances. Chemists have described the properties of certain unknown elements and predicted their occurrence on the basis of the periodic law; and their descriptions and predictions have subsequently been satisfied by the discovery of the elements in question. In the same way, palaeontologists have described certain unknown fossils on the basis of evolutionary theory and discoveries have

1. III.5.4.   2. *Ibid.*

afterwards been made conforming to their descriptions. And, on the other hand, it is not true that no mixed modes ever have any prototypes in nature. Many moral terms refer to modes of behaviour which are specially commended or reproved in a given society. And many scientific terms (*e.g.* eclipse, evolution, measurement, oxidation) are designed to refer to certain complex events and processes.

Nevertheless, it is true and important that we are very prone to forget the conventional and arbitrary element in meanings. And it is useful to bear in mind what Locke is emphasizing here, namely, that in a large and important class of words, which he calls the names of mixed modes, the conventional element is at a maximum. If we want to find out what a duck-billed platypus is like, we can consult a dictionary or a text-book of zoology. But by far the best course is to examine a specimen for ourselves. We can then have an *ostensive* definition of the name of the animal. '*That* is a duck-billed platypus.' But the vast majority of the words we use cannot be defined ostensively. If we want to know the meaning of 'cause', 'nature', or 'substance', to take only examples of philosophical terms, we can, of course, accept dictionary definitions. But these also contain no words that can be ostensively defined. In any case a dictionary is nothing but a misleadingly precise catalogue of verbal equivalents which are conventionally acceptable among users of standard English. The only way to determine meaning in such cases, is to determine how the words are used. And Locke's point is that there are no 'real meanings' which can be discovered in such cases. Not only are there no well-marked natural patterns corresponding to names of mixed modes so that ostensive definition is impossible, but the lack of such patterns renders conventional usage, which is our only criterion of 'meaning', uselessly indeterminate. The result of this, as Locke points out, is that it is easy to use such words meaninglessly or, in his terminology, 'without clear and distinct ideas' corresponding to them.

Locke does not point out the practical consequences of all this for philosophy. Philosophers are constantly tempted to use words which are vague, because the conventional rules for their use are few and inexact, as if they were precise. In order to do this, they have, in effect, to remedy the inadequacies of conventional usage by prescribing new rules of their own. But when they do this, they are not making discoveries about the 'real meanings' of their terms; they are merely recommending conventions for English usage where no such conventions exist. And they cannot, of course, then proceed to follow their own conventions in order to make discoveries about the nature of reality by metaphysical reasoning.

This last point is a vitally important one for the understanding of the futility of much of the metaphysics written in the past and also, it must be added, of some of the analytical philosophy practised in recent years. We have to remember that the gaps in our rules of usage for abstract words are nothing like the gaps on our map of the Antarctic continent or the Amazon basin. We fill these in by making discoveries about the actual facts of geography and we can then use our improved map to guide us to further discoveries. But abstract words and the relations between them do not refer to features of reality in the way that lines on a map may refer to a river system. Still less do they refer, as the translation theory suggests, to shadowy immaterial things called 'concepts' which have their existence in the mind.

Thus the philosopher who wants to construct a metaphysical theory about the nature of reality cannot rely on tracing the logical connexions between the judgements expressed in ordinary language. The meanings of abstract words are too vague and variable to offer any basis for such logical connexions. And if he makes his terms precise by definitions of his own, he is doing nothing more than tracing the logical connexions between his own definitions. And this will tell him nothing about the world. Thus Locke's theory about mixed modes points the way, though Locke himself did not stress the point, to an important limitation of human knowledge. One of the consequences of the fact that the meanings of words can be no more precise than the conventions governing their use is that deductive metaphysics of the classical type can give us no new information about reality. Whether it has other useful functions is another question.

An interesting corollary of Locke's theory of meaning is his account of definition. It had been supposed by philosophers of the Aristotelian and scholastic tradition that definitions were of things and not merely of the verbal expressions referring to things. One defined a thing by giving its 'essence' in terms of its genus and species. For example, the essential nature of man was held to be a 'rational animal' where 'animal' is the term referring to the genus of man and 'rational' the term referring to the specific difference between man and other animals. The essence of a thing was the characteristic complex of qualities in which the supposed real nature of the thing consisted. This practice was the result of two closely associated errors which it is Locke's achievement to have refuted.

The first was the belief, which we have discussed above, that words can have real meanings which are independent of conventional usage. Socrates, in Plato's dialogues, is always seeking to discover the *nature* of justice, virtue, beauty, good, and other such abstract concepts. He does this in the only way open to him by trying to find a common core of meaning in the various uses of the words which express these concepts without ever seeming to realize that where the conventional usage of the word is ambiguous or very vague, as it nearly always is with abstract words, there cannot possibly be such a common core of meaning. Associated with this Platonic superstition was the Aristotelian belief that the plants, animals, rocks and so on which make up the natural world have 'real natures' which are fixed and unalterable and which it is the object of science to discover. Every species in nature is clear-cut and distinct and there are no fuzzy edges to confuse the investigator. But it does not need a very advanced knowledge of natural history to tell us that one plant or animal does not resemble others of the same species as one Hurricane Mark I resembles another. The range of variance in any natural species is very wide and, as Locke points out, there are always hybrids, monsters, and borderline cases which we hesitate either to admit to the species or to exclude from it. It is senseless to argue whether an idiot with a mental age of six months or a monster born of human parents is to be classed as a human being as if we were arguing about a question of fact. We can know all the facts and still argue, for we are arguing only about how the conventional use of the word 'human' should be stretched or restricted. The 'real meaning' superstition and the 'fixed species' superstition reinforce each other in obvious ways and Locke's theory of nominal essences goes a long way to dispose of both.

Locke's account of definition follows naturally from this. 'A *definition* is nothing else but *the showing of the meaning of one word by several other not synonymous terms*.'[1] Thus to define an expression, for Locke, is to expand it in terms of other more familiar expressions. Names of complex ideas are shorthand modes of expression and are defined by the names of the elements from which the complex ideas are constructed. It follows, of course, that simple ideas cannot be defined verbally. 'The reason whereof is this, that the several terms of a definition, signifying several ideas, they can altogether by no means represent an idea which has no composition at all.'[2] It is necessary, in any case, that some terms in a language should be indefinable or no definitions would be possible at all. Almost all modern logicians would agree that Locke was right in suggesting that definitions are of names and not of things though they might dissent from some details of his account. The defects of the Aristotelian view are now generally recognized.

Locke ends his discussion of language with some practical recommendations for avoiding the consequences of its natural imperfections. When we use words privately 'for the recording of our own thoughts' the chief requisite is that we should use them consistently; that is, the same word should be used to stand for the same idea. But language is chiefly used for communication, and here it is necessary to establish

1. III.4.6.   2. III.4.7.

that the idea signified by a certain word in the mind of *A* is identical with the idea which the same word stands for in the mind of *B* with whom *A* is communicating. It is obviously impossible, on Locke's premises, that this should ever be established, even if it were true, as he seems to think, that he could regard the *word* as an idea common to the minds of *A* and *B*. However, it is just as difficult for him to prove that the sight or sound of the word 'green', *i.e.* the idea of the *word* 'green', is identical in my mind and in yours, as it is to prove that the sensation of green is qualitatively identical for us both. The problem is insoluble in principle and is therefore no problem. What we do in practice is to regard communication as satisfactory if the behaviour for which our words are a stimulus is substantially what we intend or expect it to be.

Locke does not try to solve the problem he sets himself. Instead, he points out some of the difficulties in the way of perfect communication and shows, in terms of his general theory of language, how the names of mixed modes and of substances are more serious sources of misunderstanding than the names of simple ideas or simple modes. These sources of difficulty arise from the nature of language and we can do little about them. But there are faults in the way in which most people use language and these faults can be corrected with care and attention. (1) We should take care not to use words meaninglessly or without corresponding ideas which are clear and distinct and, in the case of complex ideas of substances, 'conformable to things as they exist'.[1] (2) We must be careful to observe the conventions in accordance with which the words of our language are used and always indicate clearly when and how we are departing from these conventions when this is necessary. (3) We should 'use the same word constantly in the same sense'.[2] If we observe these rules in our communications with our fellows, disputes and misunderstandings will be minimized.

1. III.11.10.   2. III.11.26.

CHAPTER SEVEN

The Nature of Knowledge

WE can now pass on to the last book of the *Essay* where Locke discusses the general nature of knowing. He has here reached the point at which he can deal with the main part of the project which he outlined at the beginning of the *Essay*: 'to enquire into the original, certainty, and extent of human knowledge together with the grounds and degrees of belief, opinion and assent'.[1] In the first three books, he has been concerned with the origins alone. He has been establishing and justifying an empirical outlook which can be summarized as follows: (i) every possible object of human knowledge is either directly given in experience or can be constructed out of materials which are themselves directly experienced; (ii) such elementary materials are of two kinds, those given in sensation and those given in introspection. This then is the basic assumption on which he is going to base his theory of the nature of knowing. Now it is an unfortunate paradox that the very part of the *Essay* in which Locke proposes to solve the main problems which he set himself at the beginning is by far the least successful part of the whole work. And not only is it unsuccessful but it is, to a modern reader, difficult. It is not possible to remove the difficulties without giving a false picture of Locke's theory, but a preliminary general account of his view of knowing may be helpful.

It will be remembered that Locke proposed at the start of the *Essay* to use the word 'knowledge' in a very narrow sense in which we cannot properly be said to know anything unless (*a*) we are certain of it and (*b*) our certainty can be justified. Now there are, of course, very few items of our knowledge which we would care to say that we know, in this sense of the word. There are indeed a large number of propositions of which most people are certain; for example, 'things equal to

1. I.i.i.

the same thing are equal to one another', 'twice two are four', 'the same material thing cannot be in two places at once'. But these are not very interesting statements and, indeed, we rarely consider them unless we are talking philosophy and are trying to find examples of statements which are indubitably true. There are other more interesting statements like 'there is a God' and 'human beings have a life after death' which many people profess to be certain of but which to many others seem doubtful. And when doubt arises about such statements, it is usually because Locke's second condition is not satisfied. We may *feel* certain but it is impossible to find a universally acceptable method of proving the statement and so justifying our certainty. Only of trivial statements like 'twice two are four' and 'things equal to the same thing are equal to one another' do we usually say that the statements are 'self-evident' and therefore require no proof.

Now there is one field of human enquiry where everyone admits that we can have certain knowledge if we take the proper precautions and where there is an agreed procedure for finding out when our certainty is justified. This field is mathematics. Euclid's *Elements of Geometry* is the earliest and most famous example of this method. Euclid starts by defining terms like 'point', 'angle', 'line', and so on which he is going to need in his discussion. He then lays down certain axioms like 'the whole is greater than its part' and certain postulates like 'two straight lines cannot enclose a space'. These are taken as unproved assumptions, and on the basis of these assumptions, together with the definitions and the ordinary rules of reasoning, conclusions are drawn. These conclusions are known as 'theorems' and require for their proof no more than the original assumptions. Once a theorem has been proved, it can itself be used as an assumption for proving further theorems, and so on. Thus by starting from very obvious and 'self-evident' statements Euclid obtains a great deal of new knowledge, all of which is logically derived from his original assumptions but is by no means so obvious and trivial as they are.

Now in the seventeenth century, great advances were taking place both in mathematical knowledge and in those branches of science where mathematical methods can most easily be applied. And it was natural enough for a philosopher acquainted with these discoveries to assume that mathematics was the standard by which all other human knowledge must be judged. This is, of course, an error. But it was an error which other philosophers than Locke have made. The mistake infects only a comparatively small part of Locke's work, but it forms the underlying assumption of all the work of Descartes, Spinoza, and their followers. It is, indeed, the characteristic error of the so-called 'rationalism' of the seventeenth century. Locke, however, adopts the rationalist point of view only when he comes to discuss the nature of knowing.

There are, in fact, only certain types of subject matter which can be treated mathematically. And in mathematics, as in logic, our knowledge can never be anything more than the consequences of our original assumptions. We can never discover any new facts about the world by such reasoning; we can only make explicit the consequences of what we already know or assume. To find new facts about the world we must look to experience.

Now the whole point of Locke's argument in Book II of the *Essay* was precisely that all the materials of our knowledge are derived from experience. Yet when he turns in the fourth book to discuss the ways in which these materials can be put together into statements or propositions which alone can be said to be true or false and which alone therefore we can properly be said to know, he seems to forget Book II altogether. When we know a proposition, in his sense of 'know', we do so in virtue of a necessary relation which binds together the ideas in the proposition. Our knowledge follows from putting our ideas together just as a theorem of Euclid follows from putting together certain of the original axioms and postulates. His task, therefore, is to find out what these necessary relations are, to list them and to show how the various sorts of propositions which we can be said to know are built up from ideas derived from experience linked together by these relations of necessity.

It will make the nature of his task clearer if we take an example of a proposition which is 'necessarily true' and compare it with propositions whose truth is not of this kind, the ordinary factual propositions whose truth we have to confirm in experience. 'If, if Italy goes communist, there will be a war, and Italy will go communist, then there will be a war.' Call this compound proposition, A. Then A is a necessary proposition whose truth does not in any way depend on the truth of its component propositions, B, 'Italy will go communist' and C, 'there will be a war'. B and C may be true or false and only the actual facts of history can tell us whether they are true or not. But we know that A is true whatever the actual facts of history may be, because it is true in virtue of the logical relations between B and C. We could put any other propositions at all in place of B and C and the resulting compound proposition would still be true because any compound statement of the form 'if, if p then q, and p is true, then q is true' can be seen to hold good whatever sentences are put in the places of p and q.

We have here an example of a logical relation (and there are, of course, many other such logical relations) which binds together two statements[1] into a compound statement which is necessarily true and which we can be said to know, in Locke's sense of the word 'know'. Now Locke wants to find and classify similar relations which bind together, not *statements* into compound *statements* like A above, but *ideas* into statements. And he wants us to be able to know the resulting statements with complete certainty in virtue of the relations between the component ideas from which the statement is built up. He was, in fact, setting himself an impossible task. That the task was impossible will only be realized by following the actual details of his argument.

Yet his treatment of knowledge was valuable in that it

1. The words 'proposition' and 'statement' may be used as equivalent in this context.

explored very thoroughly one of the most tempting blind alleys in the theory of knowledge. It is very widely believed by philosophers nowadays that all propositions which are necessarily true are so in virtue of the logical relations between their components. *A* above is an example of such a necessary proposition. If this belief is true, it is very plausible to suppose that all other types of propositions can be proved, when they are provable at all, by evidence drawn from experience. Locke's resolute attempt to demonstrate the contrary was a signal failure. But we must put it to his credit that he explored the blind alley so thoroughly that reputable philosophers since his day have wasted little time on it.

Before we go on to consider the details of the argument of Book IV, there is an important point about Locke's doctrine of relations which should be noticed. He wants to explain knowledge in terms of relations between ideas. 'Some of our ideas', he says, 'have a *natural* correspondence and connexion with one another: it is the office and excellency of our reason to trace these.'[1] This supposed 'natural correspondence and connexion' between ideas gives rise, in the fourth book of the *Essay*, to a doctrine of relations which is, at first sight, at variance with the account he has already given in Book II. It will be remembered that there he seems to favour the opinion that relations are ideas which are purely mental constructions with no counterparts in reality. But when he comes in Book IV to explain knowledge in terms of relations between ideas, he has clearly to assume that our knowledge of such relations does give us some information about the world outside us. We are left to guess whether this is a genuine inconsistency in Locke's doctrine or whether he thought that relations were actually of two kinds: (i) those really grounded in the nature of the ideas which they relate; (ii) those 'not contained in the real existence of things but something extraneous and super-induced'.[2] Hume seems to have developed Locke's doctrine of relations on the second assumption when he divided what he called 'philosophical relations' into two classes, those like

1. II.33.5.   2. II.25.8.

resemblance, which depend on the nature of the ideas which we compare, and those, like relations of space and time, which do not.[1] Hume then proceeded to base our knowledge of necessary propositions on the first type. I think it is fairer to Locke to suppose that he did think that relations could be classed in this way into two radically different types. I shall therefore assume that the relations on which knowledge depends and which he discusses in Book IV, are relations which are not mere mental constructions but are really grounded in the character of the ideas which they relate. We can now turn to the details of his argument. He starts by reminding us that the materials of knowledge can be nothing else but ideas 'since the mind, in all its thoughts and reasonings, hath no other immediate object but its own ideas'.[2] And with this reminder of the basic postulate of his theory, he goes on to define knowledge as 'nothing but *the perception of the connexion of and agreement or disagreement and repugnancy of any of our ideas.* In this alone it consists.'[3] Clearly this definition needs further explanation.

What sort of 'agreement' and 'disagreement' is he talking about? He tries to answer this question by listing four types of agreement: (i) identity, (ii) relation, (iii) coexistence or necessary connexion, (iv) real existence.

(i) The examples Locke gives of this first type of agreement, 'blue is not yellow' or 'a spirit is a spirit', are not very encouraging specimens of knowledge as he defines it. It is clear, I think, that Locke is not describing a special kind of knowledge but is referring to what he thinks to be a psychological precondition of any knowledge at all. 'It is the first act of the mind, when it has any sentiments or ideas at all, to perceive its ideas; and so far as it perceives them, to know each what it is, and thereby also to perceive their difference, and that one is not another. This is so absolutely necessary, that without it there could be no knowledge, or reasoning, no imagination, no distinct thoughts at all.'[4] That is to say, knowledge would be

1. *Treatise on Human Nature*, I.3.1.
2. IV.1.1.   3. IV.1.2.   4. IV.1.4.

impossible if its objects were not to some extent, stable and distinct. But there is another point to his insistence on identity and diversity as one form of the agreement and disagreement of ideas in which knowledge consists. One of the characteristics of knowledge as Locke here describes it is that it is intuitive and carries with it a certainty that cannot be illusory. Of course, he found it difficult to provide examples of knowledge of this sort: and statements of identity are at least incorrigible in this sense, however little they merit the name of knowledge in more ordinary senses of the word. Later in the Book where Locke deals with what he calls 'trifling propositions' he recognizes, as we shall see, the defects of identical statements as expressions of 'knowledge'.

(ii) The example Locke offers of agreement in respect of relation is 'Two triangles upon equal bases between two parallels are equal'. This is a very unfortunate choice because there is, of course, no necessary connexion between 'x and y are two triangles on equal bases between parallels' and 'x and y are equal', unless we presuppose the definitions, axioms and postulates of Euclidean geometry and in particular, the notorious postulate of parallels. Locke seems to think that if we carefully inspect what we mean by 'triangle' we shall find that necessary connexions of this sort are entailed by the idea *though they are not part of it*. And this belief is certainly mistaken. In Chapter 3 where he discusses 'the extent of human knowledge' he deals with knowledge of relations in more detail. It is clear from what he says here that mathematical knowledge was for him the paradigm of relational knowledge. It is clear also that he thought that relational knowledge was especially important. 'This, as it is the largest field of our knowledge, so it is hard to determine how far it may extend: because the advances that are made in this part of knowledge, depending on our sagacity in finding intermediate ideas, that may show the relations and habitudes of ideas whose coexistence is not considered, it is a hard matter to tell when we are at an end of such discoveries.'[1] He does not confine relational

1. IV.3.18.

knowledge to mathematics which he believes to be concerned only with the simple modes of number and extension, but he finds it difficult to give convincing examples of relational knowledge of other types.

His difficulty was that the concept of relation, like some of the other basic concepts of his theory of knowledge, is one which needs very careful analysis if it is to be employed usefully in philosophical writing. Such an analysis was not even begun until the work of the symbolic logicians in the second half of the nineteenth century. In his own use of the word, Locke does not get beyond the unserviceable vagueness of everyday discourse. It is true that he admits that identity and coexistence which he lists as separate types of agreement 'are truly nothing but relations'. And he excuses their separate treatment on the ground that 'they are such peculiar ways of agreement and disagreement of our ideas, that they deserve well to be considered as distinct heads, and not under relation in general'.[1] But he does not explain in what way they are peculiar nor does he try to analyse the notion of relation any further. This was a cardinal omission, for the whole point of his account of knowledge is that it consists in our perception of relations between ideas. It is probable that Locke was misled by the delusive clarity of mathematical reasoning into believing that his concept of relation was perfectly determinate and that an analysis would be mere hairsplitting. He despised this sort of philosophizing when he found it in his scholastic contemporaries, and it was, of course, quite foreign to his practical outlook. Nevertheless, the clarification of concepts is an essential preliminary of constructive philosophical thinking and it is one of the major defects of Locke's work that he did not realize its importance. Moreover, his notions of mathematical thinking were not at all satisfactory, as we shall see.

(iii) 'The third sort of agreement or disagreement to be found in our ideas ... is *coexistence* or *non-coexistence* in the same *subject*; and this belongs particularly to substances.'[2] He mentions, as if it were an example of this sort of knowledge,

1. IV.1.7.   2. IV.1.6.

that our knowledge of the truth that gold is 'fixed' 'amounts to no more but this, that fixedness, or a power to remain in the fire unconsumed, is an idea that always accompanies and is joined with that peculiar sort of yellowness, weight, fusibility, malleableness, and solubility in *aqua regia* which make our complex idea signified by the word gold'.[1] But he later admits what obviously follows from his limited and exacting standard of knowledge, that we cannot be said strictly to *know* coexistences of this type at all. The reason for this is that 'the simple ideas whereof our complex ideas of substances are made up are, for the most part, such as carry with them, in their own nature, no *visible necessary* connexion or inconsistency with any other simple ideas'.[2] Our knowledge of coexistences is therefore meagre, as Locke admits. He can offer no examples of such knowledge other than such statements as 'shape entails extension' or 'communication of motion by impulse entails solidity'. And these statements are quite uninformative and are, indeed, purely analytic as neither term of the supposed entailment can be analysed without reference to the other.

It is, therefore, not at all clear what Locke meant by coexistence. If our knowledge of the relation is to be certain knowledge, the relation must consist in something more than two instances of a quality being 'manifested in the same spatio-temporal neighbourhood. Our knowledge of the colour of an orange, taken by itself, gives us no information about its taste or vitamin content. It does tell us that oranges are spatially extended, but this is part of the meaning of 'coloured' and is not new knowledge. Locke seems to think that this lack of necessary connexion between one simple idea and another is only a contingent defect of our knowledge which will be remedied by a deeper understanding of physical science. 'It is impossible we should know which (simple ideas) have a *necessary* union or inconsistency with one another. For, not knowing the root they spring from, not knowing what size, figure, and texture of parts they are, on which depend, and from which

1. IV.1.6.   2. IV.3.10.

result those qualities which make our complex idea of gold, it is impossible we should know what *other* qualities result from, or are incompatible with, the same constitution of the insensible parts of gold.'[1] And again: there is no discoverable connexion between any secondary quality and those primary qualities which it depends on. 'We are so far from knowing *what* figure, size, or motion of parts produce a yellow colour, a sweet taste, or a sharp sound, that we can by no means conceive how *any* size, figure, or motion of any particles, can possibly produce in us the idea of any colour, taste, or sound whatsoever: there is no conceivable connexion between the one and the other.'[2]

I think it will be clear from these passages that Locke was in a great muddle about the nature of 'coexistence' as a relation between ideas. (*a*) Our present-day knowledge of physics does tell us 'what figure, size or motion of parts produce a yellow colour' and many other facts of this kind. Nevertheless, no physicist *knows* in Locke's sense of the word any more cases of coexistence than Locke himself. The reason for this is that physical laws such as those correlating the wave frequency of light rays and the colour of our visual sense data state purely *contingent* connexions. It is false that the wave length of yellow light is 4,000 Angström units: but the statement is not self-contradictory. For the connexions between the nature of electromagnetic waves and certain colour sensations are not necessary connexions.

Notwithstanding the modest claims of his formal doctrine of causality set out in Book II, Locke seems to be supposing here that the relation between cause and effect is a *necessary* relation analogous to the connexion between premises and conclusion of a deductive argument. This is a characteristic example of the contrast between the cautious empirical attitude of Book II and the dogmatic rationalism of Book IV.

(*b*) It is very difficult to understand how there could be connexions of this kind between ideas which we could not know. We have already seen that the whole terminology of

1. IV.3.11.   2. IV.3.13.

'ideas' is hopelessly ambiguous and misleading. But one of the few virtues of substituting ideas for things as the objects of our direct knowledge is that our knowledge of ideas, unlike that of things, is intuitive, immediate and certain. And Locke admits this to be the case. 'There can be no idea in the mind, which it does not, presently, by an intuitive knowledge, perceive to be what it is, and to be different from any other.'[1] How then can we fail to perceive a relation of coexistence or, for that matter, any other relation between two ideas which are simultaneously 'present to the mind'? Locke could not answer this because he had apparently no clear definition of or criterion for coexistence. On his own premises, he was certainly quite unjustified in saying: 'Perhaps *A* coexists with *B but we cannot know that it does.*'

(iv) The last type of agreement or disagreement between ideas is 'real existence'. This is obviously very different from the first three types of agreement, as a statement affirming that something exists does not assert a relation or the lack of a relation between two ideas. The example Locke gives is 'God is'. If he intended this statement to be analysed as 'God is existent', so that existence is a predicate of God as white is a predicate of snow in 'snow is white' it can easily be shown that this analysis is false. If I say of a dog, 'Tray is not black' when, in fact, he is black, my statement is false. I am denying that a dog lacks a property which he in fact possesses. But if I say 'Tray does not exist' I am not saying that an existent dog lacks the property of existence; I am saying rather that there is nothing which has the predicates which go to constitute Tray. Similarly, to say that Tray exists does not add one more to the list of Tray's attributes like saying 'Tray is greedy'. It is to say that all Tray's properties, being black, being greedy, having big ears, short legs and so on are exemplified in a particular instance. Thus existence is not an attribute or predicate. This is, in fact, another of Locke's difficulties which arises from 'the new way of ideas'. (It will be remembered that existence is one of the ideas 'arising from all the ways of

1. IV.3.8.

sensation and reflection'.) I shall deal with this difficulty in more detail when we come to discuss his account of existential knowledge in general.

Having defined knowledge in this way, Locke now proceeds to distinguish between (a) actual knowledge which is our present intuition of the agreement and disagreement and (b) what he calls 'habitual knowledge'. Habitual knowledge is memory knowledge and there are two degrees of it: (i) where we remember both the ideas and their relation of agreement or disagreement; (ii) where we remember *that* the ideas are related but not *how* they are related. For example, we sometimes remember both a geometrical theorem and its proof and sometimes the theorem only without its proof. It is clear that the exact nature and validity of habitual knowledge depends on Locke's view of memory.

Unfortunately, his account of memory is sketchy and unsatisfactory. In the first edition of the *Essay*, he described memory as a 'storehouse' or 'repository' of ideas. But he had to withdraw this harmless if uninformative metaphor as one of his critics pointed out that the assumption that there could be ideas in the mind at any time which were not actually being thought about was at variance with his criticism of the doctrine of innate ideas. Locke therefore explained in subsequent editions that, as ideas could not be other than 'actual perceptions in the mind', to say that we lay up our ideas in the repository of memory is merely a metaphorical way of saying that 'the mind has a power in many cases to revive perceptions which it has once had, with this additional perception annexed to them, that it has had them before'.[1] And this power may be exercised either voluntarily or involuntarily.

This is, in effect, all that Locke has to say about memory. Now it is true that the most interesting and fundamental questions on the subject are physiological questions about the nature of memory traces in the brain and the way in which these are excited: and Locke has very sensibly excluded these questions from his purview. But there are important questions

1. II.10.2.

about memory which do not fall entirely within the fields of physiology and psychology and we might reasonably have expected Locke to have something to say about them. Moreover, though memory belief is like all other forms of belief in being susceptible of varying degrees of conviction from the merest suspicion to practical certainty, it differs from all other forms of belief in a very important way: it is fundamental to all of them.[1] If we had no memory beliefs, we could have no beliefs of any other kind. No mental processes are instantaneous and it follows that all our present beliefs about the world presuppose, either causally or logically, the substantial truth of certain of our memories, even if it is only our memory of how to use the English language correctly. It would therefore have been very useful for Locke to give a much fuller account of memory as a foundation for his theory of knowledge, especially for his theory of that branch of probable knowledge which he calls 'judgement'.

He should at least have tried to give an account of the special character of memory-knowledge, the belief that I have previously been acquainted with the object of my present act of memory. It is definitely misleading for him to suggest, as he does, that this consists in a *perception*, in any of the senses of that ambiguous word. Our 'perception' that a certain mental content is a memory image often consists in no more than the vaguest feeling of familiarity. And on the occasions when we can plausibly be said to 'perceive' that we have had a certain experience before, what kind of a perception is it? We cannot, by definition, directly perceive past ideas and so cannot directly compare our present experience with our past. He should also have made some attempt to distinguish the various kinds of memory knowledge. To remember how to swim or even how to recite a poem is a very different thing from remembering a name or a face, and that, in turn, is very different from remembering a proof in mathematics. But Locke does not distinguish between habit-memory and memory of events on the one hand, or between retention, recognition, and recall on the other.

1. As Locke admits (II.10.8).

Intuition and Demonstration

Locke next examines what he calls 'the degrees of our knowledge'. He first distinguishes between intuition and demonstration. In intuitive knowing, we perceive the agreement or disagreement of ideas directly and immediately and in demonstrative knowing we do so indirectly and mediately. And the different degrees of clarity with which we know anything result from and depend on the degree of immediacy of our perception of the relations between ideas. Intuition gives us our standard of certainty and anyone who demands a greater certainty than this 'demands he knows not what, and shows only that he has a mind to be a sceptic, without being able to be so'.[1] What are the examples which Locke offers of this kind of knowledge which is 'the clearest and most certain that human frailty is capable of'?[2] His examples are neither helpful nor impressive. They are trivialities like 'three is greater than two' and 'white is not black'.

It is clear, however, from what he says about demonstrative knowledge that he did not confine the function of intuition to apprehending trivialities of this sort. In demonstrative knowledge or 'reasoning' we perceive the agreement or disagreement of ideas mediately 'by the intervention of other ideas'. Here again examples would be very helpful, but Locke does not give any. It is therefore difficult to know what process he had in mind. He explains first that we cannot always immediately perceive the agreement or disagreement of two ideas, because we cannot put them together so as to make the relation between them apparent. In these cases, 'when the mind cannot so bring its ideas together as by their immediate comparison and, as it were, juxtaposition or application one to another, to perceive their agreement or disagreement, it is fain, *by the intervention of other ideas* (one or more as it happens) to discover the agreement or disagreement which it searches; and this is that which we call reasoning'.[3]

1. IV.2.1.   2. *Ibid.*   3. IV.2.2.

The disadvantages of reasoning compared with intuition are, (i) that it has not the same degree of self-evident certainty; (ii) it needs 'pains and attention'; (iii) demonstration is preceded by doubt. Intuition, being immediate, cannot be so preceded. Nevertheless demonstration is closely dependent on intuition and might be described as a series of intuitions because 'in every step reason makes in demonstrative knowledge, there is an intuitive knowledge of that agreement or disagreement it seeks with the next intermediate idea which it uses as a proof'.[1] This results in a further disadvantage of reasoning: we have to rely on memory to verify a chain of proof and memory is fallible.

This is a bare outline of what Locke has to say about the two varieties of knowledge which he has so far distinguished. Unfortunately, his treatment of this very important part of his theory of knowledge is far too concise to be clear and there are a number of awkward questions which he leaves without an answer. I shall deal here only with questions about the nature of demonstrative knowledge. The nature of 'intuition', as Locke understands the word, is best discussed after we have considered his doctrine of 'sensitive knowledge'. His view of demonstration seems to be something like this. Intuition is the immediate perception of the relation of two ideas by one of the ways of agreement or disagreement which he has already listed. If, for example, we have the idea of colour and the idea of shape, we can intuit that they are related by the relation of necessary coexistence. We then know that all coloured things have shape. We then consider the ideas of shape and extension and see that the same relation of necessary coexistence holds between these two ideas also. In other words, we see that all things which have shape are extended. We then have two statements which can be symbolized by CrS and SrE where r stands for the relation of necessary coexistence. We then see that these two statements have a common term 'shape' (S) and also that, in Locke's language, the idea of shape agrees with itself in respect of the relation of identity. Then by a further

1. IV.2.7.

intuition, we telescope *CrS* and *SrE* into *CrE*, eliminating the common term and arriving at the conclusion that all coloured things are extended.

The defects of this account of demonstration are too obvious to need much comment. (*a*) It is psychologically absurd. No one does in fact reason like that. (*b*) It is logically incomplete. The validity of relational argument of the type '*XrY* and *YrZ* together entail *XrZ*' depends on the nature of the relation *r*. Unless the relation is what is called a transitive relation like 'equal to', 'greater than' or 'subsequent to' the conclusion does not follow. For example, if *r* is 'loves' or 'greater by one than' then *XrY* and *YrZ* do *not* jointly entail *XrZ*. The example I gave is not Locke's own, for he does not provide any, but it is based on instances of coexistence which he does quote. And, of course, the relation 'necessarily coexists with' is presumed to be a transitive relation. But Locke misses the crucial point of this sort of reasoning entirely. (i) When it is valid, it is valid by virtue of the logical characters of the relations concerned. (ii) The relation must be the same in each premiss: *e.g.* from '*A* is larger than *B*' and '*B* is subsequent to *C*' I cannot validly infer anything about *A* and *C* although the relations 'larger than' and 'subsequent to' are both transitive.

So far then Locke's account of demonstration is quite unsatisfactory. And it will serve as a further criticism of it to discuss the ways in which it should be amended in order to provide an account of demonstration which is not both logically and psychologically inadequate. The main failing of his theory arises from the use of unsuitable standards. His standard type of knowledge was knowledge of mathematics and he chose this standard partly because it seemed to provide the absolute certainty which he required and partly because it was the only well developed and systematic science which was known in his time. Locke had studied some mathematics at Oxford and we might expect therefore that he would be able to illustrate and clarify his account of knowing with some mathematical examples. But the only examples he offers seem to indicate that he was under a complete misapprehension about the nature of mathematical reasoning. As we have already seen, he takes mathematical propositions to be certain and self-evident because the ideas involved 'agree in respect of relation'. In fact, of course, the propositions in question are certain only because they follow, in accordance with logical rules, from prior propositions which we have agreed to take as postulates. And these postulates are not, in every case, propositions which cannot be denied without self-contradiction. Thus we may characterize the chief failing of Locke's account of demonstration by saying that it is too narrow. If demonstrative knowledge was really confined to the narrow field prescribed by his definition, we would not only 'know' very little, in Locke's sense of the word, but we could not properly be said to know even in cases which Locke himself would have to admit as genuine cases of knowledge.

Suppose we take as examples some simple specimens of valid arguments:

(i) If the barometer falls, it will rain tomorrow.
The barometer is falling.
Therefore, it will rain to-morrow.

(ii) London is larger than Edinburgh.
Edinburgh is larger than Cambridge.
Therefore London is larger than Cambridge.

(iii) All Frenchmen are foreigners.
All foreigners are untrustworthy.
Therefore all Frenchmen are untrustworthy.

Now if ever we can know anything, in Locke's sense of the word, we know that the conclusions of these arguments are true if the premises are true and that they follow from the premises. But it is perfectly plain that this knowledge cannot be reduced to perception of the agreement or disagreement between ideas as Locke has explained these terms. In the case of (ii) and (iii), the relations between the ideas are not *necessary* relations. It is a purely contingent fact that London is larger than Edinburgh and so on. And yet the conclusion is necessarily entailed by the premises although the relations between the terms of the premises are purely contingent. Similarly in the case of (i), the compound proposition consisting of premises and conclusion is a necessary proposition. But this necessity is not a consequence of any relations between the ideas 'barometer', 'rain', etc., but is a feature of the logical rule 'if p implies q and p is true, q is true also'.

It is curious that Locke does not seem to have taken these very obvious points into account. The logical structure of the main types of proof was perfectly well known in his day although it was wrongly believed, as it was by Locke himself, that all the different types of valid argument could be reduced to the form of a syllogism. (By a 'syllogism', logicians of his day meant arguments of the type of (i) and (iii) above.) Why then does he appear to ignore demonstration in the ordinary sense and confine himself to working out a new sense from which it follows (*a*) that we can hardly ever demonstrate anything and (*b*) that what we can demonstrate we know already?

The answer to this question can only be a conjecture, but Locke's treatment of syllogistic reasoning is important here. In Book IV.17.4 he considers the question whether the syllogism is the 'proper instrument' of reason and the most useful way of reasoning. Locke answers that it is neither. It is not an aid to knowledge. 'A man knows first and then he is able to prove syllogistically.'[1] Nor is it of much use as an artificial aid in clarifying our thoughts. Its only function is to 'silence obstinate wranglers' by setting out the connexions of the argument in such a form that the objector can be taken through the argument and forced to assent at each stage. (This concession seems hardly consistent with his criticisms.)

Moreover Locke believed that the doctrine of the syllogism was actually in error on one important point. 'It is fit, before I leave this subject, to take notice of one manifest mistake in the rules of the syllogism: viz. that no syllogistical reasoning can be right and conclusive, but what has at least one *general* proposition in it.'[2] Locke is, of course, himself

1. IV.17.6.   2. IV.17.8.

mistaken here because this is a perfectly valid rule *of the syllogism*. It would be false only if it were maintained to be a universal rule of reasoning on the ground that all reasoning is syllogistic in form. Locke's belief that all reasoning could be expressed in syllogistic form probably accounts for this mistake, but his criticism shows a very imperfect acquaintance with the theory of the syllogism.

This failure to take the syllogism seriously no doubt contributes to the defects of his doctrine of inference. The theory of the syllogism is known nowadays to be only a very small part of deductive logic, but it does provide examples of important types of the logical relations involved in inference (class membership and class inclusion, for example). A study of the logical powers of these relations would have given Locke a more fertile basis for his account of inference than the one which he actually adopted.

It is interesting to notice, however, that Locke could have done justice to the actual process of inference by two adjustments to his theory of knowledge which would have been made without seriously affecting its basic principles. The two adjustments are: (i) to admit *propositions* as complex ideas; (ii) to admit the logical relations between propositions as ways of 'agreement' between ideas. His failure to make these very obvious concessions to an empirical theory of demonstration is largely responsible for the artificially restricted account of knowledge in Book IV of the *Essay*.

Objects of Knowledge

When we know, we perceive ideas as related. What does this amount to in more familiar terms? It means merely that the objects of our knowledge are propositions; these are complex mental contents whose distinguishing character is that they must be either true or false. Propositions are the units of our knowledge in the sense that we cannot know anything more primitive than a proposition. Even if our total mental furniture consisted of one idea only – say 'red', we could know the idea only as an ingredient of an identical proposition, 'red is red'.

We can raise the same question about the nature of propositions in Locke's theory of knowledge as we can about 'ideas' because, of course, a proposition is just a complex of ideas[1] related in a special way. Exactly the same ambiguities and difficulties which we find in the account of ideas we find also in the much more sketchy account of propositions and no new points of interest arise.

Yet the doctrine of propositions throws a good deal of light on Locke's theory of knowledge. This doctrine is presented in the form of an analysis of the different types of proposition. He starts with a preliminary distinction of *mental* from *verbal* propositions. This alleged distinction we have already considered in connexion with the theory of signs and we need not bother further with it here. He then goes on to classify propositions according to their logical type.

(*a*) *Maxims.* Under this heading Locke discusses propositions like 'whatever is, is' and 'it is impossible for the same thing to be and not to be'. In the logic of his day these particular tautologies were given a privileged status as two of the three 'laws of thought'. It was supposed that they had some special claim to rank as basic principles of philosophy on which the possibility and the validity of thought equally depended. Locke admits that they are self-evident but adds that they are not unique in this. Their self-evidence depends, he thinks, on the fact that we perceive the agreement or disagreement of their constituent ideas 'without the intervention or help of any other idea'. But all propositions are equally self-evident when we can know them in this way. As he points out, these maxims are just impressive ways of saying 'the same is the same' and 'the same isn't different'. And this more homely mode of expression brings out the triviality of the content. But contemporary logicians of the scholastic school claimed not only that these maxims were self-evident but also that they were the foundation of all other knowledge. They probably

1. But not 'complex ideas' in Locke's technical sense.

meant by this that if these maxims were false, both thinking and knowing would be impossible. And they were certainly correct if they meant merely that there must be a certain minimum stability about the world before it can be known. But according to Locke, they meant also (i) that maxims are those truths which are the first known to the mind and (ii) that the other parts of our knowledge depend on them. He has little difficulty in showing that (i) is absurd. As to (ii), he shows that maxims cannot serve as premises from which we arrive at new conclusions nor can they confirm the conclusions which we do reach. He concludes that their only use is 'in disputes for the silencing of obstinate wranglers'.

Locke adds that we come to know such maxims through their particular instances. 'The child, when a part of his apple is taken away, knows it better in that particular instance, than by this general proposition "The whole is equal to all its parts"; and that if one of these have need to be confirmed to him by the other, the general has more need to be let into his mind by the particular, than the particular by the general. For in particulars our knowledge begins, and so spreads itself, by degrees, to generals.'[1] Thus knowledge of general propositions, like acquaintance with general ideas, depends on our observation of particular instances. Maxims, like universals, come to be known only through the medium of everyday sense experience. We come to know that the whole is equal to the sum of its parts, for instance, by seeing individual objects taken to pieces and put together again. It is important to notice however that the individual instances do not justify the general proposition in the same way particular instances justify general propositions like 'all arsenical compounds are poisonous'. They merely *exemplify* the general principle and so enable us to grasp it. This type of rational procedure, known nowadays as 'intuitive induction', is very important in science and mathematics and we shall refer to it again below in connexion with Locke's account of human reason.

(b) *Trifling Propositions*. Another class of propositions which

1. IV.7.11

173

share with maxims the defect of adding nothing to our knowledge are what would now be called analytic propositions.
Locke calls them 'trifling propositions'. He distinguishes two
types: (i) 'purely identical propositions' in which a term is
predicated of itself like 'red is red'; (ii) the second type is a
proposition in which *a part of the complex idea is predicated of
the name of the whole*: a part of the definition of the word
defined'.

We can say no more of the first type than that they are 'true
and self-evident' and that their truth and self-evidence is a
necessary condition of human knowledge. For the perception
and discrimination of similarities and differences in our sense
fields is a precondition of knowing anything at all. 'But how
that vindicates the making use of identical propositions for the
improvement of knowledge from the imputation of trifling, I
do not see.'[1] These propositions are, of course, merely
examples or interpretations of the so-called law of identity
which Locke has already cited as a 'maxim'.

Locke gives some interesting examples of the second type
of analytic proposition. 'Lead is a metal' and 'all gold is fusible'
are both analytic *to anyone who knows what simple ideas make up
the complex ideas of lead or gold*. Of course, to someone who did
not know the meaning of the word 'lead', 'lead is a metal'
would be an informative proposition just as 'all gold is fusible'
is informative to someone who is beginning to study chemistry. But excepting such cases, 'he trifles with words who makes
such a proposition which, when it is made, contains no more
than one of the terms does and which a man was supposed
to know before; *e.g.* "A triangle hath three sides" or "saffron
is yellow".'[2] This point is a very important one and it is a
pity that Locke did not develop it further. He sketches in
outline the basic idea of what has been termed the 'functional
a priori'.[3] A proposition which at an early stage of a science
may be factual and informative may become at a later stage
an analytic proposition which expresses no more than our

1. IV.8.3.   2. IV.8.7.
3. Arthur Pap, *The* A Priori *in Physical Theory* (New York, 1946).

174

determination to use a given word in a certain way. For example, the statement that the atomic weight of gold is 197·2 originally reported a discovery of a matter of fact but, with the development of chemistry, it has become part of the *definition* of gold. In this way, inductive generalizations may become transformed into analytic statements.

(*c*) *Necessary Factual Propositions.* The third sort of proposition which Locke distinguishes may be called 'necessary factual propositions'. Locke has no special name for them, though he sometimes refers to them as 'instructive'. There are two features about them which, taken together, distinguish them from propositions of other types. (i) We can be certain of their truth. (ii) They are of the form 'all A is B' where B is a necessary consequence of the complex idea A 'but is not contained in it'. He gives as an example: 'the external angle of all triangles is bigger than either of the opposite internal angles. Which relation of the outward angle to either of the opposite internal angles, making no part of the complex idea signified by the name triangle, this is a real truth, and conveys with it instructive real knowledge.'[1] Such propositions are both certain and instructive whereas knowledge of trifling propositions, though certain, teaches us nothing. Necessary factual propositions are, for Locke, the one example of knowledge which conforms to all the standards which he specifies and it is therefore of the utmost importance for his theory that he shall give an adequate and convincing account of them. But we have already seen in the discussion of the relation of 'coexistence' that he was unable to give any examples of necessary factual propositions which will stand examination.

The Reality of Ideas

So far we have been concerned with knowledge of universal propositions and before we go on to consider Locke's account of particular existing things it will be useful to examine an important objection to the 'new way of ideas'. Locke himself

1. IV.8.8.

states the objection thus: 'But of what use is all this fine knowledge of *men's own imaginations*, to a man that inquires after the
reality of things? It matters not what men's fancies are, it is
the knowledge of things that is only to be prized: it is this
alone gives a value to our reasonings, and preference to one
man's knowledge over another's, that it is of things as they
really are, and not of dreams and fancies.'[1] Locke admits that
it would be a refutation of his position if, in knowing ideas, we
knew nothing more than the ideas themselves. But since Locke
regards ideas no less than words as *signs*, when I know an idea
I do not know just a bare mental content but a mental content
whose function it is to refer to something other than itself.
Thus the problem which Locke is concerned with here is
analogous to the problem of how we know that language is
used *significantly*, and not to the problem of how we know
when a statement is true. If I say 'whales are fishes', my statement is false. But the statement would not be false if the words
had, as we say, no meaning. 'Camaliks are sobulish' is neither
true nor false. With language, of course, the problem is not a
difficult one as we can be directly acquainted with both words
and their referents. Thus when Locke talks about 'the reality
of human knowledge' he is not primarily concerned with the
relation between our ideas and the existent states of affairs
which they represent to us. This raises quite another question
concerning what Locke calls 'knowledge of existence' which
we have still to consider.

However, as we have seen, there is no analogy between the
way in which words operate as signs and the way in which
ideas are supposed to do so. As a consequence of this mistake,
the language which Locke uses when he talks about the
'reality' of knowledge is misleading. 'It is evident', he says,
'that the mind knows not things immediately, but only by the
intervention of the ideas it has of them. Our knowledge,
therefore, is real only so far as there is a *conformity* between our
ideas and the reality of things. But what shall be here the
criterion? How shall the mind, when it perceives nothing but

1. IV.4.1.

its own ideas, know that they agree with things themselves?'[1] The use of the words 'conformity' and 'agree' in this passage suggests that there is some sort of standard relation between our ideas and the state of affairs they represent in virtue of which our ideas give us knowledge about the world, just as there is a standard set of relations between words and their referents in virtue of which language can give us information about the world. And this is quite false.

Locke goes on to consider what reasons there are for supposing that our ideas 'conform to' or 'agree with' the appropriate features of the external world. (a) He thinks there is no difficulty about our simple ideas. He believes he has established that the mind cannot make any new simple ideas and it follows that any simple idea must be the 'product of things operating on the mind'. The only 'proper conformity' which we can speak of in this connexion is the causal relation which exists between simple ideas and the extra-mental things or events which produce them. In other words, the fact that we have two different simple ideas, say, blue and sweet, is evidence that the world outside our minds has two distinct features which *correspond* to the simple ideas, though they may not *resemble* them. 'And this conformity between our simple ideas and the existence of things, is sufficient for real knowledge.'[2]

(b) Nor is there any difficulty about modes and relations. For these ideas 'being archetypes of the mind's own making, not intended to be copies of anything, nor referred to the existence of anything, as to their originals, cannot want any conformity necessary to real knowledge'.[3] As we have seen, Locke supposes that complex ideas are the product of the mental activities of combination, comparison and abstraction. He now suggests that as these complex ideas are not constructed to accord with any pattern, real or imaginary, it would be pointless to criticize them on the ground that they fail to accord with a pattern. He illustrates this point by reference to mathematics. The mathematician's ideas of a circle or a tri-

1. IV.4.3.   2. IV.4.4.   3. IV.4.5.

angle are mere mental constructions. It is probable that they are nowhere precisely exemplified in the external world, but whether this is so or not, it is irrelevant to the validity of mathematical reasoning or to the 'reality' of mathematical knowledge. 'To make our knowledge real it is requisite that the ideas answer their archetypes.'[1] And ideas of modes and relations are their own archetypes. For a mode or relation to be real, nothing more is required than that the component ideas of the complex should be mutually compatible so that 'they be so framed, that there be a possibility of existing conformable to them'.[2]

The obvious criticism of this account is that Locke is misusing his terminology when he talks of ideas being their own archetypes. The original of a picture or the prototype of a machine may properly be called an archetype, but to say that *x* is *its own* archetype is just a misleading way of saying that it has no archetype.

(*c*) But the case is quite different with our ideas of substances. These are complex ideas comprising sets of qualities coexisting in certain mutual relations and the ideas are real only if (i) these qualities have in fact existed in such a complex and (ii) we have observed them to do so. Our ideas of substances 'must not consist of ideas put together at the pleasure of our thoughts, without any real pattern they were taken from, though we can perceive no inconsistence in such a combination'.[3] The reason for this is that ideas of substances are intended to represent substances 'as they really are'. Real ideas of substances are those which conform to this standard and those which do not are dismissed by Locke as 'fantastical'.

Knowledge of Existence

Locke has so far been concerned with general and abstract knowledge. The application of his very stringent standards has had the result that we cannot say that we know any general proposition outside mathematics, except a few jejune tautolo-

1. IV.4.8.   2. II.30.4.   3. IV.4.12.

gies, 'all coloured things are extended' and the like. But Locke cannot deny that we have intuitive, certain and informative cognitions about particular matters of fact and he recognizes that he has to extend his theory in order to account for knowledge of existence. It is important to notice, however, the very sharp distinction he makes between universal and particular propositions. 'Where, by the way, we may take notice, that universal propositions of whose truth or falsehood we can have certain knowledge, concern not existence: and further, that all particular affirmations ... are only concerning existence; they declaring only the accidental union or separation of ideas in things existing, which, in their abstract natures, have no known necessary union or repugnancy.'[1] This passage is interesting because, if we allow for Locke's unduly narrow conception of a universal proposition, it makes the same sort of distinction which is now made by logicians between universal and particular statements. 'All men are mortal' is read 'for every x, if x is a man, then x is mortal'. 'Some men are bald' is read 'there is an x such that x is a man and x is bald.' The universal proposition states a universal connexion between propositions without making any affirmation of existence; the particular proposition affirms no necessary connexion but merely the accidental association of certain specified properties in a certain spatio-temporal neighbourhood. (It should be added, however, that in modern logic, $(x).(fx \supset gx)$ does not express a *necessary* connexion, in Locke's sense, between the properties f and g; it says merely that wherever the first property is found, the second is found as well.)

Locke's treatment of our knowledge of existence is in three parts: 'we have the knowledge of *our own* existence by intuition: of the existence of *God* by demonstration; and of *other things* by sensation'.[2] Intuition, in one sense of the word, and demonstration are two ways of knowing which we have already considered in connexion with abstract universal knowledge. But sensation is something new.

(*a*) What Locke has to say about our intuitive knowledge of

1. IV.9.1.   2. IV.9.2.

our own existence does not throw much light on the nature of intuition as a mental activity. His argument is substantially that by which Descartes introduces his famous maxim: 'I think, therefore I exist'. 'As for *our own existence*, we perceive it so plainly and so certainly that it neither needs nor is capable of any proof. For nothing can be more evident to us than our own existence.'[1] Even when we doubt we cannot doubt our existence, for the fact that we doubt entails that we exist.

(*b*) Locke devotes a longish chapter[2] to proving the existence of what he cautiously calls 'a God'. There is nothing original about his proof and the only surprising thing about it is that he should have thought that it was logically cogent or that it would convince anyone who did not already believe the conclusion on other grounds. It is historically interesting in that it shows the extent of his dependence on his scholastic background. And we must add in fairness to the scholastics that they did this sort of thing very much better than Locke did. He starts his argument with an empirical premiss: (1) Something exists (for I know that I myself exist). His second premiss has the appearance of an analytic proposition: (2) 'Nothing can no more produce any real being, than it can be equal to two right angles'.[3] Of course, to say that 'nothing cannot produce any real being' is merely an unusual way of saying that anything which begins to exist must have a cause for its existence. (It will be remembered that Locke regarded this as a logically certain truth.)

From (1) and (2), it follows, as Locke supposes, that something has always existed, since something does now exist and 'what was not from eternity had a beginning; and what had a beginning must be produced by something else'.[4] Having established to his satisfaction that something, x, has always existed, Locke goes on to prove that this x must have certain properties.

For this, he uses a third premiss. 'It is evident, that what had its being and beginning from another, must also have all that

1. IV.9.3.　　　　　　　2. IV.10.
3. IV.10.3.　　　　　　　4. IV.10.3.

which is in and belongs to its being from another too. All the powers it has must be owing to and received from the same source.'[1] If this premiss is accepted, it follows that the x which has always existed is the cause or source of all the qualities in the universe, and must therefore have these properties itself. Locke does not draw this, perhaps embarrassing, conclusion but contents himself with a weaker conclusion, viz. that the eternal existent being is the source of all knowledge and power in the universe and is therefore itself pre-eminently intelligent and powerful. 'Thus, from the consideration of ourselves, and what we infallibly find in our own constitutions, our reason leads us to the knowledge of this certain and evident truth, that *there is an eternal, most powerful, and most knowing Being*; which whether anyone please to call *God*, it matters not. The thing is evident; and from this idea duly considered, will easily be deduced all those other attributes, which we ought to ascribe to this eternal Being.'[2]

Locke claims that he knows the proposition italicized with a greater certainty than any proposition affirming the existence of the external world. However, he does not seem quite confident that all his readers will see the matter quite as he does, for in the second half of the chapter he reviews and enlarges on some of the main points in the argument. His review may be summarized as follows:

(i) It is obvious that something must always have existed: otherwise we have to assume that nothing can cause something, which is absurd.

(ii) Existent things can be divided exhaustively into conscious and unconscious.

(iii) Unconscious beings cannot produce conscious beings.

(iv) It follows from (i), (ii), and (iii) taken together that an eternal Mind has always existed.

He then adds some remarks on the absurdity of supposing God to be material. There is nothing of interest here except a repetition in another form of the premiss 'if A is the total cause of B, any property of B must be also a property of A'.

1. IV.10.4. 2. IV.10.6.

The defects of Locke's argument lie in the fact that even if we overlook the hopeless vagueness of some of the crucial concepts, there is no reason at all for accepting some of the premises. Consider these two propositions on which the argument depends: (*a*) If anything has a beginning it must have a cause; (*b*) if *A* is the total cause of *B*, any property of *B* must be a property of *A*. These propositions are not analytic or self-evident. They are universal factual statements which may very well be denied without any logical inconsistency. Yet it is difficult to see how they can be established or even rendered faintly probable by evidence of a factual kind.

(*a*) (i) This is a special form of the principle 'every event has a cause'. If Locke uses this principle to prove that the universe has a cause, he is guilty of an elementary type-fallacy. It has often been pointed out that the universe is just the sum total of all events and is, therefore, not itself an event. As Russell has observed,[1] anyone who claims that the universe must have a cause because every event has a cause is guilty of the same fallacy as someone who argues that because every human being must have a mother, the human race must have a mother.

(ii) In any case, (*a*) is a very dubious generalization which is not rendered very probable by the available factual evidence.

(*b*) In this case also, the available factual evidence is against the proposition. There are innumerable cases in nature of effects which have no observable similarity whatever to their causes.

Knowledge by Sensation

In his discussion of our knowledge of existence, Locke has so far made no appeal to any ways of knowing other than those which he has distinguished in his account of abstract and universal knowledge. But he has now to consider our knowledge of the existence of material objects and for this he introduces a third way of knowing, *sensation*. 'The know-

---

1. In a broadcast discussion.

ledge of the existence of *any other thing* we can have only by *sensation*: for there being no necessary connexion of real existence with any *idea* a man hath in his memory; nor of any other existence but that of God with the existence of any particular man: no particular man can know the existence of any other being, but only when, by actual operating upon him, it makes itself perceived by him. For, the having the idea of anything in our mind, no more proves the existence of that thing, than the picture of a man evidences his being in the world or the visions of a dream make thereby a true history.'[1] Now this account of knowing by sensation introduces quite a new meaning of the word 'knowledge'. Locke has defined knowledge as the perception of certain specified relations between ideas. We have seen that the definition does not account satisfactorily even for such knowledge as we have in logic and mathematics. He has now to forget his definition and it is clear from the arguments by which he supports the claim of our sensory cognitions to the name 'knowledge' that his present use of the word is very different indeed from his previous use. He admits that this is so in his discussion in Book IV.[2] where he is talking about 'the degrees of knowledge'. After dealing with intuition and demonstration he adds 'Whatever comes short of one of these, with what assurance soever embraced, is but *faith* or *opinion*, but not knowledge, at least in all general truths. There is, indeed, another perception of the mind, employed about *the particular existence of finite beings without us*; which, going beyond bare probability, and yet not reaching perfectly to either of the foregoing degrees of certainty, passes under the name of knowledge.'[2] Locke presumably does not mean that we can have a kind of knowledge which is neither certain nor yet merely probable. He no doubt intends to be taken as meaning that sensory knowledge while very different in character from the necessary propositions of logic and mathematics is yet too reliable to be sensibly stigmatized as 'merely probable'. He cannot appeal here to 'real existence' as this relation is an example of necessary connexion and could

1. IV.11.1   2. IV.2.14.

not be invoked to account for the purely contingent facts of our sense experience.

After conceding that we cannot refuse to say that there is a sense in which we really know propositions about particular existent objects, Locke proceeds to justify the claims of common sense in this respect. His arguments[1] may be summarized as follows:

(i) There is a great difference, amounting to a difference in kind, between images and sense data.

(ii) We need a causal explanation of the occurrence of our sense data because we cannot bring them in and out of existence by an act of will as we can do with images.

(iii) 'Our senses in many cases bear witness to the truth of each other's reports concerning the existence of sensible things without us.' For example, I see the glow of the fire, feel its heat and get tactual and kinaesthetic sensations when I stir it with the poker. Locke seems to regard these facts as analogous to the case of a set of witnesses who corroborate each other's story.

(iv) Sense organs are a necessary but not a sufficient condition of sense knowledge and therefore 'it is plain those perceptions are produced in us by exterior causes affecting our senses'.[2]

It is not difficult to see defects in the four reasons Locke offers above in justification of our sense knowledge. But it is more important to realize that it is not at all clear exactly what the theory is which Locke is defending here. Theories about the nature of sense perception fall rather roughly into three classes, though each class contains a good many different theories, each of which is a variation on a main theme. (A) Those philosophers who hold 'Naive Realism' and its various modifications maintain that in sense perception we are literally and directly aware of the sensible properties of the physical object. When we look at it, we actually see part of its surface; when we touch it, we literally touch part of its surface; and so on. (B) The second class of theories are of a

1. IV.2 and 11.　　　　　2. IV.11.4.

causal kind. Philosophers who hold theories of this type believe that we are *directly* aware not of physical objects but of sense data (or 'ideas of sense' in Locke's terminology) which are caused by the action of physical objects on our sense organs. (C) The third type of theory rejects a belief in physical objects as underlying or causing our sensory experience and boldly asserts that physical objects are nothing but the sense data or 'ideas' themselves combined and related in various ways. The chief difficulty in such theories is then to give a convincing account of the ways in which our sense data are related. Thus theories of type A call for minds and physical objects; theories of type B require three ingredients, minds, sense data, and physical objects, while theories of type C need only minds and sense data.[1]

Now which type of theory are we to suppose that Locke held? It is most natural to conclude that he held a theory of type B. His theory of knowledge presents what might be called a 'three-layer world'. *Minds* are directly aware of *ideas* which represent to the mind the otherwise unknown *physical objects*. And his doctrine of secondary qualities is, as we have seen, a fairly explicit causal account of sense experience. Yet, as he presents his theory above, it is so vague that it could be interpreted as a realist theory of type A. Nevertheless we cannot assume that he held such a theory without taking away one of the main points of the doctrine of ideas. It is most reasonable to assume that Locke's account of 'knowledge by sensation' is a causal theory of type B. But it is sketched in such dim and indeterminate outlines that it is not profitable to try to criticize it. All that can be done is to refer again to the general difficulty involved in all arguments which appeal to unobservable causes.[2]

I think that Locke probably felt a little unhappy about this part of his theory. In the first place, he ends with a very modest conclusion. 'In fine, then, when our senses do actually convey

1. Some theories of this type dispense with minds also and try to construct the world of experience from sense data alone.
2. See above, Chapter 3.

into our understandings any idea, we cannot but be satisfied that there doth something *at that time* really exist without us, which doth affect our senses, and by them give notice of itself to our apprehensive faculties, and actually produce that idea which we then perceive: and we cannot so far distrust their testimony, as to doubt that such collections of simple ideas as we have observed by our senses to be united together, do really exist together.'[1]

Secondly, he adds a slightly irritable postscript in which he comments on the absurdity of expecting conclusions to be logically cogent and certain where the subject matter of the argument does not permit such conclusions. 'He that, in the ordinary affairs of life, would admit of nothing but direct plain demonstration, would be sure of nothing in this world, but of perishing quickly.'[2] He falls back to his favourite last defence when combating imagined sceptics: our knowledge in this matter is at least as great as our condition demands. Our 'condition' is that of Christian men during their period of earthly probation.

Locke misses here the point of the philosophers' sceptical arguments about the existence of the external world. When they discuss the relation of sense data to physical objects and raise doubts about the 'existence' of such objects, they are not discussing a question of fact whose answer would affect our behaviour in any way. Whatever our beliefs may be about the 'existence' of physical objects and their relation to our sensory experience, they are not such as could ever be inferred by an observer from a scrutiny of our non-verbal behaviour. If this were not so, such enquiries would be scientific in character and not philosophical at all.

The upshot of Locke's discussion of knowledge is as follows. There are two sorts of propositions which can be known. The first concerns 'the existence of anything answerable' to a given idea, simple or complex. In this sort of knowledge, we are confined to particular instances, because with the exception of our knowledge of the existence of God,

1. IV.11.9.   2. IV.11.10.

our means of knowing is our sense organs. And these can reveal to us only particular matters of fact. The second sort of knowledge, which is knowledge in Locke's strict sense, gives us no assurance about the existence of anything corresponding to the ideas referred to but consists in an intuition of a necessary relation between the component ideas: *e.g.* if any figures are plane triangles, then their internal angles total 180 degrees. And the certainty and universality of these propositions depends on the intuited relations. 'In the former case, our knowledge is the consequence of the existence of things ... in the latter, knowledge is the consequence of the ideas (be they what they will) that are in our minds, producing there certain general propositions.'[1]

1. IV.11.14.

CHAPTER EIGHT

Judgement and Opinion

LOCKE has now given a complete account of those propositions which we can be said to know, in his sense of the
word. It will be seen that even his rather half-hearted extension of 'knowing' to cover some sorts of sensory cognition
leaves our stock of knowledge very meagre indeed. He is well
aware of this. 'The understanding faculties being given to
man, not barely for speculation, but also for the conduct of
his life, man would be at a great loss if he had nothing to
direct him but what has the certainty of true knowledge.'[1]
He has, therefore, to complete his account of the functions of
the human understanding by an account of judgement, 'the
faculty which God has given to man to supply the want of
clear and certain knowledge, in cases where that cannot be
had'.[2] Judgement differs from knowledge in the following
way. When we know that A is B, we directly perceive the
relation of agreement between the ideas A and B. When we
judge that A is B we presume the relation to hold or take it for
granted before we perceive it. The presumption may, of
course, be well founded or it may not. Verification of our
presumptions enables us to distinguish between right and
wrong judgement.

There are two points which have to be considered: (*a*) the
psychological differences between knowing and judging; (*b*)
the logical tests for distinguishing propositions which we can
know with certainty from those which we may assent to as
only probable. He deals with the psychological question in
terms of the degree of certainty which accompanies our
assents. In knowing, the mind 'certainly *perceives* and is undoubtedly satisfied of the agreement or disagreement of any of
its ideas'[3] while in judging the mind only *presumes* the agreement or disagreement 'which is, as the word imports, taken

1. IV.14.1.   2. IV.14.3.   3. IV.14.4.

188

to be so before it certainly appears'.[1] It is true, of course, that we assent to different propositions with different degrees of subjective certainty; but it too often happens that propositions which we suppose ourselves to know and which seem indubitable, turn out to be false. It would then follow, on Locke's premises, that we had perceived a relation of agreement between certain ideas which did not really hold between those ideas, or, in other words, that we had appeared to perceive the relation but had not really done so. But this is impossible on Locke's definition of 'idea'. It would be self-contradictory for him to maintain that we can perceive a non-existent idea, whether of relation or of any other type, in the way that a drunkard can perceive a non-existent pink rat. One of the uses of the terminology of 'ideas' is to remove, at least at one level of knowledge, the distinction between appearance and reality. And elsewhere, Locke himself admits this. 'For let any idea be what it will, it can be no other but such as the mind perceives it to be; and that very perception sufficiently distinguishes it from all ideas, which cannot be other, *i.e.* different, without being perceived to be so.'[2] The more important question concerns the nature of the logical criteria which should regulate the degree of our assent.

Locke has therefore to explain the grounds on which we are entitled to make judgements. This is a question which does not arise in the cases where we are said to know a proposition, because knowing, by Locke's definition, consists in perceiving the presence or absence of a certain relation between ideas. But this is not so with judgement. 'That which makes me believe is something extraneous to the thing I believe.'[3] Since in judging, we do not perceive the relation but presume its existence, we must have some grounds for our presumption. If this were not so, our assertion of one proposition p rather than another, q, would be merely capricious; it would be nonsense to talk of p being more probable than q; and the confirmations of our judgements by fact would be a matter of pure chance, which they are not. Though Locke does not give

1. *Ibid.*   2. II.29.5.   3. IV.15.3.

these reasons, it is clear that he had to take them into account, and he follows his short chapter on judgement by considering[1] 'the several degrees and grounds of probability and assent or faith'.

He defines probability as 'the appearance of agreement upon fallible proofs' and distinguishes two grounds for it: (*a*) the extent to which a given proposition whose truth or falsity is not self-evident conforms with our experience; (*b*) the testimony of others. Of course (*b*) has to be evaluated in the light of (*a*) and Locke gives some sensible rules for assessing the value of testimony. 'In the testimony of others is to be considered: (1) The number. (2) The integrity. (3) The skill of the witnesses. (4) The design of the author when it is a testimony out of a book cited. (5) The consistency of the parts and the circumstances of the relation. (6) Contrary testimonies.'[2] On the basis of these rules we proportion the degree of our assent to a proposition to the evidence for it. At best, our assent comes very near to certainty and propositions could, in principle at least, be arranged in an order of reliability starting 'from the very neighbourhood of certainty and demonstration quite down to improbability and unlikeliness even to the confines of impossibility'. And corresponding to degrees of probability, there are degrees of assent or belief ranging from confident assertion through doubt to disbelief. The difficulty here is to make the degree of our conviction correspond precisely with the degree of probability justified by the evidence. Locke tries to give some general rules for this but they are no more than commonsense rules of thumb in accordance with which people do in fact make judgements and assign probabilities in a rough and ready sort of way.

However, he is well aware of the difficulties in the way of obtaining reliable knowledge and points to them in support of a characteristic moral. 'Since, therefore, it is unavoidable to the greatest part of men, if not all, to have several *opinions*, without certain and indubitable proofs of their truth ... it would, methinks, become all men to maintain peace, and the

1. IV.14.   2. IV.15.4.

common offices of humanity, and friendship, in the diversity of opinions. . . . We should do well to commiserate our mutual ignorance, and endeavour to remove it in all the gentle and fair ways of information; and not instantly treat others ill, as obstinate and perverse, because they will not renounce their own, and receive our opinions.'[1] The sort of intolerance against which he is protesting here was manifested in his day, as in ours, chiefly in matters of religion and politics.

Locke divides probable propositions into two classes: (*a*) those concerning matters of fact and therefore verified by empirical evidence; (*b*) those concerning matters which cannot be supported by human testimony because there is no empirical evidence for them. We might expect that Locke would place propositions known by religious faith into class (*b*). But this is not what he does. The matters 'falling not under the reach of our senses' are (i) 'the existence, nature, and operation of finite immaterial beings without us; as spirits, angels, devils, etc. Or the existence of material beings which, either for their smallness in themselves or remoteness from us, our senses cannot take notice of . . . (ii) Concerning the manner of operation in most parts of the works of nature: wherein, though we see the sensible effects, yet their causes are unknown, and we perceive not the ways and manner how they are produced.'[2] This peculiar classification led T. H. Huxley to remark that Locke held to a sort of 'inverted agnosticism', accepting the dogmas of religion but doubting the findings of the natural sciences. Most of the questions which he believes not to be decidable by empirical evidence, are matters which have in fact been very largely determined by such evidence: for example, facts about microbes and remote nebulae and the laws of physics and chemistry. He believes that the evidence proper to such matters is evidence from analogy, a form of argument in which we infer that because two cases are alike in certain observed respects, they will also be alike in certain unobserved respects. It is true that arguments of this type do

1. IV.16.4   2. IV.16.12.

have their place in natural science in the formulation of hypo-
theses, but their field of application is not nearly so wide as
Locke thought it was. And they certainly cannot be used to
prove the existence of alleged entities like angels and devils
which are not only unobserved but also *unobservable*.

The result of this account of probable knowledge is that
Locke has given no account at all of the logical grounds of
our assent to probable conclusions. How do we justify our
conclusion that all or most A's are B's on the basis of our
acquaintance with a limited sample of A's of which all or
most have been B's? We should, for example, regard a teacher
as justified in remarking that most children who are good at
algebra are also good at geometry on the basis of his experience of several hundred children. It is useless for Locke to say
that probable knowledge is distinguished from certain knowledge in being 'nothing but the appearance of such an agreement or disagreement, by the intervention of proofs[1] whose
connexion is not constant or immutable or is at least not
perceived to be so'.[2] What can it mean to say that one idea
appears to have certain connexions with other ideas but does
not really do so, or that it has a certain connexion but not a
constant and immutable connexion? If ideas are as Locke has
defined them, it is self-contradictory for him to maintain that
they can ever appear to have certain properties or to stand in
certain relations without really doing so. Nor can they ever
have qualities or relational properties which they do not
appear to have.

Moreover, to say that an idea has a certain connexion,
which is *not* a constant and immutable connexion, with another idea is to say that, given two occurrences of ideas A and
B, they may have a certain mutual relation on the first occurrence and not on the second. This involves the type-token
confusion between two senses of 'idea'.[3] If 'idea' means whatever we are immediately acquainted with in thinking, it means

1. 'Proofs' are defined as 'the intervening ideas' in a demonstration.
(IV.2.3.)
2. IV.15.1.   3. See Chapter 2 above.

primarily a particular sense-datum occurring at a certain time
or a particular occurrence of a certain concept in the mental
history of a given individual. But if Locke talks of an idea
whose connexions are not constant, he is referring to the same
type-idea occurring on different occasions. The words 'constant' and 'immutable' are obviously applicable to connexions
of ideas only in the second of these two senses. But if the relations between the ideas are founded on the nature of the ideas
themselves, as they must be if they are to be necessary, it is
hardly possible for two type-ideas to be in a given relation on
one occasion and not on another. To suppose this would be
to suppose, for example, that a sense datum of a given shade
of crimson could be on one occasion darker than a given shade
of pink and on another occasion lighter. Locke does actually
express a doubt whether a 'mutable idea' can properly be said
to be one idea at all.[1] I think it is clear that this doubt is
justified. An idea-type could be 'mutable' only if all its idea-
tokens could fail to be identical in content.

The important problem about probable inference is to
determine how many occurrences of two given ideas in conjunction justify us in presuming that the connexion between
them is constant and immutable, to use Locke's terms, or at
least so nearly constant that we can assume their constant connexion without any serious risk. And Locke does not try to
deal with this problem. Of the two grounds of probable assent
which he mentions, the second is irrelevant. Testimony is required to establish particular facts but, in this, it is merely a
substitute for personal observation. The other criterion he proposes is the 'conformity of anything with our own knowledge,
observation and experience'.[2] This statement can be taken in
two senses. It may refer to our belief in a general statement on
the basis of our past experience of particular cases falling
under the generalization, or merely to our belief that the next
instance of A we meet with will be found conjoined with B
because all cases of A which have fallen under our notice have
been so conjoined. And in the second case, our belief rests on

1. II.29.9. 2. IV.15.4.

the assumption that the general statement is at least probable.

But Locke does not explicitly consider the case of general statements of the form 'all *A* is *B*' at all, when he is discussing knowledge. 'The propositions we receive upon inducements of *probability* are of *two sorts*: either concerning some particular existence, or, as it is usually termed, matter of fact, which, falling under observation, is capable of human testimony; or else concerning things, which falling beyond the discovery of our senses, are not capable of any such testimony.'[1] Yet in his discussion he cites as examples of truths concerning *particular matters of fact* 'all the stated constitutions and properties of bodies and all the regular proceedings of causes and effects in the ordinary course of nature',[2] all of which are statable only in general propositions. Part of the difficulty in evaluating what Locke has to say is that he makes no distinction between general and particular statements. Yet this distinction and the relation between these types of statement is crucial to a discussion of probable inference. When we infer that a given event *E* will probably happen, we do so because of an assumption about a *class* of events of which *E* is a member. We have seen, however, that Locke supposed that our knowledge of general propositions depended not on acquaintance with a sample of the members of a given class but on the basis of our intuition of 'constant and immutable' connexions between ideas. He thought, in other words, that our general knowledge of matters of fact comes from intuitive induction and not from problematic induction. And this basic error naturally disqualified him from offering a plausible account of belief and judgement.

The Nature of Reason

Locke's account of human reason throws light both on his theory of knowledge and on his philosophy of religion. For he adheres to the precedent set by the medieval philosophers

1. IV.16.5.   2. IV.16.6.

who gave Christianity a rational colouring in dividing the truths of religion into two classes, natural and revealed. Natural religion is the set of propositions about God and man's relation to God which are demonstrable by unaided human reason.

Locke points out that the word 'reason' is used ambiguously. He intends however to restrict its meaning to signify 'that faculty whereby man is supposed to be distinguished from beasts'.[1] The word 'faculty' which we have met previously means in Locke nothing more than a dispositional property of the mind. He has already discussed other faculties, perception or thinking, for example, and volition or willing. We naturally want to know what the functions of reason are and how it is related to the other powers of the mind. Now Locke comes to give his account of reason after he has dealt with the nature of human knowledge which he has explained in terms of perception and its various modes. 'What room is there for the exercise of any other faculty but *outward sense* and *inward perception*? What need is there of *reason*?'[2] He answers that reason is necessary both 'for the enlargement of our knowledge and regulating our assent'.[3] It comprises in fact, two sub-faculties which Locke calls 'sagacity' and 'illation' or 'inference'.

The function of sagacity is to discover the 'intermediate ideas' which form the links in our chains of demonstration. To take an example which will not be invalidated by Locke's peculiar theory of demonstration, suppose we are asked to prove a rider in geometry. The exercise of what Locke calls sagacity will consist in making the relevant selection of axioms and theorems which are necessary and sufficient to prove the required conclusion. The exercise of illation or inference will consist in drawing the right conclusions from the premises so provided. Obviously, these two capacities are mutually complementary. Sagacity directs the inferential process in the right way and illation is the 'perception of the connexion there is between the ideas in each step of the deduc-

1. IV.17.1.   2. IV.17.2.   3. *Ibid.*

tion'.[1] Reason, in other words, includes *reasoning* which Locke has already accounted for in terms of the perception of the relations between ideas. But he adds here that reason 'likewise perceives the probable connexion of all the ideas or proofs to one another, in every step of a discourse to which it will think assent due. This is the lowest degree of that which can truly be called reason.'[2] He adds that there are in all four functions or 'degrees' of reason: (1) sagacity or the 'discovery and finding out of proofs'; (2) the arranging of premises in a logical order 'to make their connexion and force be plainly and easily perceived'; (3) the perception of the logical connexions; (4) drawing a valid conclusion.

This classification of the functions of reason is clearly defective. In the first place, there is no real distinction between (2), (3) and (4). Drawing the right conclusion is just a special case of perceiving logical connexions. And when we set out premises in logical order, we do so in consequence of the logical connexions we perceive between them. Secondly, there are important functions of reason which Locke has omitted to mention. He is, of course, entitled to restrict the use of the word to the sense he has outlined, but the result is that there are important functions of the mind of which he has given no account at all. For example, what W. E. Johnson called 'intuitive induction' or the recognition of particular statements as *exemplifying* general statements is not covered by the account Locke has given. If an intelligent schoolboy is told that $1 + 3 = 4, 1 + 3 + 5 = 9, 1 + 3 + 5 + 7 = 16$, and so on, he will soon grasp the general statement of which these particular arithmetical statements are instances, viz. the sum of the first n odd numbers is n^2. This type of reasoning is of first-rate importance in mathematical and scientific work and it is a serious defect of Locke's doctrine of reason that it does not take account of it. We have seen that he does recognize the existence of intuitive induction when he shows that we learn general maxims like 'the whole is equal to the sum of its parts' by observing particular instances of the maxim. But

1. IV.17.2.   2. *Ibid.*

he does not give the process a name or note it as the function of any 'faculty'.

Intuitive induction is, of course, a special case of abstraction. Its specific difference is that the universal arrived at by intuitive induction is a principle or 'maxim' and not a concept or general idea. But Locke's account of abstraction is both too crude and too specialized to be extended to include intuitive induction. And, in any case, he omits, rather surprisingly, to include abstraction as a function of reason, though perhaps he admits their connexion indirectly in saying both that reason is the faculty which distinguishes men from animals and also that animals are almost certainly incapable of abstraction.[1]

Further, the formulation of statements about all the members of a given class on the evidence of a sample of the class is a form of reasoning which is fundamental to the natural sciences and, indeed, to the ordinary conduct of our lives. It is, moreover, common to animals and to man. Any animal which 'learns by experience' that fire burns or water quenches thirst is generalizing on the basis of experience, though the generalization is of a primitive kind. Yet as we have seen, Locke gives no proper account of this type of reasoning. His explanation of knowing in terms of perceiving relations between ideas leads him to talk of perceiving the 'probable connexion of ideas with one another'. But he does not try to give an account of this probable connexion nor could he have done so without exposing the basic weakness of his whole account of knowledge and judgement.

It is, in fact, difficult to see why Locke introduces this separate account of reason as a 'faculty'. The second of the two functions he assigns to it, 'illation' or inference, is merely the intuition of logical connexions which has already been explicitly assigned to the faculty of perception.[2] We are thus left to guess the relation between perception and reason. Perception can hardly be a species of reason as it has among its functions the intuiting of sense data and images. And this is an activity common to man and animals whereas reason is

1. II.11.10–11   2. II.21.5.

said to be peculiar to man. Nor can reason be a species of perception as it includes 'sagacity' which is a sort of rational imagination. This is an activity of the mind while in perception the mind is passive. Again in his discussion of the modes of thinking,[1] perception in the sense of sensation is listed as one of these modes although thinking is described as an activity of mind. The fact is that Locke was in rather a muddle about the mutual relations of the various functions of the mind. Perception, reason, knowledge, judgement, thinking—all these words he uses without exactly defining the relations between them. The only way of making sense of what he says about perception and reason, for example, is to suppose that he uses both these words as generic terms to refer to groups of mental functions. 'Perception' refers primarily to sense perception and its use is extended by analogy to cover non-sensory intuitions like the perceiving of logical connexions. 'Reason' refers primarily to *reasoning* and is extended, by analogy, to include certain ancillary mental processes. There is therefore an overlap in the denotation of these words as Locke uses them; they both refer indifferently to the intuiting of logical relations. But apart from this, 'perception' refers to dispositional properties of the mind which are lower, in the evolutionary sense, than those to which 'reason' refers. And I think it is correct to say that both perceiving and reasoning are, for Locke, forms of thinking.

The Provinces of Faith and Reason

'I find every sect, as far as reason will help them, make use of it gladly; and where it fails them, they cry out, "It is a matter of faith and above reason".'[2] This sounds like the cynical comment of an unbeliever on the intellectual vagaries of theologians, but Locke did not intend it to be taken in this way. He was most anxious to place our knowledge of the truths of religion on a firm rational basis and he thought that his first step should be to distinguish clearly the respective

1. II.19. 2. IV.18.2.

provinces of faith and reason. He proposes the following distinction. We know a truth by reason when we assent to a
conclusion as either certain or probable to some degree on the
basis of evidence derived from sensation or reflection. We
know a truth by faith, on the other hand, when we assent to
any proposition 'upon the credit of the proposer as coming
from God in some extraordinary way of communication'.[1]
The source of truths known by faith is called revelation.

But Locke observes that there are certain restrictions on the
type and scope of knowledge which can be conveyed by
revelation. It cannot, for example, enable us to know any new
simple ideas. Even if St Paul in his vision of paradise had any
qualitatively new experience, the natural deficiencies of language would have prevented him from communicating it to
his readers. And although revelation can give us knowledge
which can also be attained by natural unaided reason, it can
never provide stronger proofs of its assertions than reason can.
God could, for example, reveal geometrical truths to men if
he wished, but we would nevertheless know them more
certainly if we proved them for ourselves. It follows from this
that no alleged revelation can ever be admitted against the
clear evidence of reason. For example, no alleged revelation
should ever persuade us that the same body can be in more
than one place at the same time. (This was probably a satirical
comment on the doctrine of transubstantiation, which alleged
that the body of Christ was present, whole and entire, in each
portion of consecrated bread or wine administered in the
eucharist.) 'Since the evidence, first, that we deceive not ourselves in ascribing it to God, secondly, that we understand it
right; can never be so great as the evidence of our own
intuitive knowledge whereby we discern it impossible for the
same body to be in two places at once.'[2]

Locke goes on to point out that the genuine character of any
supposed revelation can only be established by reason. It
follows, of course, that our certainty that a given revealed
proposition is true can never justifiably exceed our certainty

1. *Ibid.*   2. IV.18.5.

that the proposition is, in fact, revealed. And since a complicated factual question about the alleged supernatural source of a given piece of information can never be established with certainty or even with a high degree of probability, it follows that faith, untempered by judicious doubt, is never logically justified. Locke does not openly draw this awkward conclusion but it is implicit in his treatment of the whole question. Nevertheless, he admits that revelation has a proper function in conveying to us truths which either cannot be established by the natural light of reason or have not, in fact, been so established. 'But yet, it still belongs to reason to judge of the truth of its being a revelation, and of the signification of the words wherein it is delivered.'[1]

Locke's rather cautious and matter of fact attitude to religious faith is due not to lack of religious sincerity on his part but to a well-grounded fear of what he called 'enthusiasm'. This is the name he gives to 'a third ground of assent', the opinionated self-confidence engendered by a supposed inner illumination 'which, laying by reason, would set up revelation without it'.[2] Enthusiasm 'takes away both reason and revelation, and substitutes in the room of them the ungrounded fancies of a man's own brain, and assumes them for a foundation both of opinion and conduct'.[3] The religious bigotry resulting from 'enthusiasm' and the consequent wars and persecutions were familiar horrors in the seventeenth century. Locke realized that a widespread belief in reason as the sole criterion of reliable knowledge is the only effective antidote to so common and virulent a social plague. 'Reason must be our last judge and guide in everything.'[4]

Conclusion

It has been shown that there are a great many defects of detail in the argument of Locke's Book IV. Yet the main defect is one of emphasis. He devoted his main attention to an

1. IV.18.8.   2. IV.19.3.   3. *Ibid.*
4. IV.19.14.

analysis of knowing in a strict sense of the word in which we know only those propositions which appear to us intuitively certain. His criterion of knowing is so exacting that we can know nothing but a few analytic trivialities and also, though he adds this as a belated concession to commonsense, a few statements established by immediate sensory observation. Thus the overwhelmingly greater part of our knowledge is probable knowledge only and Locke's treatment of this is scrappy and superficial. Now this is a very serious defect for two reasons. (i) We may reasonably require of a theory of knowledge that it shall provide a rational reconstruction of knowing in the accepted sense of the word. (ii) It is not possible to make a clear-cut distinction between what we can know with certainty and what we can assent to with some minor degree of conviction.

It is, indeed, commonly asserted by philosophers, even at the present day, that we can be quite certain only of analytic statements and that statements of contingent fact, even such apparently indubitable ones such as 'I am now writing' are never quite certain[1] because it is always possible for them to be refuted by subsequent evidence. For example, I may wake up and find that I was not really writing at all but only dreaming that I was. That factual statements are never incorrigible is true enough and if anyone wishes to use the word 'certain' in this stringent way to mean 'incorrigible' he is entitled to do so. But it should be realized that this would lead us to say that we can never be certain of any statements at all. *If we can never be certain of contingent propositions, we can never be certain of analytic propositions either.* This follows from the fact that our understanding of analytic statements like 'No material body can be in two places at once' or 'Nothing can be both red and green all over' is dependent on our correct understanding of the English language and, sometimes, of certain mathematical symbols. I cannot be certain that no material body can be in two places at once unless I can also be certain that I am remem-

---

1. To talk of a *statement* being certain is to use an elliptical expression: a certain statement is one of which we may justifiably *feel* certain.

bering correctly that 'body' means body, 'two' means two, 'at once' means at once, and so on. And these are contingent facts. Thus our certainty of logical and mathematical statements depends on our certainty as to the relevant contingent statements. We can therefore never be more certain of analytic statements than we are of the relevant contingent statements.

Had Locke realized this, he would no doubt have altered the emphasis of his last book entirely. He would first have thoroughly analysed the concepts of belief and probable knowledge and inference and only then considered our knowledge of logical and mathematical truths. And this would have accorded with the empiricist spirit of the first three books of the *Essay*. As his work stands, there is a marked change of outlook in the last book. The empiricist who tries to derive all human knowledge from sensation and reflection becomes the rationalist who bases knowledge on the intuition of self-evident relations between ideas. Professor Aaron has shown[1] how the account of knowledge given in IV.2 corresponds very closely with the intuitionism of Descartes' *Rules for the Direction of the Mind*, and gives reasons for supposing that Locke adopted this point of view from the members of the Cartesian school whom he met during his stay on the Continent. It is interesting, though idle, to speculate whether, if Locke had paid more attention to knowledge as exemplified by our memories and commonsense beliefs and less to our knowledge of logic and mathematics, he would have brought the *Essay* to a more satisfactory conclusion. Yet we must remember that Locke himself was convinced that his account of knowledge was his important contribution to philosophy. 'If I have done anything new', he wrote to Dr Stillingfleet, 'it has been to describe to others more particularly than had been done before, what it is they do when they perform that action which they call knowing.' The verdict of philosophers since his day has not confirmed this opinion.

1. *John Locke*, pp. 218–19: (London, 1937).

CHAPTER NINE

Political Theory

In the seventeenth century, writers were not expected to be narrow specialists and Locke's own interests were wide. He is best known, of course, for his theory of knowledge but his writings on political theory have had a great influence. He also published works on education, economic theory, theology and biblical criticism. We are concerned in this book only with Locke's philosophical ideas and there is little of philosophical interest in these other writings. It has, however, been traditional to regard speculations on the theoretical aspects of politics as philosophical in character and they are often referred to by the title of 'political philosophy'. For this reason and because Locke's writings on these subjects have been so influential, it will be well to mention them briefly.

Political Theory

If we look at a book on political theory such as Locke's *Second Treatise on Civil Government*, we shall find that the statements contained in it are of four different kinds. The first kind comprises judgements of value which may be explicit or, more commonly, implicit. A writer may suggest, for example, that the greatest happiness of the greatest number is the proper object of government; or that the liberty of the individual ought to be subordinate to the demands of efficient administration. It is often difficult to understand the precise meaning of such statements but it is easy to see that they are expressions of a kind very similar to moral evaluations such as 'cruelty is evil' or 'it is a duty to keep one's promises'. It is now fairly widely recognized that such statements, though important, cannot be *proved*, in any ordinary sense of the word, though people may sometimes be persuaded to accept them. Many of them indeed are so widely assented to, that they are not considered to demand any sort of justification.

The second class are statements of a purely factual kind. These are established by observation or testimony in the manner common to all factual statements. They may be statements referring to particular political facts such as 'Athens was a democracy in the time of Pericles' or, more usually, generalizations such as 'The national ownership of the means of production is essential to public welfare' or Plato's remark that democratic forms of government tend to degenerate into tyrannies. Generalizations of this kind are a stock-in-trade of political writers and are commonly made on totally inadequate evidence although they are just as much in need of empirical support as any scientific generalization.

Definitions are the third kind of statement. When Locke says, 'By *commonwealth*, I must be understood all along to mean, not a democracy or any form of government but any independent community which the Latins signified by the word *civitas*', he is making a definition to explain the sense in which he proposes to use a technical term. And a fourth type of statement, allied to the last, though differing from it in important respects, is the attempt to clarify concepts like 'political liberty' or 'the will of the people' by philosophical analysis.

Although nearly all the statements made in books on political theory fall into one of these four classes it is often very difficult to understand what the writer is saying because he does not distinguish clearly between these very different types of statement and often mixes them up together in a thoroughly confusing way. Arbitrary definitions masquerade as accepted usages, value judgements as factual statements and wild generalizations as sober matters of fact. Anyone who has tried to understand a standard work on political philosophy will be aware of the difficulty of avoiding these confusions. The philosophical elements in such writing, when they can be clearly dissected out from the remainder, are often small and are confined to statements of the fourth class. And these are by no means the most important features of political treatises.

Locke's writing on political subjects is reasonably clear and ingenuous as such books go. He was quite frankly a political apologist who wanted to make clear and justify the theoretical basis of the Revolution of 1688. Thus the *Treatises on Civil Government* are not very different in purpose, though vastly different in value, from political articles in the *New Statesman and Nation*. The first *Treatise* is an attack on the theoretical principle behind the misbehaviour of the Stuarts, the so-called 'divine right of kings'. This argument has no interest for us to-day, living as we do in an age when monarchy has barely an ornamental function.

The second *Treatise* is more important. Locke begins with the origin of society. He postulates what he calls a 'state of nature' and a 'natural law'. The former consists in 'men living together according to reason, without a common superior on earth with authority to judge between them'.[1] Man's liberty in this anarchical condition is limited only by the 'natural law' which Locke rather vaguely equates with reason. He presumably means that the natural law is a moral law self-evident to all rational creatures. Reason tells us that we must strive to preserve our own lives and those of our neighbours and refrain from acting to the detriment of the bodily welfare, liberty or property of others. Every man, in the state of nature, has to be his own policeman, judge, and executioner, and this, of course, has serious practical disadvantages. So men agree to resign certain rights proper to them in the natural state 'by agreeing with other men to join or unite into a community for their comfortable, safe and peaceable living one amongst another',[2] secure against internal and, to a lesser degree, external disorders. In return for this security, 'every man by consenting with others to make one body politic under one government, puts himself under an obligation to every one of that society to submit to the determination of the majority'.[3] If men did not contract to submit to majority rule in this way,

1. ii.19.   2. ii.95.   3. ii.97.

no civil society would outlast the first political disagreement among its citizens.

It must be noticed, however, that the only rights resigned by men on their entry into civil society are those of enforcing the natural law. Political power, which men in society resign to their government, is 'a right of making laws with penalties of death, and consequently all less penalties, for the regulating and preserving of property and of employing the force of the community in the execution of such laws and in the defence of the commonwealth from common injury and all this only for the public good'.[1] All other natural rights are retained by the individual.

Locke's version of the famous 'social contract' theory of the origin of civil government is no more satisfactory than other versions. He seems to regard it both as a factual account of the way in which society originated and as a justification of social obligation. The social contract is an historical event and because of it, we have a duty to society. He realizes that objections can be made to both these points and considers them. To the objection that there is no historical evidence for such a beginning to any civil government, Locke replies that such primitive social origins long antedated any written records. It is, therefore, in no way surprising that there should be no evidence. But this reply, though true, does not meet the real point of the objection: why does Locke hold a not very plausible theory about the origin of society for which no evidence can, in the nature of the case, be expected? I cannot help thinking that Locke was generalizing, though he does not say so, from the examples of the American colonies founded about that time. It was not an uncommon practice to draw up a constitution for such a settlement, as Locke himself had helped to do for Carolina, before any large scale emigration had taken place. It would then be plausible to regard the emigrants as parties to a social contract since they were signifying their acceptance of the new constitution by a voluntary act. Moreover, the theory is an attempt to explain

1. ii.3.

political obligation. Locke wanted to answer the question: what is the ground of our duty to society? The social contract theory does at least stress the important point that political authority depends, in some sense, on the consent of those who are governed.

Locke goes on to discuss the objection that 'all men being born under government, some or other, it is impossible any of them should ever be free and at liberty to unite together and begin a new one, or ever be able to erect a lawful government'.[1] His answer is that being born under a government does not make a man a natural subject of it. 'All men, however born, are free.' At birth, we are in the state of nature; and the social contract can be morally binding only on the actual contracting parties. No man can give away the liberty of another, to choose his own form of government. In this matter, even a son is not bound by his father's choice.

Locke is here making a moral evaluation though he appeals to the legal practice of his time in support of his opinion. It is, however, certainly not supported by present day legal practice. Governments do nowadays 'claim power over the son because of that they had over the father'. Both the *jus sanguinis* and the *jus soli* by which questions of citizenship to-day are largely decided are in conflict with what Locke calls 'the law of right reason' on this point. But does his 'theory' on the matter amount to no more than a pious sentiment? Perhaps Locke is really saying that a man's political obligations are also moral obligations only if the man himself is a party to the social contract. And indeed it seems reasonable enough to suggest that one man's obligations cannot be created by another man's acts.

So far Locke's political theory is not very original or very important. But he adds a proposal on the organization of political societies that has had a considerable influence on the development of parliamentary democracies since his time. The legislative power in the state, or the power to make laws, must not be in the hands of the same persons who hold the executive power, or the power of enforcing the laws. If this separation of powers is not ensured by the terms of the constitution, the men who form the government will have the power to exempt themselves from obedience to their own laws and the temptation to use this power will be irresistible. Thus a representative government will degenerate into a tyranny. When Locke wrote, he had in mind the recent Stuart despotism in which the king, the executive power in the land, had tried more than once to dispense with the services of parliament and arrogate its functions to himself. The sharp distinction between legislature and executive which Locke was able to draw owed much to the sharp cleavage between parliament and monarchy which was so prominent a political feature of the Stuart era. In Britain since his time, the decline of the political functions of the monarchy, the advent of party government and the cabinet system and the growing powers of the civil service have done much to blur the distinction which Locke wished to maintain. On the whole, the results have not been so subversive of parliamentary democracy as he anticipated. Nevertheless, the situation in Britain during the second world war provided some evidence in confirmation of his prophecy. The substitution of government by order in council for normal parliamentary legislation was expedient in the circumstances, but it was a mere caricature of democratic procedure. When ministers and their civil servants become in this way the effective rulers of a country there is a coalescence of the legislative and executive functions of government which can easily develop, as Locke foresaw, into a new kind of tyranny.

Locke's recommendations on the separation of political powers were taken more seriously outside his own country. But his influence here has been indirect. The French political writer, Montesquieu, developed Locke's theory of the separation of powers in his book *De l'Esprit des Lois* which was published in 1748. In the form in which it was expounded by Montesquieu, the doctrine of the separation of powers was embodied in the American constitution and has had a considerable influence on the constitutions of republican France and of other states, particularly in South America. The main difference between Locke's version of the doctrine and Montesquieu's is that Montesquieu postulated a division of the functions of the state into legislative, executive, and judiciary, in place of the division into legislative, executive, and federative, proposed by Locke.

One curious feature of Locke's political writing which has been very influential is his theory of property. It was not an entirely original theory but Locke made it famous. He starts from the premiss, which is not supported by most legal codes, that a man's own body is his own property. In consequence, 'the labour of his body and the work of his hands we may say are properly his. Whatsoever, then, he removes out of the state that nature hath provided and left it in, he hath mixed his own labour with and joined to it something that is his own, and thereby makes it his property.'[1] It looks as if he should maintain consistently with this, that there are degrees of ownership and the more labour a man 'mixes' with a product of nature, the greater his title to its possession. But this would clearly be an awkward and socially unworkable principle. In fact, Locke's criterion is whether a man by working on a natural product 'removes it out of that common state nature left it in'. Nevertheless men may not accumulate as much property as they can. 'As much as any one can make use of to any advantage of life before it spoils, so much he may by his labour fix a property in; whatever is beyond this is more than his share, and belongs to others.'[2]

Even in a primitive community employing little division of labour, so vague a theory would be a poor guide to a law of property. It is not even easy to be sure what sort of 'theory' Locke supposes it to be. He appeals to 'reason' in support of his view and we must therefore presume that he regards it as in accordance with the 'natural law', and so as embodying a value judgement about the *right* basis for a law of property. It is presumably also a recommendation for an amended use

1. ii.27.   2. ii.31.

of the word 'property' and its associated terms. But if we try to adopt the usage he recommends, we find it far too imprecise to be of any practical use. It is, perhaps, surprising that so indeterminate a doctrine should have been influential. Yet in the economic writings of Adam Smith and Ricardo, it became the basis for the labour theory of value which stated that the value of any commodity was proportionate to the amount of labour expended in its production. And this in turn developed into the theory of surplus value, one of the basic doctrines of Marxist economics. Locke would no doubt have been very distressed at the use to which his suggestion has been put. For his views on inviolability of property rights were decided even for a member of the English middle class. A government might punish a man by putting him to death but it must not deprive him of any of his property without his consent, 'the preservation of property being the end of government'.[1]

Locke tells us that a government is a trustee for its citizens with certain powers which they have relinquished to it to ensure their more efficient use. This useful notion that the relationship between the government and the governed should be analogous to that between trustee and beneficiary does something to soften the crudities of the social contract theory and draws attention to the important fact that governments have *duties*. But Locke's political theory gives little detailed guidance on the proper relations of governments and the individual citizen. As long as the government uses its powers for the purposes of its trust, it commands the allegiance of its citizens. It can however be justifiably removed by revolution if it misuses these powers, and Locke discusses the circumstances in which a government can be held to have broken its trust. The conditions permitting revolution, as he describes them, coincide strangely with the conditions leading to the Revolution of 1688. But the problem of the correct balance between the demands of public order and welfare and those of individual liberty, which is so acute to-day, are not

1. ii.138.

discussed. They were not topical in the seventeenth century except in so far as they concerned freedom of religious opinions. And the *Treatises on Civil Government* were intended to be tracts for the times. That their value has outlasted the occasion for which they were written is a measure of the intellectual fertility which characterizes so much of Locke's writing.

Religious Toleration

That every man has the right to his own opinion in matters of religion and the right to express that opinion and to choose what form of religious worship, if any, he shall adopt, seems to us, in twentieth-century England, so obvious as to be hardly worth discussion. Such freedoms have indeed been explicitly incorporated into the Charter of Human Rights drawn up by the United Nations Organization. This otherwise empty gesture is, at least, an indication of the extent to which religious toleration is nowadays generally accepted and approved. Even to-day, however, there are powerful organizations like the Roman Catholic Church and the various Communist governments which do not recognize such rights and admit them in practice, when they do, only as a measure of political expediency. In the seventeenth century, the limits of religious freedom were much narrower, both in theory and in practice. Holland was, perhaps, the only part of Europe where a man could profess and even express unorthodox opinions without serious risk of imprisonment or torture. And even there, dissenters had to be very circumspect.

Locke was not the first writer to propose a measure of religious tolerance but he was the most influential. Moreover, the reasons he gave for his opinions were derived, in some measure, from his theory of knowledge, and the success of the *Essay* may have helped to make the *Letter on Toleration* more widely acceptable. Locke's arguments for toleration are of two kinds. The first is an ethical argument to the effect that a church has no right to persecute anyone. For although a church resembles a commonwealth in being a voluntary organization, men do not renounce any of their natural rights when they join a certain church; and, in consequence, such organizations have no more power over their members than, for example, a cricket club has. The worst a church can do to an unorthodox member is to expel him from membership. Nor has the civil power any right of persecution 'because the care of souls is not committed to the civil magistrate any more than to other men'.[1] This is not so much an argument as a bare assertion which can very well be denied by an opponent who takes a different view about the nature of ecclesiastical organizations.

Locke's second argument is much stronger. The limits of human knowledge are so narrow and the probability of error on speculative matters so great that we can never know for certain that our religious opinions are correct and all others false and heretical. We have already seen how in Book IV of the *Essay* Locke showed that our confidence in any alleged revelation can never justifiably exceed our confidence that the doctrine is, in fact, revealed by God. And that any doctrine is revealed is an ordinary factual statement subject to all the natural risks of error which make such knowledge so uncertain. 'We should do well to commiserate our mutual ignorance and endeavour to remove it in all the gentle and fair ways of information; and not instantly treat others ill as obstinate and perverse because they will not renounce their own and receive our opinions.'[2] Our state of ignorance both of theology and of natural knowledge is such as to make the forcible imposition of our own opinions on others quite unjustifiable. Intolerance is, in any case, quite plainly ineffective to produce unity of religious faith. A ruler may be able to produce a semblance of outward conformity by persecuting his subjects, 'but that he principally intends by those means to compose a truly Christian church is altogether incredible'. Locke reveals the real motives behind religious persecution – arrogance, cruelty, and love of power, and adds some bitter comments on the hypocrisy of those who claim to persecute

1. *A Letter Concerning Toleration.*   2. IV.16.4.

heretics for the sake of their spiritual welfare. 'It will be very difficult to persuade men of sense that he who with dry eyes and satisfaction of mind can deliver his brother to the executioner to be burnt alive, does sincerely and heartily concern himself to save that brother from the flames of hell in the world to come.'[1]

Locke was not, however, in favour of unlimited toleration of religious opinions. The civil magistrates have the right to interfere in religious matters if the practices of any sect are unlawful in the ordinary course of life. (Human sacrifice would be an example of such a practice.) By 'unlawful' Locke appears to mean not merely 'illegal' but 'contrary to human society or to those moral rules which are necessary to the preservation of civil society'.[2] But he thinks that examples of such practices or opinions are rare in any church. Nevertheless this vague prescription gives the civil power very wide powers for the suppression of obnoxious opinions. There are no clear rules for judging when an opinion falls in this category and persecutions have often been excused on this pretext. (The inhuman treatment of the Albigenses is perhaps the best known example.) It is only too easy for a government, servile to clerical power, to claim that a common religion is the strongest bond of civil union and that, in consequence, *any* heretic holds opinions subversive of society.

But even apart from this reservation, Locke does not think that toleration should be extended to all opinions. He mentions three chief exceptions. Atheists are in no circumstances to be tolerated for the quaint reason that 'promises, covenants and oaths, which are the bonds of human society, can have no hold on an atheist'.[3] Locke did not think of investigating the purely empirical question whether atheists are, in fact, more prone to break their covenants than believers. But there are more important exceptions to be considered. Anyone whose religion involves allegiance to a foreign power or who claims a toleration for his own faith which he is not prepared

1. *A Letter Concerning Toleration.*   2. *A Letter Concerning Toleration.*
3. *A Letter Concerning Toleration.*

to extend to the faiths of others, cannot be tolerated. Locke instances the Mohammedans as an example of the first class though it is fairly clear from his discussion that he had the Roman Catholics in mind. English opposition to Roman Catholicism since the time of Mary Tudor was largely bound up with the fear that if the Catholic Church again became dominant in England, the country would be subordinate to foreign powers. At the time of the Spanish Armada such fears may have been justified but in later years the threat probably had little substance. Few people to-day would regard the fact that the Pope is the head of an independent state as an adequate ground for suppressing Roman Catholicism. (It has, however, been taken in some countries to be a justification for suppressing the Communist Party that the political allegiance of its members is given to a foreign power.)

Locke's last reservation raises a point of great importance. Should a society tolerate the opinions of a group which, were it in a position of dominance, would not grant a similar tolerance to the opinions of others? Locke is again referring primarily to the Roman Catholic Church. And we have a similar problem to-day in dealing with the secular religions of Communism and Fascism. Those who wish to defend a policy of toleration are here in an awkward dilemma which Locke does not discuss. If we tolerate a religious or political sect which does not itself tolerate opinions at variance with its own, we may soon find that sect dominant in our society. And toleration will have led to its own destruction. But if, as Locke suggests, we refuse to tolerate it, are we not sacrificing principle to expediency? We may even be accused of acting on the same principle as the Catholic or the Communist and tolerating only those who agree with us. It will no doubt be said, however, that there is a great deal of difference between refusing freedom of opinion to all but the adherents of a particular religious or political party and refusing it only to those who would not grant it to their opponents. Locke's proposal has a practical advantage in that it forces bigots to dissemble their real opinions and affect a tolerant façade. And this, in time, may mitigate their fanaticism; for it is difficult to simulate a moral attitude over a long period of time without coming to sympathize with it to some degree. Moreover, if a society professes universal toleration, it cannot refuse the claim offered by Mgr Ronald Knox on behalf of Roman Catholics.[1] When Catholics demand toleration from a non-Catholic society, he says, they are appealing not to their own principles but to those of the society in which they live. It may perhaps seem somewhat disingenuous to seek the benefit of principles which one believes to be pernicious. But the Catholic (or the Communist) would probably reply that toleration is only a bad thing when wrong opinions are tolerated. If right and salutary opinions such as those of Rome (or Moscow) are allowed free expression, then toleration is, to that extent at least, an unqualified good.

But although Locke's last reservation would withhold toleration from no one but those who would not grant it to others and would obviate the likelihood of a policy of toleration leading to its own destruction, I cannot help feeling that such a policy should admit as few exceptions as possible. It is one of the notorious embarrassments of acting on a moral principle that it puts one at a disadvantage with those who do not accept or act on the same principle. And if the proposition 'religious and political opinions should be allowed free expression' (or any other formulation of the principle of tolerance) is to be regarded as a moral judgement, I cannot see how Locke's exceptions can be justified. If, however, it is nothing but a recommendation of a social policy, its operation will properly be subject to considerations of expediency. It is one of the failings of Locke's defence of toleration that he does not make it clear how he interprets the principle in question.

1. *The Belief of Catholics* (London, 1927).

CHAPTER TEN

Conclusion

It is difficult to-day to give a just assessment of what Locke achieved in the *Essay Concerning Human Understanding*. What is valuable in it has been developed and improved by his successors and has become, to a large extent, part of an intellectual background which we accept uncritically. When our attention is drawn to those presuppositions of our ways of thinking which are derived from Locke's work, we find them obvious and even trivial. We fail to realize either that they are still important or that when they were propounded in the seventeenth century they were startling and revolutionary proposals. On the other hand, many of his mistakes seem crude and elementary and are so easy to criticize that we are tempted to wonder why he is reckoned to be a great philosopher at all. That all this is so, is a measure of his success and influence.

In writing of Locke's doctrine of nominal essences, Lord Russell remarked that 'only those who have allowed themselves to be afflicted by the scholastics will realize how much metaphysical lumber it sweeps away'.[1] The same might be said with truth of many other parts of Locke's theory of knowledge, notably the doctrines of substance and personal identity, incomplete and unsatisfactory as they are. The scholastic philosophy had originated in an attempt to provide an intellectual framework for the Christian view of the universe. Such interested speculation is perhaps not the highest form of intellectual endeavour but the ablest exponents of the scholastic philosophy had performed their task with remarkable ingenuity. But the world picture of the middle ages was very different indeed from that of the seventeenth century. The Reformation had destroyed the theological unity of Europe and the rise of natural science had provided a totally

1. *History of Western Philosophy*, p. 611 (London, 1946).

new mode of explanation of natural events. In the face of this new situation, medieval Aristotelianism was no longer able to perform its rationalizing function. Its concepts and ways of explanation had been designed to apply to a very different sort of universe and they no longer fitted. Moreover, its day of glory had departed. The exponents of scholasticism in the seventeenth century were not men of the ability of Abelard, Aquinas, and William of Ockham, but mere commentators and compilers of text books, totally lacking in originality.

The situation needed new philosophical points of view and these were offered from several sources. Descartes in France, himself a mathematician of the first rank, devised a system in which the mathematical methods of the new physics were taken as the standard for all valid thinking. He even went to the extent of setting out part of his philosophical argument in geometrical form, deriving his conclusions as theorems based on self-evident axioms. This method was later employed on a larger scale by Spinoza. Descartes' philosophy was a tribute to the success of mathematics as a language for explaining the natural world. Locke in England, professing himself an 'under-labourer' to the natural scientists, seized on the other cardinal feature of the new science, its empirical character. His philosophy is an attempt to demonstrate the extent of human knowledge, and, therefore, its limits also, by showing that all the materials of our knowledge are derived, in the last analysis, from experience, either of the world outside us or of our own mental life. 'All those sublime thoughts which tower above the clouds, and reach as high as heaven itself, take their rise and footing here; in all that great extent wherein the mind wanders in those remote speculations it may seem to be elevated with, it stirs not one jot beyond those ideas which sense or reflection have offered for its contemplation.'[1]

Of the distinguishing features of seventeenth-century natural science which are embodied in the philosophies of

1. II.i.24.

Descartes and Locke respectively, the empirical outlook has turned out to be vastly more important for philosophy than the mathematical method. (The latter was, indeed, quite unsuited to philosophy though it is now recognized as the proper method for logic.) It is not possible to give a summary description of the 'empirical outlook'. In the work of Locke and his immediate successors, it took the form of showing that there can be no genuine objects of knowledge other than those which occur in experience or can be constructed out of what occurs in experience. Contemporary empiricists tend to concentrate rather on the problem of verification of statements. They try to show how no statement can be significant unless its components refer to objects, properties or relations occurring in experience or to constructions from such empirical material. And the word 'experience' is taken to mean at least 'sense experience' and is sometimes extended, as it was by Locke, to include material provided by introspection. The value of the empirical outlook can best be demonstrated, as biochemists demonstrate the value of vitamins, by showing what happens in its absence. It is the only antidote of permanent value to the outbreaks of mysticism, irrationalism, confused verbalizing and pretentious profundity by which philosophers are infected from time to time. (Existentialism is an outstanding contemporary example.) And Locke can claim to be, if not the originator of the empirical outlook, at least its first important exponent.

And associated with his empirical outlook is Locke's belief that 'reason is our last judge and guide in everything' and that there are no other *independent* means by which reliable knowledge may be had. It would not be true to say that only empiricists are rationalists in this sense, but it is notable that a failure of confidence in the empiricist outlook is commonly accompanied by a denigration of reason and a retreat to faith, instinct, or mystical intuition as substitutes. Locke has pointed out in the *Introduction* to the *Essay*[1] how this failure of confidence in human reason is a direct result of attempting to use it

1. Intro. 7.

on insoluble or unreal problems. The metaphysicians start with an exaggerated confidence in reason but the inevitable failure of their enterprise will 'confirm them at last in perfect scepticism'.

Locke was not himself a particularly systematic or consistent thinker. This was partly due to his practical interests which made him disinclined to press an argument further than the demands of everyday living required. It was partly due, also, to a failure to be fully aware of his presuppositions. Both his scholastic training and his reading of Descartes influenced him deeply and he does not seem to have realized the wide divergence between the conclusions indicated by his own empirical premises and those entailed by the unacknowledged scholastic and Cartesian elements in this thinking. Perhaps the best example of this radical inconsistency is the contrast in outlook between the first three books of the *Essay* and the last.

Locke's greatest achievement was, then, to establish the fundamental importance of the empirical element in knowledge. But this by no means exhausts the value of the *Essay*. The application of the empirical approach to some of the traditional questions of philosophy threw a new light on the problems of substance, personal identity, and general thinking. Much of Locke's writing on special topics is undeveloped and it was left to his successors and, in particular, to David Hume, to work out the full implications of the lines of thought which Locke had suggested. His rather sketchy account of causality contains, for example, a suggestion which became in Hume's hands a classical instance of the power of the empirical outlook.

Apart from the value of Locke's incidental discussion of particular philosophical problems, he drew attention to two other topics whose importance for philosophy has not been fully realized until quite recent years. The first is the relation of language to thinking to which he devoted Book III of the *Essay*. His own treatment of the subject is subordinated to the demands of the 'new way of ideas' and, largely for that reason, is not very successful. But his suggestion that the 'doctrine of signs' is basic to other forms of knowledge, being a study of their 'instruments', has at last been taken seriously. Philosophers of nearly all schools would agree to-day that the current controversies about the limits of philosophical enquiry and the validity of metaphysics turn principally on the nature of the sign process. Even those who do not admit that the limits of expression are necessarily the limits of thinking recognize, at least, that what cannot be expressed cannot be communicated; and that until the natural history of signs has been more carefully studied and the functions of signs more thoroughly understood, it is vain to look for a solution of the problems about the limits of human knowledge. That Locke was the first to see, however dimly, that 'the original, certainty and extent of human knowledge' depends at least as much on our ways of communicating as on our ways of knowing, because the two cannot be separated, is a great part of his achievement.

The other topic of current interest to which Locke contributed is treated in the otherwise unfortunate Book IV of the *Essay*. This is the classification of different types of statement and the discussion of the different sorts of evidence appropriate to these types. He tries to distinguish statements into logical and factual, trivial and informative, general and particular, and to show the differences between the propositions of mathematics, natural science, ethics, and theology, the ways in which each is established and the degree of assent to be accorded to each kind. Locke's erroneous beliefs about the nature of knowledge and of inference make much of this discussion of little positive value. It is clear, nevertheless, that he saw some of the complexities of what has come to be known as the problem of verification far more clearly than most of his successors. Hume's rather cavalier proposal to commit to the flames all propositions which are neither the outcome of 'abstract reasoning concerning quantity or number' nor of 'experimental reasoning concerning matter of fact and existence'[1] ignores the point of Locke's patient enquiry. It may

1. *Enquiry Concerning Human Understanding*, XII.3.

well be true that statements which do not fall into one of these two categories are of no cognitive value. But it is just as important to realize that neither of these classes is homogeneous. There are many types of factual statement and many types of analytic statement. And the differences between these types may be as important as the similarities and even more illuminating.

The defects of the *Essay* are far more on the surface than its merits and therefore call for little comment here. There is no doubt that the most serious of them are consequences of the terminology of 'ideas'. The 'new way of ideas' was not Locke's invention but he endorsed it so wholeheartedly that it is now more closely associated with him than with any other philosopher. The main defect of the theory of ideas is the multiple ambiguity of the word 'idea'. One result of this ambiguity, taken together with the definition of 'idea' as 'whatsoever is the object of the understanding when a man thinks', is that Locke begs some important questions at the very outset of his enquiry. He assumes in his definition the misleading act-content analysis of thinking. He implies also the existence of a certain class-property common to all the 'objects of the understanding'. But if anything is certain in the theory of knowledge, it is that sense data, images, sensory presentations, concepts, emotions, and mental 'acts' do not resemble each other, if they can be said to do so at all, in anything like the way in which dachshunds, bull terriers, Alsatians, and Great Danes do so. They are, in no sense, species of a common genus. Yet Locke's very terminology makes this ruinous assumption. Further, the notion of ideas as signs involved Locke in all the difficulties of the 'representative theory of knowledge'. And though he could not fail to see these difficulties, he was not able to explain them away.

Lastly, we should not forget that in the very formulation of his problem, Locke opened up a whole new subject for philosophical enquiry. The problems of the theory of knowledge, which have been the principal concern of philosophers, especially in his own country, since his day, were first explicitly propounded in the *Essay*. Other philosophers had, of course, dealt with these problems but Locke was the first to insist that the nature and capacities of the human mind should be the starting point for philosophy. Philosophers are not all agreed on whether this very revolutionary change in the direction of philosophical enquiry was, on the whole, a beneficial one. At least, there can be no doubt that had Locke not redirected philosophers' interests in this way, our ideas about human knowledge and its varieties and limits would be far more confused and vague even than they are to-day. In so far as Locke has had a bad influence on philosophy it is due more to the peculiar defects of his theory of knowledge than to the fact that he made the problems of epistemology the basic questions for philosophy. Moreover, this original outlook of the *Essay*, together with its empirical basis, is the cause of its deep and lasting influence on European thought. It was, for example, this combination of interest in the problems of the human mind with the insistence on experience as the only basis for knowledge which prepared the way for the development of psychology as an independent science. Locke has sometimes been spoken of, for this reason, as the father of psychology. The philosophical works of the highest order are not those which answer the old problems in the old way but those which open up new territories or provide new techniques for exploring the old ones. Locke's *Essay* did both these things. And it has had a fertilizing influence on philosophical thinking which even to-day is not exhausted.

Index

CATALOGUE OF DOVER BOOKS

Books Explaining Science and Mathematics

WHAT IS SCIENCE?, N. Campbell. The role of experiment and measurement, the function of mathematics, the nature of scientific laws, the difference between laws and theories, the limitations of science, and many similarly provocative topics are treated clearly and without technicalities by an eminent scientist. "Still an excellent introduction to scientific philosophy," H. Margenau in PHYSICS TODAY. "A first-rate primer . . . deserves a wide audience," SCIENTIFIC AMERICAN. 192pp. 5⅜ x 8.   S43 Paperbound **$1.25**

THE NATURE OF PHYSICAL THEORY, P. W. Bridgman. A Nobel Laureate's clear, non-technical lectures on difficulties and paradoxes connected with frontier research on the physical sciences. Concerned with such central concepts as thought, logic, mathematics, relativity, probability, wave mechanics, etc. he analyzes the contributions of such men as Newton, Einstein, Bohr, Heisenberg, and many others. "Lucid and entertaining . . . recommended to anyone who wants to get some insight into current philosophies of science," THE NEW PHILOSOPHY. Index. xi + 138pp. 5⅜ x 8.   S33 Paperbound **$1.25**

EXPERIMENT AND THEORY IN PHYSICS, Max Born. A Nobel Laureate examines the nature of experiment and theory in theoretical physics and analyzes the advances made by the great physicists of our day: Heisenberg, Einstein, Bohr, Planck, Dirac, and others. The actual process of creation is detailed step-by-step by one who participated. A fine examination of the scientific method at work. 44pp. 5⅜ x 8.   S308 Paperbound **75¢**

THE PSYCHOLOGY OF INVENTION IN THE MATHEMATICAL FIELD, J. Hadamard. The reports of such men as Descartes, Pascal, Einstein, Poincaré, and others are considered in this investigation of the method of idea-creation in mathematics and other sciences and the thinking process in general. How do ideas originate? What is the role of the unconscious? What is Poincaré's forgetting hypothesis? are some of the fascinating questions treated. A penetrating analysis of Einstein's thought processes concludes the book. xiii + 145pp. 5⅜ x 8.   T107 Paperbound **$1.25**

THE NATURE OF LIGHT AND COLOUR IN THE OPEN AIR, M. Minnaert. Why are shadows sometimes blue, sometimes green, or other colors depending on the light and surroundings? What causes mirages? Why do multiple suns and moons appear in the sky? Professor Minnaert explains these unusual phenomena and hundreds of others in simple, easy-to-understand terms based on optical laws and the properties of light and color. No mathematics is required but artists, scientists, students, and everyone fascinated by these "tricks" of nature will find thousands of useful and amazing pieces of information. Hundreds of observational experiments are suggested which require no special equipment. 200 illustrations; 42 photos. xvi + 362pp. 5⅜ x 8.   T196 Paperbound **$2.00**

THE UNIVERSE OF LIGHT, W. Bragg. Sir William Bragg, Nobel Laureate and great modern physicist, is also well known for his powers of clear exposition. Here he analyzes all aspects of light for the layman: lenses, reflection, refraction, the optics of vision, x-rays, the photoelectric effect, etc. He tells you what causes the color of spectra, rainbows, and soap bubbles, how magic mirrors work, and much more. Dozens of simple experiments are described. Preface. Index. 199 line drawings and photographs, including 2 full-page color plates. x + 283pp. 5⅜ x 8.   T538 Paperbound **$1.85**

SOAP-BUBBLES: THEIR COLOURS AND THE FORCES THAT MOULD THEM, C. V. Boys. For continuing popularity and validity as scientific primer, few books can match this volume of easily-followed experiments, explanations. Lucid exposition of complexities of liquid films, surface tension and related phenomena, bubbles' reaction to heat, motion, music, magnetic fields. Experiments with capillary attraction, soap bubbles on frames, composite bubbles, liquid cylinders and jets, bubbles other than soap, etc. Wonderful introduction to scientific method, natural laws that have many ramifications in areas of modern physics. Only complete edition in print. New Introduction by S. Z. Lewin, New York University. 83 illustrations; 1 full-page color plate. xii + 190pp. 5⅜ x 8½.   T542 Paperbound **95¢**

CATALOGUE OF DOVER BOOKS

THE STORY OF X-RAYS FROM RONTGEN TO ISOTOPES, A. R. Bleich, M.D. This book, by a member of the American College of Radiology, gives the scientific explanation of x-rays, their applications in medicine, industry and art, and their danger (and that of atmospheric radiation) to the individual and the species. You learn how radiation therapy is applied against cancer, how x-rays diagnose heart disease and other ailments, how they are used to examine mummies for information on diseases of early societies, and industrial materials for hidden weaknesses. 54 illustrations show x-rays of flowers, bones, stomach, gears with flaws, etc. 1st publication. Index. xix + 186pp. 5⅜ x 8. T622 Paperbound **$1.50**

SPINNING TOPS AND GYROSCOPIC MOTION, John Perry. A classic elementary text of the dynamics of rotation — the behavior and use of rotating bodies such as gyroscopes and tops. In simple, everyday English you are shown how quasi-rigidity is induced in discs of paper, smoke rings, chains, etc., by rapid motions; why a gyrostat falls and why a top rises; precession; how the earth's motion affects climate; and many other phenomena. Appendix on practical use of gyroscopes. 62 figures. 128pp. 5⅜ x 8. T416 Paperbound **$1.25**

SNOW CRYSTALS, W. A. Bentley; M. J. Humphreys. For almost 50 years W. A. Bentley photographed snow flakes in his laboratory in Jericho, Vermont; in 1931 the American Meteorological Society gathered together the best of his work, some 2400 photographs of snow flakes, plus a few ice flowers, windowpane frosts, dew, frozen rain, and other ice formations. Pictures were selected for beauty and scientific value. A very valuable work to anyone in meteorology, cryology; most interesting to layman; extremely useful for artist who wants beautiful, crystalline designs. All copyright free. Unabridged reprint of 1931 edition. 2453 illustrations. 227pp. 8 x 10½. T287 Paperbound **$3.00**

A DOVER SCIENCE SAMPLER, edited by George Barkin. A collection of brief, non-technical passages from 44 Dover Books Explaining Science for the enjoyment of the science-minded browser. Includes work of Bertrand Russell, Poincaré, Laplace, Max Born, Galileo, Newton; material on physics, mathematics, metallurgy, anatomy, astronomy, chemistry, etc. You will be fascinated by Martin Gardner's analysis of the sincere pseudo-scientist, Moritz's account of Newton's absentmindedness, Bernard's examples of human vivisection, etc. Illustrations from the Diderot Pictorial Encyclopedia and De Re Metallica. 64 pages. **FREE**

THE STORY OF ATOMIC THEORY AND ATOMIC ENERGY, J. G. Feinberg. A broader approach to subject of nuclear energy and its cultural implications than any other similar source. Very readable, informal, completely non-technical text. Begins with first atomic theory, 600 B.C. and carries you through the work of Mendelejeff, Röntgen, Madame Curie, to Einstein's equation and the A-bomb. New chapter goes through thermonuclear fission, binding energy, other events up to 1959. Radioactive decay and radiation hazards, future benefits, work of Bohr, moderns, hundreds more topics. "Deserves special mention . . . not only authoritative but thoroughly popular in the best sense of the word," Saturday Review. Formerly, "The Atom Story." Expanded with new chapter. Three appendixes. Index. 34 illustrations. vii + 243pp. 5⅜ x 8. T625 Paperbound **$1.60**

THE STRANGE STORY OF THE QUANTUM, AN ACCOUNT FOR THE GENERAL READER OF THE GROWTH OF IDEAS UNDERLYING OUR PRESENT ATOMIC KNOWLEDGE, B. Hoffmann. Presents lucidly and expertly, with barest amount of mathematics, the problems and theories which led to modern quantum physics. Dr. Hoffmann begins with the closing years of the 19th century, when certain trifling discrepancies were noticed, and with illuminating analogies and examples takes you through the brilliant concepts of Planck, Einstein, Pauli, Broglie, Bohr, Schroedinger, Heisenberg, Dirac, Sommerfeld, Feynman, etc. This edition includes a new, long postscript carrying the story through 1958. "Of the books attempting an account of the history and contents of our modern atomic physics which have come to my attention, this is the best," H. Margenau, Yale University, in "American Journal of Physics." 32 tables and line illustrations. Index. 275pp. 5⅜ x 8. T518 Paperbound **$1.50**

SPACE AND TIME, E. Borel. Written by a versatile mathematician of world renown with his customary lucidity and precision, this introduction to relativity for the layman presents scores of examples, analogies, and illustrations that open up new ways of thinking about space and time. It covers abstract geometry and geographical maps, continuity and topology, the propagation of light, the special theory of relativity, the general theory of relativity, theoretical researches, and much more. Mathematical notes. 2 Indexes. 4 Appendices. 15 figures. xvi + 243pp. 5⅜ x 8. T592 Paperbound **$1.75**

FROM EUCLID TO EDDINGTON: A STUDY OF THE CONCEPTIONS OF THE EXTERNAL WORLD, Sir Edmund Whittaker. A foremost British scientist traces the development of theories of natural philosophy from the western rediscovery of Euclid to Eddington, Einstein, Dirac, etc. The inadequacy of classical physics is contrasted with present day attempts to understand the physical world through relativity, non-Euclidean geometry, space curvature, wave mechanics, etc. 5 major divisions of examination: Space; Time and Movement; the Concepts of Classical Physics; the Concepts of Quantum Mechanics; the Eddington Universe. 212pp. 5⅜ x 8. T491 Paperbound **$1.35**

Nature, Biology,

NATURE RECREATION: Group Guidance for the Out-of-doors, William Gould Vinal. Intended for both the uninitiated nature instructor and the education student on the college level, this complete "how-to" program surveys the entire area of nature education for the young. Philosophy of nature recreation; requirements, responsibilities, important information for group leaders; nature games; suggested group projects; conducting meetings and getting discussions started; etc. Scores of immediately applicable teaching aids, plus completely updated sources of information, pamphlets, field guides, recordings, etc. Bibliography. 74 photographs. + 310pp. 5⅜ x 8½.   T1015 Paperbound **$1.75**

HOW TO KNOW THE WILD FLOWERS, Mrs. William Starr Dana. Classic nature book that has introduced thousands to wonders of American wild flowers. Color-season principle of organization is easy to use, even by those with no botanical training, and the genial, refreshing discussions of history, folklore, uses of over 1,000 native and escape flowers, foliage plants are informative as well as fun to read. Over 170 full-page plates, collected from several editions, may be colored in to make permanent records of finds. Revised to conform with 1950 edition of Gray's Manual of Botany. xlii + 438pp. 5⅜ x 8½.   T332 Paperbound **$2.00**

HOW TO KNOW THE FERNS, F. T. Parsons. Ferns, among our most lovely native plants, are all too little known. This classic of nature lore will enable the layman to identify almost any American fern he may come across. After an introduction on the structure and life of ferns, the 57 most important ferns are fully pictured and described (arranged upon a simple identification key). Index of Latin and English names. 61 illustrations and 42 full-page plates. xiv + 215pp. 5⅜ x 8.   T740 Paperbound **$1.35**

MANUAL OF THE TREES OF NORTH AMERICA, Charles Sprague Sargent. Still unsurpassed as most comprehensive, reliable study of North American tree characteristics, precise locations and distribution. By dean of American dendrologists. Every tree native to U.S., Canada, Alaska, 185 genera, 717 species, described in detail—leaves, flowers, fruit, winterbuds, bark, wood, growth habits etc. plus discussion of varieties and local variants, immaturity variations. Over 100 keys, including unusual 11-page analytical key to genera, aid in identification. 783 clear illustrations of flowers, fruit, leaves. An unmatched permanent reference work for all nature lovers. Second enlarged (1926) edition. Synopsis of families. Analytical key to genera. Glossary of technical terms. Index. 783 illustrations, 1 map. Two volumes. Total of 982pp. 5⅜ x 8.   T277 Vol. I Paperbound **$2.25**
                                                                        T278 Vol. II Paperbound **$2.25**
                                                                                    The set **$4.50**

TREES OF THE EASTERN AND CENTRAL UNITED STATES AND CANADA, W. M. Harlow. A revised edition of a standard middle-level guide to native trees and important escapes. More than 140 trees are described in detail, and illustrated with more than 600 drawings and photographs. Supplementary keys will enable the careful reader to identify almost any tree he might encounter. xiii + 288pp. 5⅜ x 8.   T395 Paperbound **$1.35**

GUIDE TO SOUTHERN TREES, Ellwood S. Harrar and J. George Harrar. All the essential information about trees indigenous to the South, in an extremely handy format. Introductory essay on methods of tree classification and study, nomenclature, chief divisions of Southern trees, etc. Approximately 100 keys and synopses allow for swift, accurate identification of trees. Numerous excellent illustrations, non-technical text make this a useful book for teachers of biology or natural science, nature lovers, amateur naturalists. Revised 1962 edition. Index. Bibliography. Glossary of technical terms. 920 illustrations; 201 full-page plates. ix + 709pp. 4⅝ x 6⅜.   T945 Paperbound **$2.35**

FRUIT KEY AND TWIG KEY TO TREES AND SHRUBS, W. M. Harlow. Bound together in one volume for the first time, these handy and accurate keys to fruit and twig identification are the only guides of their sort with photographs (up to 3 times natural size). "Fruit Key": Key to over 120 different deciduous and evergreen fruits. 139 photographs and 11 line drawings. Synoptic summary of fruit types. Bibliography. 2 Indexes (common and scientific names). "Twig Key": Key to over 160 different twigs and buds. 173 photographs. Glossary of technical terms. Bibliography. 2 Indexes (common and scientific names). Two volumes bound as one. Total of xvii + 126pp. 5⅝ x 8⅜.   T511 Paperbound **$1.25**

INSECT LIFE AND INSECT NATURAL HISTORY, S. W. Frost. A work emphasizing habits, social life, and ecological relations of insects, rather than more academic aspects of classification and morphology. Prof. Frost's enthusiasm and knowledge are everywhere evident as he discusses insect associations and specialized habits like leaf-rolling, leaf-mining, and case-making, the gall insects, the boring insects, aquatic insects, etc. He examines all sorts of matters not usually covered in general works, such as: insects as human food, insect music and musicians, insect response to electric and radio waves, use of insects in art and literature. The admirably executed purpose of this book, which covers the middle ground between elementary treatment and scholarly monographs, is to excite the reader to observe for himself. Over 700 illustrations. Extensive bibliography. x + 524pp. 5⅜ x 8.   T517 Paperbound **$2.50**

CATALOGUE OF DOVER BOOKS

COMMON SPIDERS OF THE UNITED STATES, J. H. Emerton. Here is a nature hobby you can pursue right in your own cellar! Only non-technical, but thorough, reliable guide to spiders for the layman. Over 200 spiders from all parts of the country, arranged by scientific classification, are identified by shape and color, number of eyes, habitat and range, habits, etc. Full text, 501 line drawings and photographs, and valuable introduction explain webs, poisons, threads, capturing and preserving spiders, etc. Index. New synoptic key by S. W. Frost. xxiv + 225pp. 5⅜ x 8. T223 Paperbound **$1.45**

THE LIFE STORY OF THE FISH: HIS MANNERS AND MORALS, Brian Curtis. A comprehensive, non-technical survey of just about everything worth knowing about fish. Written for the aquarist, the angler, and the layman with an inquisitive mind, the text covers such topics as evolution, external covering and protective coloration, physics and physiology of vision, maintenance of equilibrium, function of the lateral line canal for auditory and temperature senses, nervous system, function of the air bladder, reproductive system and methods—courtship, mating, spawning, care of young—and many more. Also sections on game fish, the problems of conservation and a fascinating chapter on fish curiosities. "Clear, simple language . . . excellent judgment in choice of subjects . . . delightful sense of humor," New York Times. Revised (1949) edition. Index. Bibliography of 72 items. 6 full-page photographic plates. xii + 284pp. 5⅜ x 8. T929 Paperbound **$1.65**

BATS, Glover Morrill Allen. The most comprehensive study of bats as a life-form by the world's foremost authority. A thorough summary of just about everything known about this fascinating and mysterious flying mammal, including its unique location sense, hibernation and cycles, its habitats and distribution, its wing structure and flying habits, and its relationship to man in the long history of folklore and superstition. Written on a middle-level, the book can be profitably studied by a trained zoologist and thoroughly enjoyed by the layman. "An absorbing text with excellent illustrations. Bats should have more friends and fewer thoughtless detractors as a result of the publication of this volume," William Beebe, Books. Extensive bibliography. 57 photographs and illustrations. x + 368pp. 5⅜ x 8½.
T984 Paperbound **$2.00**

BIRDS AND THEIR ATTRIBUTES, Glover Morrill Allen. A fine general introduction to birds as living organisms, especially valuable because of emphasis on structure, physiology, habits, behavior. Discusses relationship of bird to man, early attempts at scientific ornithology, feathers and coloration, skeletal structure including bills, legs and feet, wings. Also food habits, evolution and present distribution, feeding and nest-building, still unsolved questions of migrations and location sense, many more similar topics. Final chapter on classification, nomenclature. A good popular-level summary for the biologist; a first-rate introduction for the layman. Reprint of 1925 edition. References and index. 51 illustrations. viii + 338pp. 5⅜ x 8½. T957 Paperbound **$1.85**

LIFE HISTORIES OF NORTH AMERICAN BIRDS, Arthur Cleveland Bent. Bent's monumental series of books on North American birds, prepared and published under auspices of Smithsonian Institute, is the definitive coverage of the subject, the most-used single source of information. Now the entire set is to be made available by Dover in inexpensive editions. This encyclopedic collection of detailed, specific observations utilizes reports of hundreds of contemporary observers, writings of such naturalists as Audubon, Burroughs, William Brewster, as well as author's own extensive investigations. Contains literally everything known about life history of each bird considered: nesting, eggs, plumage, distribution and migration, voice, enemies, courtship, etc. These not over-technical works are musts for ornithologists, conservationists, amateur naturalists, anyone seriously interested in American birds.

BIRDS OF PREY. More than 100 subspecies of hawks, falcons, eagles, buzzards, condors and owls, from the common barn owl to the extinct caracara of Guadaloupe Island. 400 photographs. Two volume set. Index for each volume. Bibliographies of 403, 520 items. 197 full-page plates. Total of 907pp. 5⅜ x 8½. Vol. I T931 Paperbound **$2.50**
Vol. II T932 Paperbound **$2.50**

WILD FOWL. Ducks, geese, swans, and tree ducks—73 different subspecies. Two volume set. Index for each volume. Bibliographies of 124, 144 items. 106 full-page plates. Total of 685pp. 5⅜ x 8½. Vol. I T285 Paperbound **$2.50**
Vol. II T286 Paperbound **$2.50**

SHORE BIRDS. 81 varieties (sandpipers, woodcocks, plovers, snipes, phalaropes, curlews, oyster catchers, etc.). More than 200 photographs of eggs, nesting sites, adult and young of important species. Two volume set. Index for each volume. Bibliographies of 261, 188 items. 121 full-page plates. Total of 860pp. 5⅜ x 8½. Vol. I T933 Paperbound **$2.35**
Vol. II T934 Paperbound **$2.35**

THE LIFE OF PASTEUR, R. Vallery-Radot. 13th edition of this definitive biography, cited in Encyclopaedia Britannica. Authoritative, scholarly, well-documented with contemporary quotes, observations; gives complete picture of Pasteur's personal life; especially thorough presentation of scientific activities with silkworms, fermentation, hydrophobia, inoculation, etc. Introduction by Sir William Osler. Index. 505pp. 5⅜ x 8. T632 Paperbound **$2.00**

Puzzles, Mathematical Recreations

SYMBOLIC LOGIC and THE GAME OF LOGIC, Lewis Carroll. "Symbolic Logic" is not concerned with modern symbolic logic, but is instead a collection of over 380 problems posed with charm and imagination, using the syllogism, and a fascinating diagrammatic method of drawing conclusions. In "The Game of Logic" Carroll's whimsical imagination devises a logical game played with 2 diagrams and counters (included) to manipulate hundreds of tricky syllogisms. The final section, "Hit or Miss" is a lagniappe of 101 additional puzzles in the delightful Carroll manner. Until this reprint edition, both of these books were rarities costing up to $15 each. Symbolic Logic: Index. xxxi + 199pp. The Game of Logic: 96pp. 2 vols. bound as one. 5⅜ x 8.   T492 Paperbound **$1.75**

PILLOW PROBLEMS and A TANGLED TALE, Lewis Carroll. One of the rarest of all Carroll's works, "Pillow Problems" contains 72 original math puzzles, all typically ingenious. Particularly fascinating are Carroll's answers which remain exactly as he thought them out, reflecting his actual mental process. The problems in "A Tangled Tale" are in story form, originally appearing as a monthly magazine serial. Carroll not only gives the solutions, but uses answers sent in by readers to discuss wrong approaches and misleading paths, and grades them for insight. Both of these books were rarities until this edition, "Pillow Problems" costing up to $25, and "A Tangled Tale" $15. Pillow Problems: Preface and Introduction by Lewis Carroll. xx + 109pp. A Tangled Tale: 6 illustrations. 152pp. Two vols. bound as one. 5⅜ x 8.   T493 Paperbound **$1.50**

AMUSEMENTS IN MATHEMATICS, Henry Ernest Dudeney. The foremost British originator of mathematical puzzles is always intriguing, witty, and paradoxical in this classic, one of the largest collections of mathematical amusements. More than 430 puzzles, problems, and paradoxes. Mazes and games, problems on number manipulation, unicursal and other route problems, puzzles on measuring, weighing, packing, age, kinship, chessboards, joiners', crossing river, plane figure dissection, and many others. Solutions. More than 450 illustrations. vii +. 258pp. 5⅜ x 8.   T473 Paperbound **$1.25**

THE CANTERBURY PUZZLES, Henry Dudeney. Chaucer's pilgrims set one another problems in story form. Also Adventures of the Puzzle Club, the Strange Escape of the King's Jester, the Monks of Riddlewell, the Squire's Christmas Puzzle Party, and others. All puzzles are original, based on dissecting plane figures, arithmetic, algebra, elementary calculus and other branches of mathematics, and purely logical ingenuity. "The limit of ingenuity and intricacy," The Observer. Over 110 puzzles. Full Solutions. 150 illustrations. vii + 225pp. 5⅜ x 8.
T474 Paperbound **$1.25**

MATHEMATICAL EXCURSIONS, H. A. Merrill. Even if you hardly remember your high school math, you'll enjoy the 90 stimulating problems contained in this book and you will come to understand a great many mathematical principles with surprisingly little effort. Many useful shortcuts and diversions not generally known are included: division by inspection, Russian peasant multiplication, memory systems for pi, building odd and even magic squares, square roots by geometry, dyadic systems, and many more. Solutions to difficult problems. 50 illustrations. 145pp. 5⅜ x 8.   T350 Paperbound **$1.00**

MAGIC SQUARES AND CUBES, W. S. Andrews. Only book-length treatment in English, a thorough non-technical description and analysis. Here are nasik, overlapping, pandiagonal, serrated squares; magic circles, cubes, spheres, rhombuses. Try your hand at 4-dimensional magical figures! Much unusual folklore and tradition included. High school algebra is sufficient. 754 diagrams and illustrations. viii + 419pp. 5⅜ x 8.   T658 Paperbound **$1.85**

CALIBAN'S PROBLEM BOOK: MATHEMATICAL, INFERENTIAL AND CRYPTOGRAPHIC PUZZLES, H. Phillips (Caliban), S. T. Shovelton, G. S. Marshall. 105 ingenious problems by the greatest living creator of puzzles based on logic and inference. Rigorous, modern, piquant; reflecting their author's unusual personality, these intermediate and advanced puzzles all involve the ability to reason clearly through complex situations; some call for mathematical knowledge, ranging from algebra to number theory. Solutions. xi + 180pp. 5⅜ x 8.
T736 Paperbound **$1.25**

MATHEMATICAL PUZZLES FOR BEGINNERS AND ENTHUSIASTS, G. Mott-Smith. 188 mathematical puzzles based on algebra, dissection of plane figures, permutations, and probability, that will test and improve your powers of inference and interpretation. The Odic Force, The Spider's Cousin, Ellipse Drawing, theory and strategy of card and board games like tit-tat-toe, go moku, salvo, and many others. 100 pages of detailed mathematical explanations. Appendix of primes, square roots, etc. 135 illustrations. 2nd revised edition. 248pp. 5⅜ x 8.
T198 Paperbound **$1.00**

MATHEMAGIC, MAGIC PUZZLES, AND GAMES WITH NUMBERS, R. V. Heath. More than 60 new puzzles and stunts based on the properties of numbers. Easy techniques for multiplying large numbers mentally, revealing hidden numbers magically, finding the date of any day in any year, and dozens more. Over 30 pages devoted to magic squares, triangles, cubes, circles, etc. Edited by J. S. Meyer. 76 illustrations. 128pp. 5⅜ x 8.   T110 Paperbound **$1.00**

THE BOOK OF MODERN PUZZLES, G. L. Kaufman. A completely new series of puzzles as fascinating as crossword and deduction puzzles but based upon different principles and techniques. Simple 2-minute teasers, word labyrinths, design and pattern puzzles, logic and observation puzzles — over 150 braincrackers. Answers to all problems. 116 illustrations. 192pp. 5⅜ x 8.
T143 Paperbound **$1.00**

NEW WORD PUZZLES, G. L. Kaufman. 100 ENTIRELY NEW puzzles based on words and their combinations that will delight crossword puzzle, Scrabble and Jotto fans. Chess words, based on the moves of the chess king; design-onyms, symmetrical designs made of synonyms; rhymed double-crostics; syllable sentences; addle letter anagrams; alphagrams; linkograms; and many others all brand new. Full solutions. Space to work problems. 196 figures. vi + 122pp. 5⅜ x 8.
T344 Paperbound **$1.00**

MAZES AND LABYRINTHS: A BOOK OF PUZZLES, W. Shepherd. Mazes, formerly associated with mystery and ritual, are still among the most intriguing of intellectual puzzles. This is a novel and different collection of 50 amusements that embody the principle of the maze: mazes in the classical tradition; 3-dimensional, ribbon, and Möbius-strip mazes; hidden messages; spatial arrangements; etc.—almost all built on amusing story situations. 84 illustrations. Essay on maze psychology. Solutions. xv + 122pp. 5⅜ x 8.
T731 Paperbound **$1.00**

MAGIC TRICKS & CARD TRICKS, W. Jonson. Two books bound as one. 52 tricks with cards, 37 tricks with coins, bills, eggs, smoke, ribbons, slates, etc. Details on presentation, misdirection, and routining will help you master such famous tricks as the Changing Card, Card in the Pocket, Four Aces, Coin Through the Hand, Bill in the Egg, Afghan Bands, and over 75 others. If you follow the lucid exposition and key diagrams carefully, you will finish these two books with an astonishing mastery of magic. 106 figures. 224pp. 5⅜ x 8. T909 Paperbound **$1.00**

PANORAMA OF MAGIC, Milbourne Christopher. A profusely illustrated history of stage magic, a unique selection of prints and engravings from the author's private collection of magic memorabilia, the largest of its kind. Apparatus, stage settings and costumes; ingenious ads distributed by the performers and satiric broadsides passed around in the streets ridiculing pompous showmen; programs; decorative souvenirs. The lively text, by one of America's foremost professional magicians, is full of anecdotes about almost legendary wizards: Dede, the Egyptian; Philadelphia, the wonder-worker; Robert-Houdin, "the father of modern magic;" Harry Houdini; scores more. Altogether a pleasure package for anyone interested in magic, stage setting and design, ethnology, psychology, or simply in unusual people. A Dover original. 295 illustrations; 8 in full color. Index. viii + 216pp. 8⅜ x 11¼.
T774 Paperbound **$2.25**

HOUDINI ON MAGIC, Harry Houdini. One of the greatest magicians of modern times explains his most prized secrets. How locks are picked, with illustrated picks and skeleton keys; how a girl is sawed into twins; how to walk through a brick wall — Houdini's explanations of 44 stage tricks with many diagrams. Also included is a fascinating discussion of great magicians of the past and the story of his fight against fraudulent mediums and spiritualists. Edited by W.B. Gibson and M.N. Young. Bibliography. 155 figures, photos. xv + 280pp. 5⅜ x 8.
T384 Paperbound **$1.35**

MATHEMATICS, MAGIC AND MYSTERY, Martin Gardner. Why do card tricks work? How do magicians perform astonishing mathematical feats? How is stage mind-reading possible? This is the first book length study explaining the application of probability, set theory, theory of numbers, topology, etc., to achieve many startling tricks. Non-technical, accurate, detailed! 115 sections discuss tricks with cards, dice, coins, knots, geometrical vanishing illusions, how a Curry square "demonstrates" that the sum of the parts may be greater than the whole, and dozens of others. No sleight of hand necessary! 135 illustrations. xii + 174pp. 5⅜ x 8.
T335 Paperbound **$1.00**

EASY-TO-DO ENTERTAINMENTS AND DIVERSIONS WITH COINS, CARDS, STRING, PAPER AND MATCHES, R. M. Abraham. Over 300 tricks, games and puzzles will provide young readers with absorbing fun. Sections on card games; paper-folding; tricks with coins, matches and pieces of string; games for the agile; toy-making from common household objects; mathematical recreations; and 50 miscellaneous pastimes. Anyone in charge of groups of youngsters, including hard-pressed parents, and in need of suggestions on how to keep children sensibly amused and quietly content will find this book indispensable. Clear, simple text, copious number of delightful line drawings and illustrative diagrams. Originally titled "Winter Nights Entertainments." Introduction by Lord Baden Powell. 329 illustrations. v + 186pp. 5⅜ x 8½.
T921 Paperbound **$1.00**

STRING FIGURES AND HOW TO MAKE THEM, Caroline Furness Jayne. 107 string figures plus variations selected from the best primitive and modern examples developed by Navajo, Apache, pygmies of Africa, Eskimo, in Europe, Australia, China, etc. The most readily understandable, easy-to-follow book in English on perennially popular recreation. Crystal-clear exposition; step-by-step diagrams. Everyone from kindergarten children to adults looking for unusual diversion will be endlessly amused. Index. Bibliography. Introduction by A. C. Haddon. 17 full-page plates. 960 illustrations. xxiii + 401pp. 5⅜ x 8½.
T152 Paperbound **$2.00**

Entertainments, Humor

ODDITIES AND CURIOSITIES OF WORDS AND LITERATURE, C. Bombaugh, edited by M. Gardner. The largest collection of idiosyncratic prose and poetry techniques in English, a legendary work in the curious and amusing bypaths of literary recreations and the play technique in literature—so important in modern works. Contains alphabetic poetry, acrostics, palindromes, scissors verse, centos, emblematic poetry, famous literary puns, hoaxes, notorious slips of the press, hilarious mistranslations, and much more. Revised and enlarged with modern material by Martin Gardner. 368pp. 5⅜ x 8. T759 Paperbound **$1.75**

A NONSENSE ANTHOLOGY, collected by Carolyn Wells. 245 of the best nonsense verses ever written, including nonsense puns, absurd arguments, mock epics and sagas, nonsense ballads, odes, "sick" verses, dog-Latin verses, French nonsense verses, songs. By Edward Lear, Lewis Carroll, Gelett Burgess, W. S. Gilbert, Hilaire Belloc, Peter Newell, Oliver Herford, etc., 83 writers in all plus over four score anonymous nonsense verses. A special section of limericks, plus famous nonsense such as Carroll's "Jabberwocky" and Lear's "The Jumblies" and much excellent verse virtually impossible to locate elsewhere. For 50 years considered the best anthology available. Index of first lines specially prepared for this edition. Introduction by Carolyn Wells. 3 indexes: Title, Author, First lines. xxxiii + 279pp. T499 Paperbound **$1.35**

THE BAD CHILD'S BOOK OF BEASTS, MORE BEASTS FOR WORSE CHILDREN, and A MORAL ALPHABET, H. Belloc. Hardly an anthology of humorous verse has appeared in the last 50 years without at least a couple of these famous nonsense verses. But one must see the entire volumes—with all the delightful original illustrations by Sir Basil Blackwood—to appreciate fully Belloc's charming and witty verses that play so subacidly on the platitudes of life and morals that beset his day—and ours. A great humor classic. Three books in one. Total of 157pp. 5⅜ x 8. T749 Paperbound **$1.00**

THE DEVIL'S DICTIONARY, Ambrose Bierce. Sardonic and irreverent barbs puncturing the pomposities and absurdities of American politics, business, religion, literature, and arts, by the country's greatest satirist in the classic tradition. Epigrammatic as Shaw, piercing as Swift, American as Mark Twain, Will Rogers, and Fred Allen, Bierce will always remain the favorite of a small coterie of enthusiasts, and of writers and speakers whom he supplies with "some of the most gorgeous witticisms of the English language" (H. L. Mencken). Over 1000 entries in alphabetical order. 144pp. 5⅜ x 8. T487 Paperbound **$1.00**

THE PURPLE COW AND OTHER NONSENSE, Gelett Burgess. The best of Burgess's early nonsense, selected from the first edition of the "Burgess Nonsense Book." Contains many of his most unusual and truly awe-inspiring pieces: 36 nonsense quatrains, the Poems of Patagonia, Alphabet of Famous Goops, and the other hilarious (and rare) adult nonsense that place him in the forefront of American humorists. All pieces are accompanied by the original Burgess illustrations. 123 illustrations. xiii + 113pp. 5⅜ x 8. T772 Paperbound **$1.00**

MY PIOUS FRIENDS AND DRUNKEN COMPANIONS and MORE PIOUS FRIENDS AND DRUNKEN COMPANIONS, Frank Shay. Folksingers, amateur and professional, and everyone who loves singing: here, available for the first time in 30 years, is this valued collection of 132 ballads, blues, vaudeville numbers, drinking songs, sea chanties, comedy songs. Songs of pre-Beatnik Bohemia; songs from all over America, England, France, Australia; the great songs of the Naughty Nineties and early twentieth-century America. Over a third with music. Woodcuts by John Held, Jr. convey perfectly the brash insouciance of an era of rollicking unabashed song. 12 illustrations by John Held, Jr. Two indexes (Titles and First lines and Choruses). Introductions by the author. Two volumes bound as one. Total of xvi + 235pp. 5⅜ x 8½. T946 Paperbound **$1.25**

HOW TO TELL THE BIRDS FROM THE FLOWERS, R. W. Wood. How not to confuse a carrot with a parrot, a grape with an ape, a puffin with nuffin. Delightful drawings, clever puns, absurd little poems point out far-fetched resemblances in nature. The author was a leading physicist. Introduction by Margaret Wood White. 106 illus. 60pp. 5⅜ x 8. T523 Paperbound **75¢**

PECK'S BAD BOY AND HIS PA, George W. Peck. The complete edition, containing both volumes, of one of the most widely read American humor books. The endless ingenious pranks played by bad boy "Hennery" on his pa and the grocery man, the outraged pomposity of Pa, the perpetual ridiculing of middle class institutions, are as entertaining today as they were in 1883. No pale sophistications or subtleties, but rather humor vigorous, raw, earthy, imaginative, and, as folk humor often is, sadistic. This peculiarly fascinating book is also valuable to historians and students of American culture as a portrait of an age. 100 original illustrations by True Williams. Introduction by E. F. Bleiler. 347pp. 5⅜ x 8. T497 Paperbound **$1.50**

THE HUMOROUS VERSE OF LEWIS CARROLL. Almost every poem Carroll ever wrote, the largest collection ever published, including much never published elsewhere: 150 parodies, burlesques, riddles, ballads, acrostics, etc., with 130 original illustrations by Tenniel, Carroll, and others. "Addicts will be grateful . . . there is nothing for the faithful to do but sit down and fall to the banquet," N. Y. Times. Index to first lines. xiv + 446pp. 5⅜ x 8.
T654 Paperbound **$2.00**

DIVERSIONS AND DIGRESSIONS OF LEWIS CARROLL. A major new treasure for Carroll fans! Rare privately published humor, fantasy, puzzles, and games by Carroll at his whimsical best, with a new vein of frank satire. Includes many new mathematical amusements and recreations, among them the fragmentary Part III of "Curiosa Mathematica." Contains "The Rectory Umbrella," "The New Belfry," "The Vision of the Three T's," and much more. New 32-page supplement of rare photographs taken by Carroll. x + 375pp. 5⅜ x 8.
T732 Paperbound **$2.00**

THE COMPLETE NONSENSE OF EDWARD LEAR. This is the only complete edition of this master of gentle madness available at a popular price. A BOOK OF NONSENSE, NONSENSE SONGS, MORE NONSENSE SONGS AND STORIES in their entirety with all the old favorites that have delighted children and adults for years. The Dong With A Luminous Nose, The Jumblies, The Owl and the Pussycat, and hundreds of other bits of wonderful nonsense. 214 limericks, 3 sets of Nonsense Botany, 5 Nonsense Alphabets, 546 drawings by Lear himself, and much more. 320pp. 5⅜ x 8.
T167 Paperbound **$1.00**

THE MELANCHOLY LUTE, The Humorous Verse of Franklin P. Adams ("FPA"). The author's own selection of light verse, drawn from thirty years of FPA's column, "The Conning Tower," syndicated all over the English-speaking world. Witty, perceptive, literate, these ninety-six poems range from parodies of other poets, Millay, Longfellow, Edgar Guest, Kipling, Masefield, etc., and free and hilarious translations of Horace and other Latin poets, to satiric comments on fabled American institutions—the New York Subways, preposterous ads, suburbanites, sensational journalism, etc. They reveal with vigor and clarity the humor, integrity and restraint of a wise and gentle American satirist. Introduction by Robert Hutchinson. vi + 122pp. 5⅜ x 8½.
T108 Paperbound **$1.00**

SINGULAR TRAVELS, CAMPAIGNS, AND ADVENTURES OF BARON MUNCHAUSEN, R. E. Raspe, with 90 illustrations by Gustave Doré. The first edition in over 150 years to reestablish the deeds of the Prince of Liars exactly as Raspe first recorded them in 1785—the genuine Baron Munchausen, one of the most popular personalities in English literature. Included also are the best of the many sequels, written by other hands. Introduction on Raspe by J. Carswell. Bibliography of early editions. xliv + 192pp. 5⅜ x 8.
T698 Paperbound **$1.00**

THE WIT AND HUMOR OF OSCAR WILDE, ed. by Alvin Redman. Wilde at his most brilliant, in 1000 epigrams exposing weaknesses and hypocrisies of "civilized" society. Divided into 49 categories—sin, wealth, women, America, etc.—to aid writers, speakers. Includes excerpts from his trials, books, plays, criticism. Formerly "The Epigrams of Oscar Wilde." Introduction by Vyvyan Holland, Wilde's only living son. Introductory essay by editor. 260pp. 5⅜ x 8.
T602 Paperbound **$1.00**

MAX AND MORITZ, Wilhelm Busch. Busch is one of the great humorists of all time, as well as the father of the modern comic strip. This volume, translated by H. A. Klein and other hands, contains the perennial favorite "Max and Moritz" (translated by C. T. Brooks), Plisch and Plum, Das Rabennest, Eispeter, and seven other whimsical, sardonic, jovial, diabolical cartoon and verse stories. Lively English translations parallel the original German. This work has delighted millions since it first appeared in the 19th century, and is guaranteed to please almost anyone. Edited by H. A. Klein, with an afterword. x + 205pp. 5⅝ x 8½.
T181 Paperbound **$1.15**

HYPOCRITICAL HELENA, Wilhelm Busch. A companion volume to "Max and Moritz," with the title piece (Die Fromme Helena) and 10 other highly amusing cartoon and verse stories, all newly translated by H. A. Klein and M. C. Klein: Adventure on New Year's Eve (Abenteuer in der Neujahrsnacht), Hangover on the Morning after New Year's Eve (Der Katzenjammer am Neujahrsmorgen), etc. English and German in parallel columns. Hours of pleasure, also a fine language aid. x + 205pp. 5⅝ x 8½.
T184 Paperbound **$1.00**

THE BEAR THAT WASN'T, Frank Tashlin. What does it mean? Is it simply delightful wry humor, or a charming story of a bear who wakes up in the midst of a factory, or a satire on Big Business, or an existential cartoon-story of the human condition, or a symbolization of the struggle between conformity and the individual? New York Herald Tribune said of the first edition: ". . . a fable for grownups that will be fun for children. Sit down with the book and get your own bearings." Long an underground favorite with readers of all ages and opinions. v + 51pp. Illustrated. 5⅜ x 8½.
T939 Paperbound **75¢**

RUTHLESS RHYMES FOR HEARTLESS HOMES and MORE RUTHLESS RHYMES FOR HEARTLESS HOMES, Harry Graham ("Col. D. Streamer"). Two volumes of Little Willy and 48 other poetic disasters. A bright, new reprint of oft-quoted, never forgotten, devastating humor by a precursor of today's "sick" joke school. For connoisseurs of wicked, wacky humor and all who delight in the comedy of manners. Original drawings are a perfect complement. 61 illustrations. Index. vi + 69pp. Two vols. bound as one. 5⅜ x 8½.
T930 Paperbound **75¢**

Say It language phrase books

These handy phrase books (128 to 196 pages each) make grammatical drills unnecessary for an elementary knowledge of a spoken foreign language. Covering most matters of travel and everyday life each volume contains:

> Over 1000 phrases and sentences in immediately useful forms — foreign language plus English.

> Modern usage designed for Americans. Specific phrases like, "Give me small change," and "Please call a taxi."

> Simplified phonetic transcription you will be able to read at sight.

> The only completely indexed phrase books on the market.

> Covers scores of important situations: — Greetings, restaurants, sightseeing, useful expressions, etc.

These books are prepared by native linguists who are professors at Columbia, N.Y.U., Fordham and other great universities. Use them independently or with any other book or record course. They provide a supplementary living element that most other courses lack. Individual volumes in:

Russian 75¢	Italian 75¢	Spanish 75¢	German 75¢
Hebrew 75¢	Danish 75¢	Japanese 75¢	Swedish 75¢
Dutch 75¢	Esperanto 75¢	Modern Greek 75¢	Portuguese 75¢
Norwegian 75¢	Polish 75¢	French 75¢	Yiddish 75¢
Turkish 75¢		English for German-speaking people 75¢	
English for Italian-speaking people 75¢		English for Spanish-speaking people 75¢	

Large clear type. 128-196 pages each. 3½ x 5¼. Sturdy paper binding.

Listen and Learn language records

LISTEN & LEARN is the only language record course designed especially to meet your travel and everyday needs. It is available in separate sets for FRENCH, SPANISH, GERMAN, JAPANESE, RUSSIAN, MODERN GREEK, PORTUGUESE, ITALIAN and HEBREW, and each set contains three 33⅓ rpm long-playing records—1½ hours of recorded speech by eminent native speakers who are professors at Columbia, New York University, Queens College.

Check the following special features found only in LISTEN & LEARN:

- **Dual-language recording. 812 selected phrases and sentences,** over 3200 words, spoken first in English, then in their foreign language equivalents. A suitable pause follows each foreign phrase, allowing you time to repeat the expression. You learn by unconscious assimilation.

- **128 to 206-page manual** contains everything on the records, plus a simple phonetic pronunciation guide.

- **Indexed for convenience. The only set on the market** that is completely indexed. No more puzzling over where to find the phrase you need. Just look in the rear of the manual.

- **Practical.** No time wasted on material you can find in any grammar. LISTEN & LEARN covers central core material with phrase approach. Ideal for the person with limited learning time.

- **Living, modern expressions,** not found in other courses. Hygienic products, modern equipment, shopping—expressions used every day, like "nylon" and "air-conditioned."

- **Limited objective.** Everything you learn, no matter where you stop, is immediately useful. You have to finish other courses, wade through grammar and vocabulary drill, before they help you.

- **High-fidelity recording.** LISTEN & LEARN records equal in clarity and surface-silence any record on the market costing up to $6.

"Excellent . . . the spoken records . . . impress me as being among the very best on the market," **Prof. Mario Pei,** Dept. of Romance Languages, Columbia University. "Inexpensive and well-done . . . it would make an ideal present," CHICAGO SUNDAY TRIBUNE. "More genuinely helpful than anything of its kind which I have previously encountered," **Sidney Clark,** well-known author of "ALL THE BEST" travel books.

UNCONDITIONAL GUARANTEE. Try LISTEN & LEARN, then return it within 10 days for full refund if you are not satisfied.

Each set contains three twelve-inch 33⅓ records, manual, and album.

SPANISH	the set $5.95	GERMAN	the set $5.95
FRENCH	the set $5.95	ITALIAN	the set $5.95
RUSSIAN	the set $5.95	JAPANESE	the set $6.95
PORTUGUESE	the set $5.95	MODERN GREEK	the set $5.95
MODERN HEBREW	the set $5.95		

Americana

THE EYES OF DISCOVERY, J. Bakeless. A vivid reconstruction of how unspoiled America appeared to the first white men. Authentic and enlightening accounts of Hudson's landing in New York, Coronado's trek through the Southwest; scores of explorers, settlers, trappers, soldiers. America's pristine flora, fauna, and Indians in every region and state in fresh and unusual new aspects. "A fascinating view of what the land was like before the first highway went through," Time. 68 contemporary illustrations, 39 newly added in this edition. Index. Bibliography. x + 500pp. 5⅜ x 8.   T761 Paperbound $2.25

AUDUBON AND HIS JOURNALS, J. J. Audubon. A collection of fascinating accounts of Europe and America in the early 1800's through Audubon's own eyes. Includes the Missouri River Journals —an eventful trip through America's untouched heartland, the Labrador Journals, the European Journals, the famous "Episodes", and other rare Audubon material, including the descriptive chapters from the original letterpress edition of the "Ornithological Studies", omitted in all later editions. Indispensable for ornithologists, naturalists, and all lovers of Americana and adventure. 70-page biography by Audubon's granddaughter. 38 illustrations. Index. Total of 1106pp. 5⅜ x 8.   T675 Vol I Paperbound $2.25
T676 Vol II Paperbound $2.25
The set $4.50

TRAVELS OF WILLIAM BARTRAM, edited by Mark Van Doren. The first inexpensive illustrated edition of one of the 18th century's most delightful books is an excellent source of first-hand material on American geography, anthropology, and natural history. Many descriptions of early Indian tribes are our only source of information on them prior to the infiltration of the white man. "The mind of a scientist with the soul of a poet," John Livingston Lowes. 13 original illustrations and maps. Edited with an introduction by Mark Van Doren. 448pp. 5⅜ x 8.
T13 Paperbound $2.00

GARRETS AND PRETENDERS: A HISTORY OF BOHEMIANISM IN AMERICA, A. Parry. The colorful and fantastic history of American Bohemianism from Poe to Kerouac. This is the only complete record of hoboes, cranks, starving poets, and suicides. Here are Pfaff, Whitman, Crane, Bierce, Pound, and many others. New chapters by the author and by H. T. Moore bring this thorough and well-documented history down to the Beatniks. "An excellent account," N. Y. Times. Scores of cartoons, drawings, and caricatures. Bibliography. Index. xxviii + 421pp. 5⅝ x 8⅜.   T708 Paperbound $1.95

THE EXPLORATION OF THE COLORADO RIVER AND ITS CANYONS, J. W. Powell. The thrilling first-hand account of the expedition that filled in the last white space on the map of the United States. Rapids, famine, hostile Indians, and mutiny are among the perils encountered as the unknown Colorado Valley reveals its secrets. This is the only uncut version of Major Powell's classic of exploration that has been printed in the last 60 years. Includes later reflections and subsequent expedition. 250 illustrations, new map. 400pp. 5⅝ x 8⅜.
T94 Paperbound $2.25

THE JOURNAL OF HENRY D. THOREAU, Edited by Bradford Torrey and Francis H. Allen. Henry Thoreau is not only one of the most important figures in American literature and social thought; his voluminous journals (from which his books emerged as selections and crystallizations) constitute both the longest, most sensitive record of personal internal development and a most penetrating description of a historical moment in American culture. This present set, which was first issued in fourteen volumes, contains Thoreau's entire journals from 1837 to 1862, with the exception of the lost years which were found only recently. We are reissuing it, complete and unabridged, with a new introduction by Walter Harding, Secretary of the Thoreau Society. Fourteen volumes reissued in two volumes. Foreword by Henry Seidel Canby. Total of 1888pp. 8⅜ x 12¼.   T312-3 Two volume set, Clothbound $20.00

GAMES AND SONGS OF AMERICAN CHILDREN, collected by William Wells Newell. A remarkable collection of 190 games with songs that accompany many of them; cross references to show similarities, differences among them; variations; musical notation for 38 songs. Textual dis-cussions show relations with folk-drama and other aspects of folk tradition. Grouped into categories for ready comparative study: Love-games, histories, playing at work, human life, bird and beast, mythology, guessing-games, etc. New introduction covers relations of songs and dances to timeless heritage of folklore, biographical sketch of Newell, other pertinent data. A good source of inspiration for those in charge of groups of children and a valuable reference for anthropologists, sociologists, psychiatrists. Introduction by Carl Withers. New indexes of first lines, games. 5⅜ x 8½. xii + 242pp.   T354 Paperbound $1.75

Art, History of Art, Antiques, Graphic Arts, Handcrafts

ART STUDENTS' ANATOMY, E. J. Farris. Outstanding art anatomy that uses chiefly living objects for its illustrations. 71 photos of undraped men, women, children are accompanied by carefully labeled matching sketches to illustrate the skeletal system, articulations and movements, bony landmarks, the muscular system, skin, fasciae, fat, etc. 9 x-ray photos show movement of joints. Undraped models are shown in such actions as serving in tennis, drawing a bow in archery, playing football, dancing, preparing to spring and to dive. Also discussed and illustrated are proportions, age and sex differences, the anatomy of the smile, etc. 8 plates by the great early 18th century anatomic illustrator Siegfried Albinus are also included. Glossary. 158 figures, 7 in color. x + 159pp. 5⅝ x 8⅜.   T744 Paperbound **$1.50**

AN ATLAS OF ANATOMY FOR ARTISTS, F Schider. A new 3rd edition of this standard text enlarged by 52 new illustrations of hands, anatomical studies by Cloquet, and expressive life studies of the body by Barcsay. 189 clear, detailed plates offer you precise information of impeccable accuracy. 29 plates show all aspects of the skeleton, with closeups of special areas, while 54 full-page plates, mostly in two colors, give human musculature as seen from four different points of view, with cutaways for important portions of the body. 14 full-page plates provide photographs of hand forms, eyelids, female breasts, and indicate the location of muscles upon models. 59 additional plates show how great artists of the past utilized human anatomy. They reproduce sketches and finished work by such artists as Michelangelo, Leonardo da Vinci, Goya, and 15 others. This is a lifetime reference work which will be one of the most important books in any artist's library. "The standard reference tool," AMERICAN LIBRARY ASSOCIATION. "Excellent," AMERICAN ARTIST. Third enlarged edition. 189 plates, 647 illustrations. xxvi + 192pp. 7⅞ x 10⅝.   T241 Clothbound **$6.00**

AN ATLAS OF ANIMAL ANATOMY FOR ARTISTS, W. Ellenberger, H. Baum, H. Dittrich. The largest, richest animal anatomy for artists available in English. 99 detailed anatomical plates of such animals as the horse, dog, cat, lion, deer, seal, kangaroo, flying squirrel, cow, bull, goat, monkey, hare, and bat. Surface features are clearly indicated, while progressive beneath-the-skin pictures show musculature, tendons, and bone structure. Rest and action are exhibited in terms of musculature and skeletal structure and detailed cross-sections are given for heads and important features. The animals chosen are representative of specific families so that a study of these anatomies will provide knowledge of hundreds of related species. "Highly recommended as one of the very few books on the subject worthy of being used as an authoritative guide," DESIGN. "Gives a fundamental knowledge," AMERICAN ARTIST. Second revised, enlarged edition with new plates from Cuvier, Stubbs, etc. 288 illustrations. 153pp. 11⅜ x 9.   T82 Clothbound **$6.00**

THE HUMAN FIGURE IN MOTION, Eadweard Muybridge. The largest selection in print of Muybridge's famous high-speed action photos of the human figure in motion. 4789 photographs illustrate 162 different actions: men, women, children—mostly undraped—are shown walking, running, carrying various objects, sitting, lying down, climbing, throwing, arising, and performing over 150 other actions. Some actions are shown in as many as 150 photographs each. All in all there are more than 500 action strips in this enormous volume, series shots taken at shutter speeds of as high as 1/6000th of a second! These are not posed shots, but true stopped motion. They show bone and muscle in situations that the human eye is not fast enough to capture. Earlier, smaller editions of these prints have brought $40 and more on the out-of-print market. "A must for artists," ART IN FOCUS. "An unparalleled dictionary of action for all artists," AMERICAN ARTIST. 390 full-page plates, with 4789 photographs. Printed on heavy glossy stock. Reinforced binding with headbands. xxi + 390pp. 7⅞ x 10⅝.
T204 Clothbound **$10.00**

ANIMALS IN MOTION, Eadweard Muybridge. This is the largest collection of animal action photos in print. 34 different animals (horses, mules, oxen, goats, camels, pigs, cats, guanacos, lions, gnus, deer, monkeys, eagles—and 21 others) in 132 characteristic actions. The horse alone is shown in more than 40 different actions. All 3919 photographs are taken in series at speeds up to 1/6000th of a second. The secrets of leg motion, spinal patterns, head movements, strains and contortions shown nowhere else are captured. You will see exactly how a lion sets his foot down; how an elephant's knees are like a human's—and how they differ; the position of a kangaroo's legs in mid-leap; how an ostrich's head bobs; details of the flight of birds—and thousands of facets of motion only the fastest cameras can catch. Photographed from domestic animals and animals in the Philadelphia zoo, it contains neither semiposed artificial shots nor distorted telephoto shots taken under adverse conditions. Artists, biologists, decorators, cartoonists, will find this book indispensable for understanding animals in motion. "A really marvelous series of plates," NATURE (London). "The dry plate's most spectacular early use was by Eadweard Muybridge," LIFE. 3919 photographs; 380 full pages of plates. 440pp. Printed on heavy glossy paper. Deluxe binding with headbands. 7⅞ x 10⅝.   T203 Clothbound **$10.00**

CATALOGUE OF DOVER BOOKS

THE AUTOBIOGRAPHY OF AN IDEA, Louis Sullivan. The pioneer architect whom Frank Lloyd Wright called "the master" reveals an acute sensitivity to social forces and values in this passionately honest account. He records the crystallization of his opinions and theories, the growth of his organic theory of architecture that still influences American designers and architects, contemporary ideas, etc. This volume contains the first appearance of 34 full-page plates of his finest architecture. Unabridged reissue of 1924 edition. New introduction by R. M. Line. Index. xiv + 335pp. 5⅜ x 8.   T281 Paperbound **$2.00**

THE DRAWINGS OF HEINRICH KLEY. The first uncut republication of both of Kley's devastating sketchbooks, which first appeared in pre-World War I Germany. One of the greatest cartoonists and social satirists of modern times, his exuberant and iconoclastic fantasy and his extra-ordinary technique place him in the great tradition of Bosch, Breughel, and Goya, while his subject matter has all the immediacy and tension of our century. 200 drawings. viii + 128pp. 7¾ x 10¾.   T24 Paperbound **$1.85**

MORE DRAWINGS BY HEINRICH KLEY. All the sketches from Leut' Und Viecher (1912) and Sammel-Album (1923) not included in the previous Dover edition of Drawings. More of the bizarre, mercilessly iconoclastic sketches that shocked and amused on their original publica-tion. Nothing was too sacred, no one too eminent for satirization by this imaginative, in-dividual and accomplished master cartoonist. A total of 158 illustrations. Iv + 104pp. 7¾ x 10¾.   T41 Paperbound **$1.85**

PINE FURNITURE OF EARLY NEW ENGLAND, R. H. Kettell. A rich understanding of one of America's most original folk arts that collectors of antiques, interior decorators, craftsmen, woodworkers, and everyone interested in American history and art will find fascinating and immensely useful. 413 illustrations of more than 300 chairs, benches, racks, beds, cupboards, mirrors, shelves, tables, and other furniture will show all the simple beauty and character of early New England furniture. 55 detailed drawings carefully analyze outstanding pieces. "With its rich store of illustrations, this book emphasizes the individuality and varied design of early American pine furniture. It should be welcomed," ANTIQUES. 413 illustrations and 55 working drawings. 475. 8 x 10¾.   T145 Clothbound **$10.00**

THE HUMAN FIGURE, J. H. Vanderpoel. Every important artistic element of the human figure is pointed out in minutely detailed word descriptions in this classic text and illustrated as well in 430 pencil and charcoal drawings. Thus the text of this book directs your attention to all the characteristic features and subtle differences of the male and female (adults, children, and aged persons), as though a master artist were telling you what to look for at each stage. 2nd edition, revised and enlarged by George Bridgman. Foreword. 430 illustrations. 143pp. 6⅛ x 9¼.   T432 Paperbound **$1.50**

LETTERING AND ALPHABETS, J. A. Cavanagh. This unabridged reissue of LETTERING offers a full discussion, analysis, illustration of 89 basic hand lettering styles — styles derived from Caslons, Bodonis, Garamonds, Gothic, Black Letter, Oriental, and many others. Upper and lower cases, numerals and common signs pictured. Hundreds of technical hints on make-up, construction, artistic validity, strokes, pens, brushes, white areas, etc. May be reproduced without permission! 89 complete alphabets; 72 lettered specimens. 121pp. 9⅜ x 8.   T53 Paperbound **$1.35**

STICKS AND STONES, Lewis Mumford. A survey of the forces that have conditioned American architecture and altered its forms. The author discusses the medieval tradition in early New England villages; the Renaissance influence which developed with the rise of the merchant class; the classical influence of Jefferson's time; the "Mechanicsvilles" of Poe's generation; the Brown Decades; the philosophy of the Imperial facade; and finally the modern machine age. "A truly remarkable book," SAT. REV. OF LITERATURE. 2nd revised edition. 21 illustra-tions. xvii + 228pp. 5⅜ x 8.   T202 Paperbound **$1.75**

THE STANDARD BOOK OF QUILT MAKING AND COLLECTING, Marguerite Ickis. A complete easy-to-follow guide with all the information you need to make beautiful, useful quilts. How to plan, design, cut, sew, appliqué, avoid sewing problems, use rag bag, make borders, tuft, every other aspect. Over 100 traditional quilts shown, including over 40 full-size patterns. At-home hobby for fun, profit. Index. 483 illus. 1 color plate. 287pp. 6¾ x 9½.   T582 Paperbound **$2.00**

THE BOOK OF SIGNS, Rudolf Koch. Formerly $20 to $25 on the out-of-print market, now only $1.00 in this unabridged new edition! 493 symbols from ancient manuscripts, medieval cathe-drals, coins, catacombs, pottery, etc. Crosses, monograms of Roman emperors, astrological, chemical, botanical, runes, housemarks, and 7 other categories. Invaluable for handicraft workers, illustrators, scholars, etc., this material may be reproduced without permission. 493 illustrations by Fritz Kredel. 104pp. 6½ x 9¼.   T162 Paperbound **$1.00**

PRIMITIVE ART, Franz Boas. This authoritative and exhaustive work by a great American anthropologist covers the entire gamut of primitive art. Pottery, leatherwork, metal work, stone work, wood, basketry, are treated in detail. Theories of primitive art, historical depth in art history, technical virtuosity, unconscious levels of patterning, symbolism, styles, litera-ture, music, dance, etc. A must book for the interested layman, the anthropologist, artist, handicrafter (hundreds of unusual motifs), and the historian. Over 900 illustrations (50 ceramic vessels, 12 totem poles, etc.). 376pp. 5⅜ x 8.   T25 Paperbound **$2.25**

Fiction

FLATLAND, E. A. Abbott. A science-fiction classic of life in a 2-dimensional world that is also a first-rate introduction to such aspects of modern science as relativity and hyperspace. Political, moral, satirical, and humorous overtones have made FLATLAND fascinating reading for thousands. 7th edition. New introduction by Banesh Hoffmann. 16 illustrations. 128pp. 5⅜ x 8. **T1 Paperbound $1.00**

THE WONDERFUL WIZARD OF OZ, L. F. Baum. Only edition in print with all the original W. W. Denslow illustrations in full color—as much a part of "The Wizard" as Tenniel's drawings are of "Alice in Wonderland." "The Wizard" is still America's best-loved fairy tale, in which, as the author expresses it, "The wonderment and joy are retained and the heartaches and nightmares left out." Now today's young readers can enjoy every word and wonderful picture of the original book. New introduction by Martin Gardner: A Baum bibliography. 23 full-page color plates. viii + 268pp. 5⅜ x 8. **T691 Paperbound $1.50**

THE MARVELOUS LAND OF OZ, L. F. Baum. This is the equally enchanting sequel to the "Wizard," continuing the adventures of the Scarecrow and the Tin Woodman. The hero this time is a little boy named Tip, and all the delightful Oz magic is still present. This is the Oz book with the Animated Saw-Horse, the Woggle-Bug, and Jack Pumpkinhead. All the original John R. Neill illustrations, 10 in full color. 287 pp. 5⅜ x 8. **T692 Paperbound $1.50**

28 SCIENCE FICTION STORIES OF H. G. WELLS. Two full unabridged novels, MEN LIKE GODS and STAR BEGOTTEN, plus 26 short stories by the master science-fiction writer of all time! Stories of space, time, invention, exploration, future adventure—an indispensable part of the library of everyone interested in science and adventure. PARTIAL CONTENTS: Men Like Gods, The Country of the Blind, In the Abyss, The Crystal Egg, The Man Who Could Work Miracles, A Story of the Days to Come, The Valley of Spiders, and 21 more! 928pp. 5⅜ x 8. **T265 Clothbound $4.50**

THREE MARTIAN NOVELS, Edgar Rice Burroughs. Contains: Thuvia, Maid of Mars; The Chessmen of Mars; and The Master Mind of Mars. High adventure set in an imaginative and intricate conception of the Red Planet. Mars is peopled with an intelligent, heroic human race which lives in densely populated cities and with fierce barbarians who inhabit dead sea bottoms. Other exciting creatures abound amidst an inventive framework of Martian history and geography. Complete unabridged reprintings of the first edition. 16 illustrations by J. Allen St. John. vi + 499pp. 5⅜ x 8½. **T39 Paperbound $1.85**

SEVEN SCIENCE FICTION NOVELS, H. G. Wells. Full unabridged texts of 7 science-fiction novels of the master. Ranging from biology, physics, chemistry, astronomy to sociology and other studies, Mr. Wells extrapolates whole worlds of strange and intriguing character. "One will have to go far to match this for entertainment, excitement, and sheer pleasure . . . ," NEW YORK TIMES. Contents: The Time Machine, The Island of Dr. Moreau, First Men in the Moon, The Invisible Man, The War of the Worlds, The Food of the Gods, In the Days of the Comet. 1015pp. 5⅜ x 8. **T264 Clothbound $4.50**

THE LAND THAT TIME FORGOT and THE MOON MAID, Edgar Rice Burroughs. In the opinion of many, Burroughs' best work. The first concerns a strange island where evolution is individual rather than phylogenetic. Speechless anthropoids develop into intelligent human beings within a single generation. The second projects the reader far into the future and describes the first voyage to the Moon (in the year 2025), the conquest of the Earth by the Moon, and years of violence and adventure as the enslaved Earthmen try to regain possession of their planet. "An imaginative tour de force that keeps the reader keyed up and expectant," NEW YORK TIMES. Complete, unabridged text of the original two novels (three parts in each). 5 illustrations by J. Allen St. John. vi + 552pp. 5⅜ x 8½. **T1020 Clothbound $3.75**
T358 Paperbound $2.00

3 ADVENTURE NOVELS by H. Rider Haggard. Complete texts of "She," "King Solomon's Mines," "Allan Quatermain." Qualities of discovery; desire for immortality; search for primitive, for what is unadorned by civilization, have kept these novels of African adventure exciting, alive to readers from R. L. Stevenson to George Orwell. 636pp. 5⅜ x 8. **T584 Paperbound $2.00**

A PRINCESS OF MARS and A FIGHTING MAN OF MARS: TWO MARTIAN NOVELS BY EDGAR RICE BURROUGHS. "Princess of Mars" is the very first of the great Martian novels written by Burroughs, and it is probably the best of them all; it set the pattern for all of his later fantasy novels and contains a thrilling cast of strange peoples and creatures and the formula of Olympian heroism amidst ever-fluctuating fortunes which Burroughs carries off so successfully. "Fighting Man" returns to the same scenes and cities—many years later. A mad scientist, a degenerate dictator, and an indomitable defender of the right clash—with the fate of the Red Planet at stake! Complete, unabridged reprinting of original editions. Illustrations by F. E. Schoonover and Hugh Hutton. v + 356pp. 5⅜ x 8½. **T1140 Paperbound $1.75**

Music

A GENERAL HISTORY OF MUSIC, Charles Burney. A detailed coverage of music from the Greeks up to 1789, with full information on all types of music: sacred and secular, vocal and instrumental, operatic and symphonic. Theory, notation, forms, instruments, innovators, composers, performers, typical and important works, and much more in an easy, entertaining style. Burney covered much of Europe and spoke with hundreds of authorities and composers so that this work is more than a compilation of records . . . it is a living work of careful and first-hand scholarship. Its account of thoroughbass (18th century) Italian music is probably still the best introduction on the subject. A recent NEW YORK TIMES review said, "Surprisingly few of Burney's statements have been invalidated by modern research . . . still of great value." Edited and corrected by Frank Mercer. 35 figures. Indices. 1915pp. 5⅜ x 8. 2 volumes.   T36 The Set, Clothbound **$12.50**

A DICTIONARY OF HYMNOLOGY, John Julian. This exhaustive and scholarly work has become known as an invaluable source of hundreds of thousands of important and often difficult to obtain facts on the history and use of hymns in the western world. Everyone interested in hymns will be fascinated by the accounts of famous hymns and hymn writers and amazed by the amount of practical information he will find. More than 30,000 entries on individual hymns, giving authorship, date and circumstances of composition, publication, textual variations, translations, denominational and ritual usage, etc. Biographies of more than 9,000 hymn writers, and essays on important topics such as Christmas carols and children's hymns, and much other unusual and valuable information. A 200 page double-columned index of first lines — the largest in print. Total of 1786 pages in two reinforced clothbound volumes. 6¼ x 9¼.
The set, T333 Clothbound **$17.50**

MUSIC IN MEDIEVAL BRITAIN, F. Ll. Harrison. The most thorough, up-to-date, and accurate treatment of the subject ever published, beautifully illustrated. Complete account of institutions and choirs; carols, masses, and motets; liturgy and plainsong; and polyphonic music from the Norman Conquest to the Reformation. Discusses the various schools of music and their reciprocal influences; the origin and development of new ritual forms; development and use of instruments; and new evidence on many problems of the period. Reproductions of scores, over 200 excerpts from medieval melodies. Rules of harmony and dissonance; influence of Continental styles; great composers (Dunstable, Cornysh, Fairfax, etc.); and much more. Register and index of more than 400 musicians. Index of titles. General Index. 225-item bibliography. 6 Appendices. xix + 491pp. 5⅝ x 8¾.   T705 Clothbound **$10.00**

THE MUSIC OF SPAIN, Gilbert Chase. Only book in English to give concise, comprehensive account of Iberian music; new Chapter covers music since 1941. Victoria, Albéniz, Cabezón, Pedrell, Turina, hundreds of other composers; popular and folk music; the Gypsies; the guitar; dance, theatre, opera, with only extensive discussion in English of the Zarzuela; virtuosi such as Casals; much more. "Distinguished . . . readable," Saturday Review. 400-item bibliography. Index. 27 photos. 383pp. 5⅜ x 8.   T549 Paperbound **$2.25**

ON STUDYING SINGING, Sergius Kagen. An intelligent method of voice-training, which leads you around pitfalls that waste your time, money, and effort. Exposes rigid, mechanical systems, baseless theories, deleterious exercises. "Logical, clear, convincing . . . dead right," Virgil Thomson, N.Y. Herald Tribune. "I recommend this volume highly," Maggie Teyte, Saturday Review. 119pp. 5⅜ x 8.   T622 Paperbound **$1.35**

Prices subject to change without notice.

Dover publishes books on art, music, philosophy, literature, languages, history, social sciences, psychology, handcrafts, orientalia, puzzles and entertainments, chess, pets and gardens, books explaining science, intermediate and higher mathematics, mathematical physics, engineering, biological sciences, earth sciences, classics of science, etc. Write to:

Dept. catrr.
Dover Publications, Inc.
180 Varick Street, N.Y. 14, N.Y.